THANK YOU
SUPPORT O
SERVICES!

P9-CFE-214

Larry N. McAllister
PRESIDENT - EAGLE GROUP

COOKBOOK

150 GREAT FAMILY RECIPES FROM AMERICA'S PRO CHEFS AND NFL PLAYERS

Introductions by **FAITH HILL** and **JOHN MADDEN**

Chefs' Recipes Courtesy of **TASTE OF THE NFL**

RECIPE NOTES AND EDITING BY LIANA KRISSOFF AND LEDA SCHEINTAUB

CONTENTS

CONTENTS

WELCOME

THE **SUNDAY NIGHT FOOTBALL COOKBOOK** IS THE RESULT OF ALMOST TWO DECADES OF GREAT FOOTBALL COOKING.

Many of the talented chefs who have contributed to Taste of the NFL—an annual celebration of food and football that benefits America's food banks—are featured here. They are a diverse group from all over the country, serving up a wide variety of regional cuisine—from Kansas City barbecue sauce to Philly's famous cheese steak, from Seattle favorite Dungeness crab to Miami's South Beach–worthy guava shrimp. Also included are unique signature dishes from such culinary superstars as Emeril Lagasse and Bobby Flay, as well as sure crowd-pleasers from John Madden's kitchen. The recipes range from simple to ambitious, but the one thing they have in common is that they're best enjoyed with family and friends.

We football fans are a loyal bunch, and it's only natural that we'd turn first to the recipes from our home teams, but there's no need for rivalry in the kitchen. If you like good food, you're going to love all the recipes in this collection, from your favorite team and your biggest opponent alike. The recipes are organized by region, and within each region you'll find appetizers, main dishes, and desserts to make a meal with. But feel free to mix and match to come up with a meal of your own creation.

The grand finale is an indispensable Super Bowl guide with three different menus to suit any style of gathering, whether you're throwing the traditional dips-and-chips bash, hosting a fancier get-together, or enjoying a special evening with close family. Because even the most dedicated fans don't necessarily want to tailgate every weekend, and because sometimes the best way to experience a Sunday night game is in your own home, surrounded by the people you care about most.

Peppered with regional food finds and a diverse selection of NFL player favorites, *The Sunday Night Football Cookbook* will inspire you to get cooking throughout the football season and beyond.

FAITH HILL
GRAMMY AWARD WINNER & MULTI-PLATINUM SELLING COUNTRY SUPERSTAR

I'VE BEEN A FOOTBALL FAN SINCE JUNIOR HIGH. MY FAMILY AND I ROOT FOR OUR HOME TEAM, THE TENNESSEE TITANS.

On Sunday nights during football season, dinner has to be planned around the game . . . we have a routine. It's an all-gather-around the television time.

Sunday has always been a special day for me, and Sunday nights are a unique time to get the family together. My parents brought me up in a home that was dedicated to family, religion, and hard work. We never wasted food, and we never had what we didn't need. My mom still uses the pots and pans that she cooked with when I was a child. I think my parents' lessons rubbed off on me; the iron skillet that I cook in is 25 years old and was a gift from my mom.

Another lesson that my parents imparted to me is the importance of helping those who are not able to provide for themselves. Today, many people in this country are hungry and our food banks are strapped to the limits.

The Sunday Night Football Cookbook benefits Feeding America, a network of food banks around the country. I hope you enjoy this collection of great recipes for your family's football nights and thanks for helping America's food banks.

— *Faith Hill*

JOHN MADDEN
ANALYST, NBC SUNDAY NIGHT FOOTBALL, AND MEMBER OF THE PRO FOOTBALL HALL OF FAME

OVER THE YEARS, I'VE SEEN HOW PEOPLE COME TOGETHER AT BIG COOKOUTS TO SHARE THEIR FAVORITE RECIPES, WHETHER

it's a bunch of bundled-up Packers fans grilling bratwurst in December outside Lambeau Field in Green Bay or a group of friends cooking duck a dozen different ways in their backyard.

A big outdoor feast is a great thing, but making dinner with your family in the kitchen is really special. Because I've been playing, coaching, or broadcasting most of my life, I never get a chance to make a Sunday night meal, complete with family, food, and football. We get to participate in some great football games, sure, but one of the best ways to enjoy the big game is by making it a true family night.

I hope this cookbook sparks a lot of family dinners. We have some great recipes written by the best chefs from all over the country. We have family favorites from the players themselves. We have a collection of incredible tastes from around America, from Kansas

City barbecue to Louisiana gumbo to Wisconsin cheese. Best of all, this cookbook directly benefits others through Feeding America and food banks across the country.

I have never been a finicky eater. My favorite is Mexican food. The only things I don't like are sushi and liver.

Here's where you come in. Turn the page and give a few of these recipes a try, and know that by purchasing this cookbook, you are helping to fight hunger in America through the nation's largest food bank, Feeding America. I hope you'll find the perfect dinner for your family, your friends, and for Football Night in America.

— *John Madden*

EAST

NEW ENGLAND BAKED STUFFED CLAMS

THE BOSTON PATRIOTS BECAME THE NEW ENGLAND PATRIOTS AFTER MOVING TO FOXBOROUGH, MASS., IN 1971.

CHEF: Paul O'Connell, Chez Henri, Cambridge

WINE SUGGESTION: Maso Canali

SERVES 6

PREP TIME
00:30+

---

2 cups white wine

12 cherrystone clams (see *Notes*)

2 tablespoons unsalted butter

1 onion, minced

2 teaspoons minced Anaheim or other mild chile

2 garlic cloves, minced

½ cup minced celery

½ cup diced chorizo

½ cup toasted Portuguese sweet bread crumbs (see *Notes*)

½ cup toasted corn bread crumbs

1 teaspoon smoked paprika

2 tablespoons minced scallion

2 tablespoons minced fresh parsley

Salt and freshly ground black pepper

Lemon wedges

Preheat the oven to 350°F.

In a large saucepan, bring the wine and 1 quart water to a boil. Add the clams, cover, and cook until clams open, 3 to 5 minutes. Transfer the clams to a large bowl. Strain the cooking liquid through a cheesecloth-lined sieve into a bowl and set aside.

Shuck the clams, reserving half the shells. Mince the clams and set aside.

In a large skillet, melt the butter over medium heat. Add the onion, chile, garlic, celery, and chorizo and cook until the onion and celery are softened, about 5 minutes. Add the minced clams, bread crumbs, and enough of the clam broth to lightly moisten the mixture. Add ½ teaspoon of the smoked paprika, the scallion, and parsley, and season with salt and pepper to taste.

Spoon the mixture into the shells, place them on a baking sheet, and bake until lightly browned, about 30 minutes.

Place 1 stuffed clam on each of 6 serving plates, sprinkle with the remaining ½ teaspoon smoked paprika, and garnish with lemon wedges. Serve immediately.

NOTES: *Cherrystone clams are an East Coast variety, about 2½ inches in diameter with a hard shell. If unavailable, you can substitute any medium-sized hard-shell clam.*

Portuguese sweet bread, made with milk and sugar and traditionally eaten around Christmas and Easter, is common in New England cooking, reflecting the influence of the region's Portuguese immigrants. The bread also makes great French toast—a good way to use any leftovers. If unavailable, substitute another sweet bread such as brioche or challah.

SEARED SALMON
WITH JALAPEÑO DRESSING

THE NEW YORK TITANS BECAME THE
JETS WHEN THEY MOVED NEAR
LAGUARDIA AIRPORT IN 1963.

CHEF: Shin Tsujimura, Nobu New York, New York City

WINE SUGGESTION: Martin Codax Albarino

SERVES 4

PREP TIME
00:30

SALMON

8   ounces sashimi-grade salmon

    Salt and freshly ground
    black pepper

2   teaspoons olive oil

JALAPEÑO DRESSING

¼   cup rice vinegar

1   jalapeño chile, finely chopped

½   teaspoon finely grated garlic

½   teaspoon salt, or to taste

5   tablespoons grapeseed oil
    (see page 178)

    Mixed salad greens

MAKE THE SALMON: Slice the salmon into 16 equal pieces and season lightly with salt and pepper. Heat 1 teaspoon of the oil in a medium sauté pan over high heat. Add half the salmon pieces and sear for 10 seconds on each side. Add the remaining 1 teaspoon oil and repeat with the rest of the salmon. Set aside.

MAKE THE JALAPEÑO DRESSING: In a food processor, combine the vinegar, chile, garlic, and salt and purée until smooth. With the motor running, slowly add the oil through the feed tube and process until thickened.

Place a small amount of salad greens on each of 4 serving plates. Top with 4 pieces of salmon and drizzle with the dressing.

RADICCHIO AND ENDIVE SALAD
WITH ROASTED PEARS AND GORGONZOLA

IN 1966, THE REDSKINS SCORED THE MOST POINTS EVER IN A REGULAR SEASON GAME—72 AGAINST THE GIANTS.

PREP TIME 01:00

CHEF: Bob Kinkead, Kinkead's, Washington, D.C.

WINE SUGGESTION: Martin Codax Albarino

SERVES 6

VINAIGRETTE

¼ cup red wine vinegar

2 tablespoons port wine

¼ teaspoon honey

1 shallot, minced

¼ teaspoon salt

¼ teaspoon freshly ground black pepper

6 tablespoons olive oil

¼ cup walnut oil

2 tablespoons grapeseed oil (see page 178)

1 teaspoon chopped fresh chives

SALAD

30 walnut halves

4 ounces Gorgonzola or Roquefort cheese

4 tablespoons cream cheese

3 ripe Bosc pears (see *Note*)

2 Belgian endives

1 head radicchio

¼ teaspoon salt

¼ teaspoon freshly ground black pepper

MAKE THE VINAIGRETTE: In a medium bowl, whisk together the vinegar, port, honey, shallot, salt, and pepper. Slowly add the olive oil, walnut oil, and grapeseed oil, one at a time, whisking until emulsified. Add the chives.

MAKE THE SALAD: Preheat the oven to 350°F. Spread the walnuts over a baking sheet and toast until lightly browned, about 10 minutes. Remove from the oven and raise the oven temperature to 400°F. Let the walnuts cool and chop 24 of them, reserving the remaining 6 for garnish. In a mixer fitted with the paddle attachment, combine the Gorgonzola cheese, cream cheese, and half of the chopped walnuts and mix until incorporated.

Peel and core the pears and cut in half, working quickly so they don't discolor. Pat the pears dry with paper towels and place core side up on the baking sheet. Divide the cheese mixture among the pear halves. Bake until the pears are tender and the cheese mixture starts to melt, about 20 minutes.

Meanwhile, reserve 6 of the outer endive leaves for garnish and cut the rest into thin strips. Core the radicchio and cut into thin strips. In a large bowl, toss together the endive, radicchio, salt, pepper, and remaining chopped walnuts. Add the vinaigrette and toss to coat.

Divide the salad among 6 serving plates and place the reserved endive leaves at the sides of the plates. Place a pear half on top of each salad and garnish with a walnut half.

NOTE: *If you can't find ripe Bosc pears, or if you are using another variety such as Anjou, Comice, or Bartlett, you will need to poach them briefly. Peel the pears, leaving them whole. Fill a medium saucepan with enough water to cover the pears and add 2 tablespoons sugar and 1 teaspoon salt. Bring to a boil, stirring until the sugar is dissolved. Add the pears in one layer, reduce the heat to low, and cook, turning a couple of times, until slightly softened but not fully poached—the pears will continue to soften in the oven. Using a slotted spoon, remove the pears from the liquid, cool slightly, pat dry with paper towels, and proceed with the recipe.*

SIZZLE AND SPICE SHRIMP
WITH WATERMELON AND MANGO SALAD

THE DOLPHINS COMPLETED THE NFL'S
FIRST PERFECT SEASON, CULMINATING
WITH A SUPER BOWL WIN, IN 1972.

PREP TIME
00:30+
MARINATE 20 MINUTES

CHEF: **Allen Susser,** Chef Allen's, Aventura

WINE SUGGESTION: Martin Codax Albarino

SERVES 6

SIZZLE AND SPICE SHRIMP

Juice of 3 large limes

2 teaspoons soy sauce

1 teaspoon sugar

1½ teaspoons salt

1 pound large shrimp, preferably wild, peeled and deveined

3 star anise pods

2 tablespoons fennel seeds

1 teaspoon ground cinnamon

1 teaspoon ground cayenne pepper

1 teaspoon finely minced Kaffir lime leaves (see *Note*)

1 teaspoon dried mint

WATERMELON AND MANGO SALAD

2 cups seeded watermelon cut into 1-inch cubes

2 cups mango cut into 1-inch cubes

1 bunch frisée, trimmed

¼ cup fresh lemon juice, or to taste

¼ cup fresh orange juice

2 tablespoons chopped fresh tarragon

½ cup extra-virgin olive oil

Salt and freshly ground black pepper

2 tablespoons olive oil

1 tablespoon black sesame seeds

Wild Florida shrimp aren't always available outside the region but are well worth going out of your way to find. They're fresher, more flavorful, and more ecologically sound than the farmed shrimp that have become standard in most stores these days.

MAKE THE SIZZLE AND SPICE SHRIMP: In a large bowl, combine the lime juice, soy sauce, 1 tablespoon water, the sugar, and ½ teaspoon of the salt and whisk to dissolve the sugar and salt. Add the shrimp, toss to coat, and marinate at room temperature for 20 minutes.

Meanwhile, in a spice grinder, combine the star anise pods and fennel seeds and pulse until coarsely ground. Transfer to a small bowl and add the cinnamon, cayenne pepper, lime leaves, mint, and remaining 1 teaspoon salt. Set aside.

MAKE THE WATERMELON AND MANGO SALAD: In a large bowl, combine the watermelon and mango. Toss gently with the frisée. In a medium bowl, whisk together the lemon juice, orange juice, and tarragon. Add the extra-virgin olive oil in a slow stream, whisking until thickened. Season with salt and pepper to taste. Gently toss the salad with the dressing.

COOK THE SHRIMP: Remove the shrimp from the marinade and pat with paper towels to remove most of the marinade. Place on a plate and toss to coat with the spice mixture. Heat the oil in a large skillet over medium-high heat. Add the shrimp and sauté until cooked through and pink, about 5 minutes.

Divide the salad among 6 serving plates and place the shrimp in the center of the bowls. Sprinkle with the sesame seeds and serve immediately.

NOTE: *Both the fruit and the leaves of the Kaffir lime plant are highly aromatic and are integral to Thai, Cambodian, and Indonesian cooking. The fruit itself is tiny with bumpy skin, and the leaves are dark green and glossy. You can find lime leaves in Asian markets and some specialty grocers. If fresh leaves aren't available, you can substitute frozen. In a pinch you can use dried lime leaves or regular lime zest— you'll need to double the quantity called for.*

TIKI BARBER'S
KALBI
KOREAN-STYLE SHORT RIBS

TIKI BARBER SET VIRTUALLY EVERY CAREER OFFENSIVE RECORD FOR THE GIANTS.

PREP TIME
00:30
MARINATE 3+ HOURS

CHEF: Tiki Barber, Analyst, Football Night in America

SERVES 4 TO 6

2 pounds boneless beef short ribs (kalbi), very thinly sliced lengthwise (see *Note*)

2 tablespoons toasted sesame oil

6 tablespoons soy sauce

2 tablespoons sugar

1 tablespoon honey

6 tablespoons water

2 scallions, minced

3 garlic cloves, minced

2 teaspoons sesame seeds

Freshly ground black pepper to taste

2 heads red leaf lettuce, leaves separated

Kalbi is the Korean word for ribs, and this popular barbecue dish is cooked right at the table on countertop grills in Korean restaurants. It's served with whole lettuce leaves, which are used to wrap the meat.

Pat the short ribs dry with paper towels. In a medium bowl, combine the remaining ingredients except the lettuce and stir to dissolve the sugar. Add the short ribs to the marinade and turn to coat the meat. Cover with plastic and refrigerate for 3 to 4 hours.

Heat a large nonstick skillet over medium-high heat. Remove the meat from the marinade and cook for 1 to 2 minutes on each side, to desired doneness. Serve immediately, with lettuce leaves for wrapping.

NOTE: *The thinner the meat the better. To make your life easier, ask your butcher to slice the meat, or look for precut kalbi, available at Korean groceries.*

"When I was playing, I'd be so nervous I wouldn't eat much on game days. Maybe a waffle with some bananas or strawberries. After games, I was starving. My wife and I and some teammates always went out to a place called Primola on the Upper East Side of Manhattan. We would pig out on veal and pasta for what seemed like hours. That was a fun time."

TIKI BARBER WAS VOTED TO 3 NFL
PRO BOWLS DURING HIS ILLUSTRIOUS
10-YEAR PLAYING CAREER.

TIKI BARBER'S
CHAP CHE
KOREAN-STYLE VERMICELLI

CHEF: Tiki Barber, Analyst, Football Night in America

SERVES 4 TO 6

PREP TIME
01:00

- 8 ounces Korean vermicelli
- 4 teaspoons toasted sesame oil
- 2 teaspoons plus 2 tablespoons soy sauce
- 1½ teaspoons fish sauce
- ½ teaspoon sugar
- 1 garlic clove, minced
- 4 ounces chicken breast, diced
- 4 ounces spinach leaves
- 2 tablespoons plus 1 teaspoon vegetable oil
- ½ cup thinly sliced onion
- ½ cup thinly sliced red bell pepper
- ½ cup thinly sliced carrot
- ½ cup thinly sliced mushrooms
- Salt and freshly ground black pepper

Tiki says, "My wife is half-Korean, half-Vietnamese, so my diet is diverse. My favorite foods have become dishes like bi bim bop and Korean beef. That's become my comfort food. My mother-in-law makes these cellophane noodles with all kinds of vegetables, asparagus, or herbs and a little bit of chicken or beef. Nobody that we've ever brought to our house has not liked it."

Bring a large pot of water to a boil. Add the noodles and cook until softened, about 5 minutes. Drain, rinse, and drain again. (You can toss with a little vegetable oil to prevent them from sticking together.) Cool, then cut into 3-inch pieces using kitchen shears.

Meanwhile, combine 2 teaspoons of the sesame oil, 2 teaspoons of the soy sauce, the fish sauce, sugar, and garlic in a medium bowl, stirring to dissolve the sugar. Add the chicken and toss to coat in the marinade. Let sit for 20 minutes at room temperature.

Blanch the spinach in a pan of salted boiling water for 30 seconds. Drain, rinse in cold water, and drain again. Squeeze the spinach to remove excess water, then chop the spinach.

In a large skillet, heat 2 tablespoons of the vegetable oil over medium heat. Add the onion, pepper, carrot, and mushrooms and sauté until just starting to soften, about 3 minutes.

Meanwhile, in a separate skillet, heat the remaining 1 teaspoon vegetable oil over medium heat. Add the chicken and cook for about 2 minutes, until just cooked through. Add the chicken to the vegetables, along with the noodles, remaining 2 tablespoons soy sauce, and 2 teaspoons sesame oil. Cook, stirring, until the mixture is heated through. Taste and adjust the seasoning, adding salt, if needed, and pepper to taste. Serve immediately.

SPICY SEAFOOD SOUP

THE JETS SHARE TEAM COLORS
WITH FORMER OWNER LEON HESS'S
HESS GAS STATIONS.

PREP TIME
00:30+

CHEF: Shin Tsujimura, Nobu New York, New York City

WINE SUGGESTION: McWilliam's Shiraz

SERVES 2

DASHI

One 3-inch strip kombu

1 ounce bonito flakes

SEAFOOD SOUP

1 cup chopped bok choy

½ small corn cob

2 large shrimp, peeled and deveined

2 small sea eel fillets, cut into 1-inch pieces

2 razor clams

2 large mussels

2 asari clams (see *Note*)

2 ounces cleaned squid, thinly sliced

One 5-ounce skinless sea bass fillet, bones removed and cut into chunks

2 tablespoons light soy sauce, or to taste

2 tablespoons sake

1 teaspoon chile-garlic sauce

Salt

Fresh cilantro leaves

The base for this signature Nobu dish is dashi, a Japanese stock made up of just two ingredients: kombu, a long, dark seaweed, and bonito flakes, made from dried tuna. This simple stock is packed with flavor and nutrients and is the foundation for many Japanese dishes, including miso soup. Both kombu and bonito flakes can be found in Asian markets.

MAKE THE DASHI: Lightly wipe the kombu with a dry cloth to remove the white powder. Place in a medium saucepan with 1 quart water. Bring to a boil over high heat. Remove the kombu and discard. Return the water to a boil, add the bonito flakes, and remove from the heat. Let stand for 3 minutes, then strain through a cheesecloth-lined sieve into a bowl and return the stock to the saucepan. Discard the bonito flakes.

MAKE THE SEAFOOD SOUP: Bring a large pot of water to a boil. One ingredient at a time, blanch the bok choy, corn, shrimp, and eel for 1 to 2 minutes, until just cooked, removing with a slotted spoon to a bowl and letting the water return to a boil after each ingredient has cooked.

Remove the meat from the razor clams and thinly slice. Discard the shells. Rinse the mussels and asari clams well.

Bring the dashi back to a boil. Add the razor clams, mussels, asari clams, squid, and sea bass and return to a boil. Cover the pot, lower the heat, and cook until the clams open and the squid and sea bass are cooked through, about 5 minutes. Add the soy sauce, sake, chile-garlic sauce, and salt to taste.

Ladle the soup into 2 bowls, dividing the ingredients equally. Garnish with cilantro and serve immediately.

NOTE: *Asari clams, also known as Manila clams, are a sweet, tender variety grown in the Pacific Northwest. If not available, littleneck clams can be substituted.*

BRAISED SHORT RIB MEATBALLS
WITH TOMATO AND WILD MUSHROOM SAUCE

PREP TIME
03:00+
MARINATE OVERNIGHT

CHEF: **Stephen Lewandowski,** Tribeca Grill, New York City

WINE SUGGESTION: LMM Napa Cabernet

BRAISED SHORT RIBS

	One 750-ml bottle red wine
	One 750-ml bottle port wine
6	shallots, chopped
6	garlic cloves, crushed
3	sprigs fresh rosemary
3	sprigs fresh thyme
3	pounds beef short ribs, well trimmed
	Salt and freshly ground black pepper
2	tablespoons olive oil
3	white onions, chopped
2	carrots, chopped
2	celery stalks, chopped
4	cups low-sodium beef broth, plus more as needed

MEATBALLS

½	pound ground pork
½	pound ground beef
½	pound ground veal
2	small white onions, diced
3	large eggs
2	tablespoons Dijon-style mustard
2	tablespoons ketchup
½	cup fine bread crumbs
1	cup finely grated Parmesan cheese
2	tablespoons minced fresh oregano

3	tablespoons minced fresh basil
3	tablespoons minced fresh parsley
1	cup beer, preferably lager
½	cup milk, plus more as needed
	Salt and freshly ground black pepper to taste

TOMATO AND WILD MUSHROOM SAUCE

¼	cup olive oil, plus 1 tablespoon, plus more as needed
2	cups diced white onions
¼	cup chopped garlic
3	cups mixed wild mushrooms (such as cremini, portobello, and oyster)
1	cup red wine
	One 28-ounce can chopped tomatoes with juices
	One 32-ounce can tomato purée
1	tablespoon dried oregano
1	tablespoon dried basil
1	tablespoon dried parsley
2	teaspoons sugar, or to taste
	Salt and freshly ground black pepper
2	tablespoons heavy cream
1	tablespoon unsalted butter
	Grated pecorino toscano cheese

THE GIANTS HAVE MANY NICKNAMES, INCLUDING "BIG BLUE," THE "JERSEY GIANTS," THE "G-MEN," AND THE "JINTS."

SERVES 4

This is no ordinary meatball, and you'll need a little skill in the kitchen and a good chunk of time to execute this dish. Make it for a special occasion, like when your team makes the playoffs.

MAKE THE BRAISED SHORT RIBS: In a large bowl, combine the red wine, port, shallots, garlic, rosemary, and thyme. Place the short ribs in a heavy-duty zip-top bag and pour the marinade over the ribs. Seal the bag and refrigerate overnight.

Preheat the oven to 350°F.

Remove the short ribs from the marinade and pat dry with paper towels. Reserve the marinade. Season with salt and pepper to taste. In a large, heavy pot, heat the oil over medium-high heat. Brown the short ribs on all sides, about 8 minutes, turning with tongs. Transfer to a plate. Add the onions, carrots, and celery to the pot and sauté for about 5 minutes, or until softened. Return the short ribs to the pot. Add the reserved marinade and enough broth to cover the meat and bring to a boil. Remove the pan from the heat, cover, and place in the oven to braise for 3 to 3½ hours,

or until the meat is very tender. Remove the ribs from the pot, reserving the liquid. Cool briefly, then finely mince the meat.

MAKE THE MEATBALLS: In a large bowl, combine the minced short ribs with all the ingredients, mixing well, adding more milk if necessary. The mixture should be slightly loose. Take a small amount of the mixture and cook it so you can taste; adjust the seasonings if necessary. Form the mixture into 2-inch balls and put them on a baking sheet. Refrigerate while you make the sauce.

MAKE THE TOMATO AND WILD MUSHROOM SAUCE: Heat the ¼ cup of the oil in a large saucepan over medium heat. Add the onions, garlic, and mushrooms and sauté for about 5 minutes, or until softened. Add the wine and cook until reduced by two-thirds. Add the tomatoes, tomato purée, oregano, basil, parsley, sugar, and salt and pepper to taste. Bring to a simmer, then reduce the heat and simmer for 1½ hours. Add the cream and butter and remove from the heat.

COOK THE MEATBALLS: During the last 30 minutes of cooking the sauce, in a large skillet, heat the remaining 1 tablespoon oil over medium-high heat. Add the meatballs in batches, shaking the skillet frequently and adding more oil as needed. Cook each batch for about 5 minutes, or until browned all over. Using a slotted spoon, transfer the meatballs to a bowl.

Add the meatballs to the sauce, place over medium heat, and bring to a simmer. Reduce the heat, cover, and simmer, stirring occasionally, until the meatballs are cooked through, about 15 minutes.

Divide the meatballs and sauce among serving plates, sprinkle with cheese, and serve immediately.

BUFFALO'S FAMOUS BEEF ON WECK

THE BILLS ARE THE ONLY NEW YORK
TEAM TO PLAY HOME GAMES
WITHIN NEW YORK STATE.

PREP TIME

02:00+

CHEF: Frank DiVincenzo, Billy Ogden's, Buffalo

WINE SUGGESTION: Red Rock Merlot

SERVES 6 TO 8

BEEF

One 5-pound top round beef roast

Salt and freshly ground
black pepper

GRAVY

½ cup (1 stick) unsalted butter

⅔ cup all-purpose flour

Beef soup base paste

2 teaspoons granulated garlic
(or garlic powder)

2 teaspoons granulated onion
(or onion powder)

½ teaspoon ground white pepper

6 to 8 kümmelweck, Kaiser,
or hard rolls (see *Note*)

Dill pickle spears

Prepared horseradish

MAKE THE BEEF: Preheat the oven to 350°F.

Put the roast on a metal rack in a roasting pan with the fat side up and season generously with salt and pepper. Roast for about 1¾ hours, or until the internal temperature registers 140°F on a meat thermometer for medium-rare.

Let the roast rest, loosely covered with aluminum foil, for 20 minutes, then thinly slice.

MAKE THE GRAVY: Meanwhile, in a medium saucepan, melt the butter over medium-low heat until just bubbling. Add the flour and whisk until smooth, creating a roux. Cook, stirring constantly, for about 10 minutes, or until the roux is lightly colored. Remove from the heat.

In a separate medium saucepan over medium heat, bring 4 cups water to a boil. Add the beef base in the amount called for on the jar. Add the garlic, onion, and white pepper. Return to a boil and slowly add the roux, whisking until blended and smooth. Reduce the heat to medium-low and cook for about 20 minutes, stirring constantly, until thickened. Taste and adjust the seasonings if necessary. Transfer the gravy to a shallow pan and add the beef, stirring until the beef is well coated.

Split the rolls in half and fill with the beef. Serve with the pickle spears and horseradish.

NOTE: *This sandwich—rare roast beef dipped in gravy and piled high—is found in restaurants and bars throughout the Buffalo area. Natives will tell you it's not Beef on Weck if it's not served on a kümmelweck roll—a type of hard roll topped with lots of pretzel salt and caraway seeds. If you can't find kümmelweck rolls, make your own by brushing Kaiser or hard rolls with a thin cornstarch slurry, sprinkling with caraway seeds and coarse salt, and baking at 400°F until nicely browned.*

PHILLY CHEEZ STEAK SANDWICH

ON OCTOBER 22, 1939, THE EAGLES PLAYED
THE BROOKLYN DODGERS IN THE FIRST
TELEVISED NFL GAME, WHICH AIRED ON NBC.

CHEF: Jack McDavid, Jack's Firehouse, Philadelphia

WINE SUGGESTION: DaVinci Chianti

SERVES 4

PREP TIME
00:30

¼ cup peanut oil

1 pound Spanish onions, peeled and thinly sliced

2 jalapeño chiles, seeded and thinly sliced

8 ounces Cheez Whiz or other processed cheese spread

2 pounds rib-eye steak, cut into ¼-inch-thick slices

   Salt and freshly ground black pepper

4 Italian or hoagie rolls, split in half

No visit to Philadelphia is complete without sampling the city's most celebrated dish: the steak and cheese sandwich, or Philly cheese steak. Although Cheez Whiz hadn't been invented when the first cheese steak was introduced in the 1930s, for many fans it has since become a favorite topping.

In a medium saucepan, heat the oil over medium heat. Add the onions and chiles and cook for about 20 minutes, stirring often, until the onions are caramelized. Remove the onion and chile mixture to a bowl and stir in the Cheez Whiz.

Heat a large skillet over medium-high heat. Season the steak with salt and pepper. Sear the steak for 2 to 3 minutes on each side, until browned and to desired doneness.

Place a roll half on each of 4 plates. Divide the steak among the rolls and top with the onion mixture. Top with the remaining roll halves.

SKEWERED LAMB TENDERLOIN

IN 2007 THE GIANTS BECAME THE
THIRD NFL FRANCHISE
TO WIN AT LEAST 600 GAMES.

PREP TIME

01:00

MARINATE 4 HOURS

CHEF: Bobby Flay, Mesa Grill, New York City

WINE SUGGESTION: MacMurray SC Pinot Noir

SERVES 4

LAMB SKEWERS

- 1 pound boneless lamb tenderloin, cut into 2-inch pieces
- 1 cup olive oil
- 1 head garlic, peeled and crushed
- 3 fresh rosemary sprigs, bruised with the back of a chef's knife, plus more for garnish

    Salt and freshly ground black pepper

- 8 roasted shallots or pearl onions

CRACKED WHEAT SALAD

- 1½ cups cooked cracked wheat
- 2 tablespoons diced red bell peppers
- 2 tablespoons diced yellow bell peppers
- 3 tablespoons chopped fresh tarragon
- ¼ to ½ cup fresh lemon juice, to taste
- 2 tablespoons honey

    Salt and freshly ground black pepper to taste

RED WINE SAUCE

- ½ bottle Rioja red wine
- 1 teaspoon Dijon-style mustard
- ½ cup olive oil

    Salt and freshly ground black pepper

If you'd like to prepare the lamb on an outdoor barbecue, fire up a charcoal or wood grill at least 30 minutes before you're ready to grill and let it burn until the coals glow or it burns down to embers, then grill for 3 to 4 minutes on each side, basting and turning as you go.

MAKE THE LAMB SKEWERS: In a large bowl, combine the lamb, oil, garlic, rosemary, and salt and pepper to taste, turning to fully coat the lamb. Cover with plastic wrap and marinate for 4 hours in the refrigerator, turning occasionally.

MAKE THE CRACKED WHEAT SALAD: In a large bowl, combine all the ingredients well. Set aside until ready to serve.

MAKE THE RED WINE SAUCE: In a medium saucepan, bring the wine to a simmer over medium heat. Simmer until reduced to a syrup, watching carefully toward the end so it doesn't burn or become sticky. In a food processor, combine the wine syrup and mustard and process to combine. With the motor running, slowly add the oil through the feed tube and process until thickened. Season with salt and pepper to taste. Set aside until ready to serve.

COOK THE LAMB: Preheat the broiler and line a broiler pan with aluminum foil. Remove the lamb from the marinade and thread onto 4 metal skewers (if using wooden skewers, soak them in water for 30 minutes first), alternating with the shallots, and leaving a couple of inches free on both ends. Broil for 3 to 4 minutes on each side, basting with the marinade a few times, until the meat is seared on the outside and just cooked through.

Divide the salad among 4 serving plates. Top each with a lamb skewer, drizzle with the sauce, and serve garnished with rosemary sprigs.

BRAISED VEAL CHEEKS
WITH FRIED LEEKS

THE BILLS' 32-POINT COMEBACK IN A
41–38 PLAYOFF WIN OVER HOUSTON IN 1993
WAS THE BIGGEST EVER IN NFL HISTORY.

CHEF: Andy DiVincenzo, Billy Ogden's, Buffalo

WINE SUGGESTION: Red Rock Merlot

SERVES 6

PREP TIME
02:30+

BRAISED VEAL CHEEKS

2   tablespoons olive oil

1   cup all-purpose flour

    Salt and freshly ground black pepper

12 veal cheeks (about 3 pounds), cleaned and trimmed

4   cups red wine

3   cups low-sodium veal broth or beef broth

½   cup balsamic vinegar

12 garlic cloves, peeled and left whole

FRIED LEEKS

    Vegetable oil for frying

4   small leeks, white and light green parts only, cleaned and cut into thin strips

    Salt

3   cups cooked couscous

MAKE THE VEAL CHEEKS: Preheat the oven to 325°F.

In a large, heavy saucepan or Dutch oven, heat the oil over medium-high heat. Spread the flour over a large plate and season with salt and pepper. Dredge the veal cheeks in the flour and shake to remove excess. Add the veal cheeks to the pan and brown on all sides, about 5 minutes. Remove to a large plate and set aside. Add the wine, broth, and vinegar and bring to a boil, stirring to break up any browned bits from the bottom of the pan. Add the garlic and season with salt and pepper to taste. Return the veal cheeks to the pan, cover, place in the oven, and braise for 2½ to 3 hours, until very tender.

MAKE THE FRIED LEEKS: Meanwhile, heat about 1 inch of oil in a medium saucepan to 350°F. Add the leeks in batches and fry for about 30 seconds, until golden brown, watching carefully that they don't burn. Using a slotted spoon, transfer to paper towels to drain and sprinkle with salt.

Divide the couscous among 6 serving plates and top with 2 veal cheeks. Garnish with the fried leeks and serve immediately.

THAI-STYLE BRAISED PORK SHANK
WITH CHIVE PANCAKES

PREP TIME
02:30+

CHEF: **David Holben,** Bistral, Dallas

WINE SUGGESTION: Bridlewood Syrah

PORK SHANKS

Four 1-pound pork shanks, trimmed of fat

Salt and freshly ground black pepper

1 cup white vinegar

1 sprig fresh rosemary

1 sprig fresh thyme

2 quarts low-sodium chicken broth

¼ cup peeled and chopped ginger

6 Kaffir lime leaves (see page 20)

1 cup soy sauce

1 tablespoon unsalted butter

1 large onion, diced

2 garlic cloves, minced

2 tablespoons palm sugar (see *Notes*)

6 plum tomatoes, coarsely chopped

4 tablespoons ketchup

2 tablespoons honey

1 teaspoon ground cayenne pepper

4 teaspoons chili powder

4 teaspoons paprika

4 teaspoons Worcestershire sauce

2 tablespoons sambal oelek (see *Notes*)

¼ cup tahini (see page 199)

¼ cup tamarind paste

CHIVE PANCAKES

1¼ cups all-purpose flour, plus more for kneading

1 cup boiling water

2 teaspoons sesame oil, plus more for brushing the dough

2 tablespoons finely chopped fresh chives

VEGETABLES

2 tablespoons peanut oil

1 yellow squash, diced

1 zucchini, diced

¼ head napa cabbage

Salt and freshly ground black pepper

2 tablespoons black sesame seeds

2 tablespoons tan sesame seeds

MAKE THE PORK SHANKS: Pat the pork shanks dry with paper towels and season with salt and pepper. Put them in a large saucepan and add the vinegar and enough water to cover. Add the rosemary and thyme. Bring to a boil over medium-high heat, then reduce the heat and simmer for 1 hour. Remove the pork shanks from the heat and cool to room temperature in the liquid.

THE COWBOYS HAVE APPEARED
IN AN NFL-RECORD EIGHT
SUPER BOWLS, WINNING FIVE.

SERVES 4

Preheat the oven to 350°F.

Combine the broth, ginger, lime leaves, and soy sauce in a braising pan just large enough to hold the pork shanks and bring to a boil over medium-high heat. Add the pork shanks, cover, place in the oven, and braise for about 1 hour, basting every 10 minutes, until the meat is just falling off the bones. Remove the pork shanks to a plate and cover loosely with foil. Reserve the cooking liquid.

In a medium saucepan, heat the butter over medium heat until melted. Add the onion, reduce the heat to medium-low, cover, and cook until softened but not colored, about 5 minutes. Add the garlic and cook for 1 minute. Raise the heat to medium and add the palm sugar, tomatoes, ketchup, honey, cayenne pepper, chili powder, paprika, Worcestershire sauce, and sambal oelek. Bring to a simmer and simmer for 15 to 20 minutes, until the sauce has thickened. Add the tahini, tamarind, and reserved braising liquid from the pork shanks and bring to a boil, then reduce the heat and simmer for 10 to 20 minutes, until thickened.

MAKE THE CHIVE PANCAKES:
Sift the flour into a medium bowl and make a well in the center. Pour in the boiling water and mix quickly with a wooden spoon. Remove the dough from the bowl and knead on a lightly floured surface for 10 minutes. Cover with plastic wrap and let rest in a warm place for 10 minutes. Roll out the dough into a long cylinder shape and cut into 16 pieces. Using a rolling pin, roll each piece into a ball and flatten slightly. Brush one side of half of the balls with oil and sprinkle with chives. Place a plain pancake on top of each oiled pancake, then roll out the two pieces together on a lightly floured surface until paper-thin. Heat 2 teaspoons oil in a medium skillet over medium-high heat. Cook the pancakes, flipping once, until lightly browned, about 5 minutes, adding more oil to the skillet as needed and wrapping the pancakes in foil as they are cooked to keep warm. Set aside.

MAKE THE VEGETABLES: In a large skillet, heat the oil over medium heat. Add the squash and zucchini and cook for about 2 minutes, until slightly softened. Add the napa cabbage and

cook until the vegetables are crisp-tender, about 5 minutes. Season with salt and pepper to taste.

Reheat the pork shanks and sauce. Divide the vegetables among 4 serving plates. Stand the pork shanks up in the center of the vegetables. Drizzle with the sauce and sprinkle with the sesame seeds. Serve 2 pancakes with each plate.

NOTES: *Palm sugar, also known as jaggery in India, is a dark, unrefined sugar made from the sap of the palm tree or from sugar cane. It comes in a solid cone-shaped form or as easier-to-use soft, crumbly pieces and can be found in Asian and Indian markets.*

Sambal oelek is a condiment made from chiles, salt, and sometimes sugar and is commonly used in Indonesian cooking. It is often served as a condiment in small bowls at the table so diners can adjust the heat level of their food. It is available in Asian markets.

MAPLE AND CHILE-GLAZED PORK CHOPS

THE EAGLES ARE THE ONLY TEAM EVER TO WIN BACK-TO-BACK CHAMPIONSHIPS BY SHUTOUTS, IN 1948 AND 1949.

CHEF: Jack McDavid, Jack's Firehouse, Philadelphia

WINE SUGGESTION: Frei Brothers RR Chardonnay

SERVES 4

PREP TIME
00:30
REFRIGERATE 4 HOURS

½   cup ancho chili powder

Salt

Four 16-ounce porterhouse pork chops

2   cups apple juice

½   cup maple syrup

2   tablespoons lemon juice, or to taste

Freshly ground black pepper

Combine the chili powder and 2 teaspoons salt and spread over a large plate. Rub the pork chops with the mixture, place on a plate, and cover with plastic. Refrigerate for 4 hours.

Meanwhile, in a medium saucepan, combine the apple juice, maple syrup, and lemon juice over medium-high heat. Season lightly with salt and pepper. Bring to a boil and cook until reduced to a glaze, about 10 minutes.

Preheat the oven to 400°F. Line a baking sheet with aluminum foil.

Remove the pork chops from the refrigerator and brush with glaze on both sides. Place on the baking sheet and bake until a meat thermometer registers 150°F for medium, about 20 minutes. Let stand for 5 minutes, then place on serving plates and serve.

ANDRE TIPPETT'S
LOBSTER AND ONION PIZZA

#56 LINEBACKER (RETIRED)
UNIVERSITY OF IOWA, b. 12-27-59
2008 INDUCTEE, PRO FOOTBALL HALL OF FAME

PREP TIME
00:30+

CHEFS: **Andre Tippett** and his wife, **Rhonda Tippett**

SERVES 4 TO 6

- 2 tablespoons unsalted butter
- 1 large Vidalia onion, thinly sliced
- 2 garlic cloves
- Pinch of brown sugar
- Salt and freshly ground black pepper
- 8 ounces cooked lobster meat, cut into bite-size pieces
- 8 ounces prepared pizza dough
- ½ cup ricotta cheese
- 1 scallion, chopped
- ½ cup shredded mozzarella cheese
- 2 tablespoons grated Parmesan cheese

Andre's wife, Rhonda, says, "This recipe was inspired by a friend of ours who is a well-known chef in Boston, and also a huge Patriots fan. We created our own version and simplified it a bit since we are not gourmet chefs. We make this pizza often when we are having friends over—everyone loves our pizzas!"

Preheat the oven to 450°F.

In a large skillet, melt the butter over medium heat. Add the onion and sauté until translucent, about 10 minutes. Add the garlic, brown sugar, and salt and pepper to taste. Cook for an additional 10 minutes, or until the onion is caramelized. Add the lobster and remove from the heat.

Lightly sprinkle a work surface with flour. Using a rolling pin, roll the pizza dough out into a very thin 12-inch circle. (This is where a big football player comes in handy.) Stretch the dough out onto a large rimless baking sheet.

Spread the ricotta cheese over the pizza dough, leaving a 1-inch border around the edges. Spread the lobster and onion mixture over the ricotta and scatter the scallion over the top. Sprinkle with the mozzarella and Parmesan cheeses.

Bake the pizza until the cheese melts and the crust is golden brown and crisp, about 12 minutes. Slice using a pizza wheel and serve immediately.

NICK MANGOLD'S
SPAGHETTI AND MEATBALLS

#74 CENTER
6'4", 300 POUNDS
OHIO STATE, b. 1-13-84

CHEF: Nick Mangold

SERVES 4

PREP TIME
03:00+

SAUCE

2	tablespoons extra-virgin olive oil
3	garlic cloves, finely chopped
	Two 28-ounce cans crushed tomatoes, preferably San Marzano
2	tablespoons sugar
1	teaspoon dried oregano
1	teaspoon Italian seasoning
2	teaspoons salt
1	teaspoon red pepper flakes, or to taste
½	cup dry red wine

MEATBALLS

	One 1-ounce packet Good Seasons Italian salad dressing mix
1	pound lean ground sirloin
¼	cup Italian-style seasoned bread crumbs
2	tablespoons grated Parmesan cheese
¼	teaspoon dried oregano
¼	teaspoon Italian seasoning
½	teaspoon salt
¼	teaspoon freshly ground black pepper
1	pound hot cooked spaghetti

Nick says, *"No matter who makes it or where I get it, there's something about spaghetti and meatballs that is comfort food for me. A nice home-cooked meal, I really don't think anything could beat that."*

MAKE THE SAUCE: In a large saucepan, heat the oil over medium heat. Add the garlic and sauté for 2 minutes, until softened and aromatic. Add the remaining ingredients and bring to a simmer.

MAKE THE MEATBALLS: Meanwhile, in a large bowl, combine all the ingredients and mix well with a wooden spoon or your hands. Roll into sixteen 1½-inch meatballs. Place the meatballs in the sauce and bring back to a simmer. Reduce the heat to low, cover the pan, and cook for 3 hours, stirring occasionally and adding a little water if the sauce gets too thick.

Serve the sauce and meatballs over the spaghetti.

ROCKFISH WITH BABY ARTICHOKES,
OVEN-DRIED TOMATOES, AND PRESERVED LEMON

PREP TIME 02:00+

CHEF: **Jeffrey "J.G." Gaetjen,** Kinkead's, Washington, D.C.

WINE SUGGESTION: McWilliam's Shiraz

OVEN-DRIED TOMATOES

4	plum tomatoes, halved
1	tablespoon olive oil
	Salt and freshly ground black pepper

ARTICHOKES

18	baby artichokes
3	lemons, halved
¼	cup plus 2 tablespoons extra-virgin olive oil
6	garlic cloves, sliced
3	sprigs fresh thyme
1	cup dry white wine
4	cups low-sodium chicken or vegetable broth or water
	Salt and freshly ground black pepper
1	teaspoon fresh thyme leaves
½	cup (1 stick) unsalted butter

ROCKFISH

	Four 5½- to 6-ounce rockfish fillets
	Salt and freshly ground black pepper
½	cup buttermilk
½	cup bread crumbs, seasoned with salt and pepper
4	tablespoons vegetable oil
2	tablespoons extra-virgin olive oil, plus more for the olives
4	fresh basil sprigs
18	pitted niçoise olives
1	tablespoon julienned preserved lemon rind (see *Note*)
2	tablespoons capers, drained

MAKE THE OVEN-DRIED TOMATOES: Preheat the oven to 300°F.

Toss the tomatoes with the oil, and season with salt and pepper to taste. Put them cut side down on a wire rack set over a baking sheet. Roast for 1 hour, or until the skins wrinkle. Cool for at least 1 hour, then peel and set aside.

MAKE THE ARTICHOKES: Trim away the outer tough skin on the artichoke stems with a sharp paring knife. Tear away the tough outer leaves,

FORMER HEAD COACH JOE GIBBS LED
THE REDSKINS TO 3 SUPER BOWL WINS
BETWEEN 1983 AND 1992.

SERVES 4

down to the pale yellow center, then trim the tops off the pale leaves. As you are working, put the trimmed artichokes in a bowl of water with the juice and halves of 1 of the lemons.

In a sauté pan with steep sides, combine the ¼ cup oil and the garlic and sauté over medium-high heat until starting to brown, about 3 minutes. Add the artichokes and sauté until lightly browned on all sides. Add the thyme sprigs, wine, and broth and bring to a boil. Reserve 1 of the lemon halves and squeeze the rest into the cooking liquid; season lightly with salt and pepper. Reduce the heat and simmer until tender, about 20 minutes. A wooden skewer inserted into an artichoke should slide in and out smoothly. Remove and discard the thyme sprigs. Remove 6 of the nicest artichokes, cut in half, and reserve for garnish.

Add the thyme leaves to the sauté pan and continue to boil the artichokes in the braising liquid until very soft, 5 to 8 minutes. Put a fine-mesh sieve over a small saucepan and pour in the braised artichokes and their liquid, saving the liquid in the saucepan. Boil

the liquid over high heat until reduced by half; set aside.

Transfer the braised artichokes to a blender, along with a few tablespoons of the cooking liquid, and purée, adding more liquid a little at a time to make a very smooth purée. Push the purée through the sieve and return it to the blender. Add the butter and purée again. Season with salt and pepper to taste and more lemon juice if necessary. Cover to keep warm, and set aside.

MAKE THE ROCKFISH: Preheat the oven to 375°F.

Sprinkle each fillet lightly with salt and pepper; dip the top side in the buttermilk and then the bread crumbs. In a large, ovenproof sauté pan, heat the vegetable oil over medium-high heat. Carefully place the fillets in the pan, breaded side down. Cook until browned and crisp on the bottom, about 3 minutes, then turn the fillets over and put the pan in the oven for about 3 minutes, until cooked through.

In a medium sauté pan, heat 1 tablespoon of the olive oil over medium heat and add the reserved artichoke halves, cut

side down. Cook until browned, about 3 minutes, then turn over and cook for 1 minute. Remove from the pan and set aside. Add the remaining 1 tablespoon olive oil to the pan, along with the dried tomato halves, and cook until warmed through.

Mound the artichoke purée in the center of each of 4 warmed serving plates. Top with a rockfish fillet. Garnish each plate with 3 artichoke halves and 2 tomato halves. In a small bowl, toss the olives with the preserved lemon, a drizzle of olive oil, and the capers and add some of the mixture to each plate. Garnish with basil sprigs and serve immediately.

NOTE: *Preserved lemons can be found in jars in Moroccan and Middle Eastern markets. You can substitute seeded diced lemon, or strips of lemon zest.*

NEW YORK STRIP STEAKS

SOY-MARINATED

BEGINNING IN 2008, THE BILLS WILL
PLAY ONE REGULAR SEASON GAME
PER YEAR IN TORONTO.

PREP TIME

00:30

MARINATE 4 TO 6 HOURS

CHEF: Andy DiVincenzo, Billy Ogden's, Buffalo

SERVES 6 TO 8

Four 14- to 16-ounce center-cut
New York strip steaks

½ cup Chinese light soy sauce
(see *Notes*)

½ cup Worcestershire sauce

¼ cup kecap manis (see *Notes*)

½ cup sugar

Salt and freshly ground
black pepper

These intensely flavorful steaks can also be cooked on a hot grill outdoors: Set the grill grate about 6 inches from the heat and wait until the coals are ashed over. If you prefer to serve the steaks unsliced, cook one 12-ounce steak per person.

With the tip of a paring knife, poke holes in the steaks on both sides. In a medium bowl, combine the soy sauce, Worcestershire sauce, and kecap manis; divide the mixture between 2 large heavy-duty zip-top bags. Sprinkle the steaks with sugar on both sides and place them in the marinade. Seal the bags and put the steaks in the refrigerator to marinate for 4 to 6 hours. Let sit at room temperature for 30 minutes before proceeding.

Heat a large cast-iron skillet or flat griddle over high heat until very hot. One or two at a time, remove the steaks from the marinade and put them in the pan; cook for 3 to 4 minutes per side. The steaks will be very black. Transfer to a carving board and cover loosely with aluminum foil as they are done. Season with salt and pepper. Starting with the steaks you cooked first, cut across the grain into thin slices. Serve immediately.

NOTES: *Chinese light soy sauce, not to be confused with low-sodium (or "lite") soy sauce, is actually less salty than dark soy sauce. Its flavor is more delicate than that of the Japanese soy sauces ubiquitous in U.S. supermarkets, but those are fine substitutes.*

Kecap manis is a thick, dark Indonesian soy sauce sweetened with palm sugar. It's available at Asian markets.

SCOTTISH LENTIL SOUP

#9 PLACE KICKER
6'1", 202 POUNDS
TROY, b. 5-3-78

CHEF: Lawrence Tynes

SERVES 8

PREP TIME
02:00

---

2   smoked ham hocks

1   large leek, chopped

4   carrots, diced

¼   cup chopped fresh parsley

1   pound red lentils

     Salt and freshly ground black pepper

Lawrence says, "My mom is Scottish and I grew up eating a lot of traditional Scottish food. Like sausage rolls wrapped in puff pastry with baked beans and chips, which are French fries. This soup is my favorite—the recipe has been in our family for more than 50 years." Served with a green salad and crusty bread, it becomes a hearty, complete meal.

In a large pot, bring 12 cups water and the ham hocks to a boil. Reduce the heat, cover, and simmer, occasionally skimming the foam and impurities from the top, about 1 ½ hours, or until the meat is tender and falling off the bone. Remove the ham hocks from the broth, cool, then pull the meat from the bones, discarding the skin and bones. Set aside.

Add the leek, carrots, and parsley to the broth and return to a boil. Reduce the heat and simmer, partially covered, for about 20 minutes, or until the vegetables have softened. Add the lentils, return to a boil, then simmer, partially covered, for 20 to 30 minutes, until the lentils have softened. Return the ham to the pot and cook to heat through. Season with salt and pepper to taste and serve immediately.

GARLICKY GUAVA SHRIMP

THE DOLPHINS WERE THE FIRST TEAM TO
ADVANCE TO THE SUPER BOWL FOR
THREE CONSECUTIVE SEASONS.

PREP TIME
00:30

CHEF: **Allen Susser,** Chef Allen's, Aventura

WINE SUGGESTION: Martin Codax Albarino

SERVES 4

- 1 cup extra-virgin olive oil
- 4 garlic cloves, minced
- 6 whole dried red chiles
- 2 pounds medium shrimp, peeled and deveined
- 2 large guavas, peeled, seeded, and diced
- ¼ cup minced fresh flat-leaf parsley
- 1 teaspoon salt
- 2 tablespoons chopped green onions

Shrimp and guava together make this a uniquely Florida entrée. The guava is a fist-sized tropical fruit with yellow, red, or greenish-white skin, flesh that ranges in color from yellow to red, a musky perfumy flavor, and lots of seeds—usually more than 100 in each small fruit. Guavas are common in Florida; in cooler climates you can find them in better supermarkets and specialty produce stores.

In a deep, heavy skillet, heat the oil over medium heat. Add the garlic and chiles and cook for 10 seconds. Add the shrimp, raise the heat to medium-high, and cook for about 5 minutes, or until the shrimp curl and turn pink. Add the guava, parsley, and salt and cook to heat through.

Divide the shrimp among 4 serving plates and top with the green onions.

SEARED SCALLOPS WITH ZUCCHINI PICCALILLI
AND SPICY CORN TARTAR SAUCE

WHENEVER THE PATRIOTS SCORE AT HOME, MEN IN REVOLUTIONARY WAR GARB FIRE A SALUTE WITH FLINTLOCK MUSKETS.

PREP TIME
00:30+
MARINATE OVERNIGHT

CHEF: **Chris Schlesinger**, East Coast Grill & Raw Bar, Cambridge

WINE SUGGESTION: McWilliam's Riesling

SERVES 2

ZUCCHINI PICCALILLI

- 1 zucchini, diced
- ½ red onion, diced
- ¼ cup finely chopped seedless green grapes
- Tabasco sauce to taste
- ½ cup cider vinegar
- ⅓ cup granulated sugar
- 2 teaspoons ground coriander
- Salt and freshly ground black pepper

SPICY CORN TARTAR SAUCE

- ½ cup mayonnaise
- 2 tablespoons sweet pickle relish
- ½ cup cooked corn kernels
- 1 teaspoon chipotle chile purée, or more to taste
- 2 tablespoons chopped fresh chervil (see *Note*)
- Juice of 1 lemon, or to taste
- Salt and freshly ground black pepper to taste

SCALLOPS

- 2 teaspoons salt
- 1 tablespoon cracked black pepper
- 1 pound large scallops, cleaned and trimmed
- 1 tablespoon olive oil

A piccalilli is a flavorful pickled vegetable relish, here made from zucchini, but it can include peppers, onions, or virtually any other vegetables. Preparation styles vary from country to country, the most popular American version being the stadium food staple, sweet pickle relish, served with hot dogs.

MAKE THE ZUCCHINI PICCALILLI: In a large bowl, combine all the ingredients except the salt and pepper. Cover and refrigerate overnight, then season with salt and pepper to taste just before serving.

MAKE THE SPICY CORN TARTAR SAUCE: In a medium bowl, combine all the ingredients. Cover and refrigerate until ready to serve. Taste and adjust the seasonings just before serving.

MAKE THE SCALLOPS: Combine the salt and pepper and spread out over a large plate. Rub the scallops all over to coat with the mixture and create a thin crust. Heat the oil in a large nonstick skillet over medium-high heat until very hot but not smoking. Sear the scallops, turning once, until golden brown and just cooked through, about 5 minutes.

Place a mound of piccalilli in the center of 2 large plates. Top with the scallops and a spoonful of the tartar sauce. Serve immediately.

NOTE: *Chervil, a feathery green herb in the parsley family, tastes like a cross between parsley and anise. Fresh chervil is much more flavorful than dried, so seek it out in farmers' markets in the summer. If chervil is unavailable, parsley will work equally well in this recipe.*

WHOLE CRISP SEA BASS
WITH FRIED RICE NOODLES

BUFFALO IS THE ONLY TEAM TO WIN FOUR CONSECUTIVE AFC CHAMPIONSHIPS.

CHEF: Andy DiVincenzo, Billy Ogden's, Buffalo

WINE SUGGESTION: Frei Brothers RR Chardonnay

SERVES 4

PREP TIME
00:30+

SAUCE

1 **cup hoisin sauce**

2 **tablespoons soy sauce**

2 **tablespoons honey, or to taste**

1 **tablespoon grated fresh ginger**

1 **teaspoon Chinese five-spice powder (see Note)**

 Chile oil to taste

¼ **cup sesame oil**

FRIED RICE NOODLES

 Peanut oil for frying

8 **ounces rice vermicelli (mai fun noodles), cut into 2-inch pieces with kitchen shears**

 Salt

SEA BASS

 One 20- to 28-ounce black sea bass, scaled and gutted

 Salt

 Cornstarch for dredging

 Soy sauce

MAKE THE SAUCE: In a food processor, combine the hoisin sauce, soy sauce, honey, ginger, five-spice powder, and chile oil and process until smooth. With the motor running, slowly add the oil through the feed tube and process until thickened. Pour into a squirt bottle and set aside.

MAKE THE FRIED RICE NOODLES: In a large Dutch oven or deep-fryer, heat 3 inches of oil over medium-high heat until it reaches 350°F. Add the rice noodles, a few at a time, and fry until crisp and golden, 3 to 5 minutes. Remove with a slotted spoon and drain on paper towels. Sprinkle lightly with salt.

MAKE THE SEA BASS: Increase the heat under the oil and raise the temperature of the oil to 375°F. Cut 3 slits down to the bone and on an angle on either side of the fish. Season with salt and dredge in cornstarch, rubbing the cornstarch into the cuts and on the fins. Place the fish, standing upright and curled, head to tail, in a fryer basket. Deep-fry for 7 to 8 minutes, until golden brown and crisp and cooked through. Remove from the oil and brush the fish all over with soy sauce. Return to the oil and fry for 1 minute.

Arrange a bed of rice noodles on a serving platter and place the fish on top. Drizzle with the sauce from head to tail and serve immediately.

NOTE: *Chinese five-spice powder is a seasoning made up of equal parts ground cinnamon, cloves, fennel, star anise, and Sichuan peppercorns. You can find premixed jars in Asian markets.*

JASON CAMPBELL'S
CHICKEN CASSEROLE

#17 QUARTERBACK
6'5", 230 POUNDS
AUBURN, b. 12-31-81

PREP TIME
01:30+

CHEF: Jason Campbell

SERVES 6 TO 8

1	teaspoon salt
4	bone-in chicken thighs
1	pound small elbow noodles
½	cup (1 stick) unsalted butter
1	onion, chopped
1	green bell pepper, chopped
4	celery stalks, chopped
	One 10¾-ounce can cream of chicken soup
	One 10¾-ounce can cream of celery soup
	One 10¾-ounce can cream of mushroom soup
8	ounces cheddar cheese, grated

Jason says, "A lot of the food I ate growing up was fresh from the garden. Peas, corn, collard greens, butter beans, okra. Pretty much everything we ate, we went out and picked. Even in a dish like this, I like my veggies to be as fresh as possible."

Bring a large pot of water to a boil. Add the salt and chicken thighs, bring back to a boil, then reduce the heat and simmer about 45 minutes, until the meat is very tender and falling off the bone. Using tongs, remove the chicken from the pot (reserving the cooking liquid) and cool, then remove the meat from the bones and shred it.

Preheat the oven to 375°F.

Return the cooking water to a boil, adding more water to fill the pot if needed. Add the noodles and cook until al dente, about 5 minutes. Drain in a colander placed over a large bowl, reserving the cooking liquid.

In a large saucepan, melt the butter over medium heat. Add the onion, pepper, and celery and sauté until softened, about 5 minutes. Add the chicken and cook for 2 minutes. Add

the soups and 2 cups of the reserved cooking liquid. Bring to a simmer and simmer for 2 minutes.

Spread one-third of the macaroni in a 9-by-13-inch casserole dish. Top with one-third of the chicken mixture. Sprinkle one-third of the cheese over the chicken. Repeat the layers twice, ending with the cheese. Bake until lightly browned, about 20 minutes.

Cut into serving portions and serve immediately.

TREVOR LAWS's
CORN BREAD CASSEROLE

#93 DEFENSIVE TACKLE
6'1", 295 POUNDS
NOTRE DAME, b. 1-14-85

CHEF: Trevor Laws

SERVES 6

PREP TIME
00:30

One 8½-ounce package corn muffin mix

One 8¾-ounce can whole-kernel corn, drained

One 8¼-ounce can cream-style corn

One 8-ounce carton plain yogurt

2   large eggs

4   tablespoons unsalted butter, melted

Trevor says, "This casserole is really moist, it's not dry like regular corn bread. You can eat it with a little bit of jam or even a little bit of homemade barbecue sauce. Oftentimes, if I'm making something on the grill, I'll serve it as a side dish."

Preheat the oven to 350°F.

Coat an 8-inch pie dish with nonstick cooking spray.

Combine all the ingredients in a bowl and stir well to blend. Pour the mixture into the pie dish and bake for 40 to 45 minutes, until the top is lightly golden and crisp.

ASPARAGUS AND SHIITAKE MUSHROOM RISOTTO
WITH BLUE CHEESE

PREP TIME

02:00+

CHEF: Jack McDavid, Jack's Firehouse, Philadelphia

WINE SUGGESTION: Frei Brothers RR Chardonnay

ASPARAGUS AND MUSHROOM STOCK

1	tablespoon olive oil
1	onion, chopped
	Reserved mushroom stems (from risotto)
	Reserved asparagus stems (from risotto)
2	garlic cloves, peeled and left whole
3	fresh bay leaves
2	fresh thyme sprigs
1	cup white wine
6	whole black peppercorns

MUSHROOM SAUCE

1	tablespoon olive oil
15	shiitake mushrooms, stems removed and reserved, caps thinly sliced
1	shallot, minced
1	teaspoon minced garlic
2	tablespoons sherry vinegar
2	tablespoons unsalted butter
½	teaspoon dried thyme
	Salt and freshly ground black pepper

RISOTTO

1	pound (about 35) thin asparagus, ends snapped off and reserved
3	tablespoons olive oil
½	pound (about 10) shiitake mushrooms, stems removed and reserved
4	chives, blanched, chilled in ice water, and dried
3	shallots, chopped
2	garlic cloves, minced
1½	cups Arborio rice
¾	cup white wine
2	tablespoons sherry vinegar
4	ounces blue cheese, such as Maytag
	Salt and freshly ground black pepper

Though any crumbly blue cheese will work, Maytag blue cheese—a rich and piquant cow's milk variety—is a favorite for this dish, as its assertive bite contrasts with the smoothness of the risotto and the earthiness of the asparagus and shiitakes.

MAKE THE ASPARAGUS AND MUSHROOM STOCK: In a large saucepan, heat the oil over medium heat. Add the onion, mushroom stems, asparagus stems, garlic, bay leaves, and thyme and sauté until the onion and mushroom stems are caramelized, about 20 minutes. Add the wine and stir, scraping up the browned bits from the bottom of the pan, until almost evaporated. Add 8 cups water and the peppercorns, raise the heat to medium-high, and bring to a boil. Reduce the heat and simmer for 45 minutes, then strain and return to the saucepan. Keep at a bare simmer over low heat.

IN 1976, AT AGE 30, BARTENDER VINCE PAPALE JOINED THE EAGLES, BECOMING THE OLDEST ROOKIE IN NFL HISTORY.

SERVES 4

MAKE THE MUSHROOM SAUCE: In a medium sauté pan, heat the oil over medium heat. Add the mushrooms, shallot, and garlic and cook until softened, about 5 minutes. Add ½ cup of the stock and the vinegar and stir, scraping up the browned bits from the pan. Bring to a boil, then reduce the heat to a simmer. Swirl in the butter and add the thyme and salt and pepper to taste. Set aside and reheat just before serving.

MAKE THE RISOTTO: In a large bowl, toss the asparagus with ½ tablespoon of the oil. In a separate bowl, toss the mushroom caps with ½ tablespoon of the remaining oil. Heat a stovetop grill pan over medium-high heat until hot. Put the asparagus and mushroom caps on the grill pan and cook until browned and tender, about 5 minutes, then remove from the pan. Dice the mushroom caps and set aside. Gather 8 asparagus spears and tie them together with a blanched chive. Repeat to make 4 asparagus bundles. Slice any leftover asparagus spears on the diagonal and set aside.

In a medium heavy saucepan, heat the remaining 2 tablespoons oil over medium heat. Add the shallots and garlic and sauté until softened, about 5 minutes. Add the rice and stir with a wooden spoon to coat with the oil, about 1 minute. Add the wine and vinegar and cook, stirring, until absorbed, about 2 minutes. Add ½ cup of the simmering mushroom stock and cook, stirring constantly, until the broth is absorbed. Continue simmering and adding broth, about ½ cup at a time, stirring constantly and letting each addition be absorbed before adding the next, until the rice is creamy but still al dente, 18 to 22 minutes. (You may have leftover stock.) Remove from the heat and stir in the diced mushroom caps, sliced asparagus, and half of the blue cheese. Season with salt and pepper to taste.

Spoon the risotto into the center of each of 4 serving plates and spoon the sauce around the risotto. Top with the asparagus bundles and crumble the remaining blue cheese on top.

EGGPLANT AND SWISS CHARD CRÊPES
WITH TOMATO-BASIL COULIS

PREP TIME
01:00+
LET STAND 1 HOUR

CHEF: Paul O'Connell, Chez Henri, Cambridge

WINE SUGGESTION: Whitehaven Sauvignon Blanc

TOMATO-BASIL COULIS

- 2 pounds tomatoes, peeled (see page 181)
- ½ cup chopped fresh basil
- 2 tablespoons olive oil
  Salt and freshly ground black pepper

CRÊPES

- 2 large eggs
- ¼ teaspoon salt
- 1 cup all-purpose flour
- 1¼ cups milk
  Melted unsalted butter

FILLING

- 3 pounds eggplant
- ½ cup olive oil
- 1 cup diced onions
- 2 teaspoons ground cardamom
  Salt and freshly ground black pepper
- 2 tablespoons fresh lemon juice
- 2 tablespoons chopped fresh cilantro
- 2 tablespoons minced scallion
- ½ cup soft goat cheese, at room temperature
- ¼ cup ricotta cheese
- 1 large egg yolk
- 2 tablespoons fines herbes (see *Note*)
- ½ teaspoon grated lemon zest
- 4 cups Swiss chard cut into chiffonade

- 1 cup grated Parmesan cheese

MAKE THE TOMATO-BASIL COULIS: Cut the tomatoes in half crosswise and use a spoon to remove the core and seeds. Put the tomatoes in a food processor and process until smooth. Add the basil and pulse to combine. Transfer to a bowl, stir in the oil, and season with salt and pepper to taste. Let stand, stirring occasionally, for the flavors to develop while you complete the recipe.

MAKE THE CRÊPE BATTER: Beat the eggs and salt in a large bowl. Gradually beat in the flour, followed by the milk. Strain through a fine-mesh sieve into a bowl. Cover and refrigerate for 1 hour.

MAKE THE FILLING: Meanwhile, preheat the oven to 450°F. Puncture each eggplant a few times with the tip of a small knife and put on a baking sheet. Roast for about 40 minutes, or until the eggplant is very soft and collapsed. Remove from the oven and let cool to room temperature. Lower the oven temperature to 375°F.

COOK THE CRÊPES: Heat a medium nonstick skillet over medium-high heat and brush with butter. Pour a scant ¼ cup of the batter into the skillet and quickly swirl to coat the bottom. Cook until set and lightly golden underneath, about 45 seconds, then flip and cook on the other side until lightly golden, 15 to 30 seconds. Repeat with the remaining batter, brushing the skillet with butter between crêpes. Transfer the crêpes to a plate, stacking them as they are cooked, and set aside.

FINISH THE FILLING: In a sauté pan, heat 2 tablespoons of the oil over medium heat. Add the onions and sauté until softened, about 5 minutes. Add the cardamom and salt and pepper to taste and cook for an additional 5 minutes, or until the onions are very soft and the mixture is aromatic. Remove from the heat and transfer to a food processor.

Split each eggplant open and scoop

SERVES 4

out the pulp. Add the eggplant pulp and lemon juice to the food processor and purée. With the motor running, slowly add ¼ cup of the remaining oil through the feed tube and process until smooth. Add the cilantro and scallion and pulse a few times to combine. Transfer to a bowl.

Clean the food processor bowl and add the goat cheese, ricotta cheese, and egg yolk and pulse to combine, scraping down the sides of the bowl if necessary. Transfer to a bowl and fold in the fines herbes and lemon zest. Season with salt and pepper to taste.

In a large sauté pan, heat the remaining 2 tablespoons olive oil over medium heat. Add the Swiss chard and cook, tossing with tongs, until softened, about 5 minutes. Season with salt and pepper to taste. Remove from the pan to a sieve to drain and cool.

ASSEMBLE AND BAKE THE CRÊPES: Spread most of the tomato-basil coulis over a large casserole dish, reserving some for topping. Place the crêpes on a flat surface and spoon the eggplant filling evenly over the crêpes. At one end of each crêpe, place some of the Swiss chard in a cigar shape, followed by some of the cheese mixture. Roll the crêpes up jelly-roll style. Arrange the crêpes seam side down over the coulis, sprinkle with Parmesan cheese, and bake until heated through and the cheese is melted, about 30 minutes.

Spoon some of the sauce over each of 4 serving plates. Top each plate with 2 crêpes and serve immediately.

NOTE: *Fines herbes is a classic French mixture of herbs, usually including parsley, tarragon, chervil, and chives. Dried fines herbes is available in the spice section of most markets.*

DEMARCUS WARE'S
CHEESY CHICKEN AND BROCCOLI CASSEROLE

#94 LINEBACKER
6'4", 257 POUNDS
TROY UNIVERSITY, b. 7-31-82

PREP TIME

00:30+

CHEF: **DeMarcus Ware**

SERVES 8

One 6-ounce Stove Top Stuffing Mix for Chicken

1½ pounds boneless, skinless chicken breast, cut into 1-inch pieces

One 16-ounce bag frozen broccoli florets, thawed and drained

One 10¾-ounce can cream of chicken soup

8 ounces processed American cheese, cut into ½-inch cubes

DeMarcus Ware is a big fan of broccoli. This dish, adapted from a signature Kraft recipe, is one of his favorites, and DeMarcus's wife, Taniqua, makes it for them often.

Preheat the oven to 400°F.

Prepare the stuffing mix according to the package directions. Set aside to cool.

Meanwhile, combine the chicken, broccoli, soup, ½ cup water, and cheese in a 9-by-13-inch baking dish. Top with the stuffing, spreading evenly over the chicken mixture.

Bake for about 30 minutes, until the chicken is cooked through and the topping is lightly browned.

Cut into serving portions while still hot and serve immediately.

LEE EVANS's
BANANA PUDDING

#83 WIDE RECEIVER
5'10", 197 POUNDS
UNIVERSITY OF WISCONSIN, b. 3-11-81

CHEF: Lee Evans

SERVES 8 TO 10

PREP TIME
00:30
CHILL 4 HOURS

Half of a 12-ounce box vanilla wafers

4 large egg yolks

¾ cup sugar

¼ cup cornstarch

¼ teaspoon salt

3 cups milk

4 tablespoons (½ stick) unsalted butter, cut into pieces

1 teaspoon vanilla extract

4 ripe bananas

Whipped cream (optional)

When Lee Evans was a boy growing up in northern Ohio, comfort food meant his aunt's silky-smooth banana pudding. For best results, make sure your bananas are ripe but still firm and you cover them completely with pudding to prevent browning.

Line the bottom of a 2-quart baking dish with vanilla wafers and set aside.

In a medium bowl, lightly beat the egg yolks and set aside. In the top of a double boiler over simmering water, whisk together the sugar, cornstarch, and salt. Slowly add the milk, whisking to dissolve the sugar and cornstarch, then whisk constantly until hot and slightly thickened, 5 to 7 minutes. Slowly add some of the heated milk mixture to the eggs to temper them, then pour the mixture back into the double boiler. Add the butter and stir constantly until the mixture thickens enough to coat the back of a spoon, 2 to 3 minutes. Remove from the heat and stir in the vanilla. Pour half the pudding into the wafer-lined pan while still hot, then quickly slice half the bananas directly into the baking dish.

Arrange a layer of wafers over the bananas, then top with half of the remaining pudding and the remaining bananas. Finish with the remaining pudding, spreading it over the bananas to fully cover them. Cover with plastic, pressing the plastic directly onto the surface of the pudding if you don't want a skin. Cool to room temperature, then refrigerate for at least 4 hours or overnight.

Spoon into dessert bowls and top with whipped cream if you like.

CHOCOLATE-PECAN TOFFEE TORTE

PREP TIME

02:00+

LET SET AT LEAST 4 HOURS

CHEF: **Jack McDavid,** Jack's Firehouse, Philadelphia

WINE SUGGESTION: Barefoot Bubbly

PECAN LAYER

1½ cups pecan halves

½ cup packed light brown sugar

2 tablespoons all-purpose flour

2 tablespoons unsalted butter, chilled and cut into pieces

CHOCOLATE LAYER

¾ cup heavy cream

6 ounces semisweet chocolate, cut into small pieces

1 tablespoon corn syrup

1 tablespoon unsalted butter

TOFFEE CREAM LAYER

½ cup plus 1½ tablespoons granulated sugar

2 tablespoons corn syrup

2 cups half-and-half

2 teaspoons vanilla extract

1½ tablespoons instant espresso or coffee granules

2 large eggs

2 large egg yolks

4 tablespoons cornstarch

1 cup confectioners' sugar

1½ cups (3 sticks) unsalted butter, cut into pieces, at room temperature

Whipped cream

Chopped toasted pecans

Each layer of this torte requires time for setting, so if you're serving it the same day, tackle the first layer early on. Or plan ahead and divide your time evenly, making each layer on a separate day.

MAKE THE PECAN LAYER: Preheat the oven to 350°F. Coat a 9-inch springform pan with cooking spray.

In a food processor, combine the pecans, sugar, flour, and butter and pulse until the mixture resembles coarse crumbs. Press the mixture into the bottom of the pan, place the pan on a baking sheet, and bake for about 10 minutes, until light golden and set. Remove from the oven and cool completely on a wire rack. Set aside.

IN 1943, THE EAGLES BRIEFLY MERGED WITH THE STEELERS TO FORM THE PHIL-PITT STEAGLES.

SERVES 8

MAKE THE CHOCOLATE LAYER: In a medium saucepan, heat the cream over medium heat until bubbles form around the edges. Remove from the heat, add the chocolate, and whisk until the chocolate melts. Add the corn syrup and butter and whisk until the mixture is smooth. Pour the mixture over the cooked pecan layer, cool, then cover with plastic wrap and refrigerate until set, at least 2 hours or overnight.

MAKE THE TOFFEE CREAM LAYER: In a medium saucepan, combine ½ cup granulated sugar, the corn syrup, and 1 tablespoon water over medium heat and stir until the sugar dissolves. Increase the heat and bring to a boil without stirring until the mixture turns a deep red-brown, 5 to 7 minutes. Reduce heat and slowly add half-and-half; heat until small bubbles form around the edges. Remove from the heat and add the vanilla.

Combine the instant espresso granules with 3 tablespoons hot water and stir to dissolve. Set aside. In a large bowl, beat the eggs and egg yolks. Beat in the remaining 1½ tablespoons granulated sugar and the cornstarch until smooth. Whisking constantly, slowly pour in ½ cup of the hot caramel mixture to temper the eggs. Slowly return the mixture to the saucepan, whisk until smooth, and place the pan over medium heat. Whisking constantly, bring the mixture to a boil. Remove from the heat and transfer to a bowl.

Using an electric mixer on medium speed, beat the mixture for 1 minute to cool slightly. Lower the mixer speed and add the confectioners' sugar and dissolved espresso. When the mixture has cooled slightly but is still warm, beat in the butter, bit by bit, until all the butter is incorporated and the mixture is smooth with no lumps of butter remaining.

Spread the toffee cream over the chocolate layer and smooth with a spatula. Cool, then cover with plastic and refrigerate until set, at least 2 hours or overnight.

Carefully release the clip on the rim of the pan and lift it off the torte. Cut into 8 slices and serve topped with whipped cream and chopped pecans.

ERNEST WILFORD'S
APPLE SURPRISE

#18 WIDE RECEIVER
6'4", 223 POUNDS
VIRGINIA TECH, b. 1-14-79

PREP TIME
01:00+

CHEF: **Ernest Wilford**

SERVES 12 TO 16

1	box yellow cake mix
⅓	cup margarine or unsalted butter, softened
2	large eggs
	One 21-ounce can apple pie filling
½	cup firmly packed brown sugar
1	teaspoon ground cinnamon
½	cup coarsely chopped almonds or walnuts
1	cup sour cream
1	teaspoon vanilla extract

Preheat the oven to 350°F.

In a large bowl using an electric mixer on low, beat together the cake mix, margarine, and 1 of the eggs, until crumbly. Press into an ungreased 9-by-13-inch baking pan. Spread the apple pie filling evenly over the top.

In a small bowl, combine the brown sugar, cinnamon, and almonds; sprinkle the mixture over the apple layer.

In another small bowl, beat the sour cream, remaining egg, and vanilla. Pour over the brown sugar mixture.

Place in the oven and bake until a toothpick inserted in the center comes out clean, 50 to 60 minutes. Cool completely on a wire rack before serving.

FROZEN ORANGE SOUFFLÉ

FORMER DOLPHINS' HEAD COACH DON SHULA IS THE MOST SUCCESSFUL COACH IN NFL HISTORY, WITH 24 WINNING SEASONS.

CHEF: Allen Susser, Chef Allen's, Aventura

WINE SUGGESTION: Barefoot Bubbly

SERVES 6

PREP TIME
00:30+
FREEZE AT LEAST 4 HOURS

1½ teaspoons unflavored gelatin

Juice of 2 large oranges, preferably Valencia (about ¾ cup)

4 large egg whites

Pinch of salt

⅔ cup granulated sugar

1 cup heavy cream

1 tablespoon vodka

Confectioners' sugar

Candied orange slices

Fresh mint sprigs

Wrap parchment paper or foil around six 4-ounce soufflé molds to form a 1-inch collar and tape the overlapping ends together if necessary.

In a medium heatproof bowl set over a pan of simmering water, dissolve the gelatin in the orange juice. Set the bowl in an ice bath until the mixture is chilled and slightly thick, about 20 minutes, stirring frequently.

Meanwhile, place the egg whites and salt in a large bowl and set aside while you make the sugar syrup.

In a medium saucepan, combine the granulated sugar with 2 tablespoons water over medium heat and stir until the sugar dissolves. Bring to a boil without stirring, washing down any sugar crystals from the sides of the pan with a pastry brush dipped in cold water. When the mixture reaches 230°F, using an electric mixer, begin beating the egg whites on high speed until stiff peaks form. Continue boiling the syrup until it reaches 240°F. Remove the syrup from the heat and lower the mixer speed to medium. Pour the syrup into the egg whites in a thin, steady stream between the beater and the side of the bowl. Turn the mixer speed back to high and continue to beat the meringue until it cools to room temperature and forms stiff peaks, about 10 minutes.

In a medium bowl using the clean beaters of an electric mixer, beat the cream until soft peaks form. Fold in the vodka.

Beat one fourth of the meringue into the gelatin mixture to lighten, then fold the gelatin mixture into the meringue, along with the whipped cream.

Spoon the mixture into the ramekins, filling them ⅓ to 1 inch above the rims. Freeze until firm, then cover with plastic wrap and freeze at least 4 hours, or overnight.

Remove the soufflés from the freezer and let stand at room temperature for about 15 minutes before serving. Remove the collars and dust with confectioners' sugar. Top with candied orange slices, garnish with mint sprigs, and serve.

ANGEL FOOD CAKES
WITH STRAWBERRY SORBET
AND RHUBARB COMPOTE

THE REDSKINS ARE ONE OF ONLY TWO
TEAMS IN THE NFL WITH AN OFFICIAL
MARCHING BAND.

PREP TIME
02:00+
CHILL 1 HOUR

CHEF: Jeffrey "J.G." Gaetjen, Kinkead's, Washington, D.C.

WINE SUGGESTION: Barefoot Bubbly

SERVES 4

STRAWBERRY SORBET

1	cup mineral water (not sparkling)
½	cup sugar
¼	cup light corn syrup
2	cups strawberry purée (see *Note*)

RHUBARB COMPOTE

½	cup sugar
1	pound rhubarb, peeled and diced
2	teaspoons kirsch (cherry brandy)

ANGEL FOOD CAKES

½	cup cake flour
¼	cup plus 2 tablespoons sugar
	Pinch of salt
6	large egg whites
½	teaspoon cream of tartar
¾	teaspoon fresh lemon juice
½	teaspoon grated orange zest
½	teaspoon vanilla extract
	Fresh mint sprigs

MAKE THE STRAWBERRY SORBET: In a medium saucepan, bring the mineral water, sugar, and corn syrup to a boil over medium heat, stirring until the sugar is dissolved. Remove from the heat and transfer to a medium bowl to cool. Add the strawberry purée, cover, and refrigerate until cold, at least 1 hour. Transfer to an ice cream machine and churn according to the manufacturer's instructions.

MAKE THE RHUBARB COMPOTE: Meanwhile, in a medium saucepan, bring ½ cup water and the sugar to a boil over medium heat, stirring until the sugar is dissolved. Add the rhubarb, lower the heat, and simmer until softened, about 3 minutes. Add the kirsch. Remove from the heat and transfer to a bowl to cool. Cover and refrigerate until cold, at least 1 hour.

MAKE THE ANGEL FOOD CAKES: Preheat the oven to 375°F. In a medium bowl, sift together the flour, 2 tablespoons sugar, and the salt. In a separate bowl with an electric mixer, beat the egg whites and cream of tartar until soft peaks form. Add the ¼ cup sugar in 3 parts, beating in each addition before adding the next. Turn the mixer speed down, add the lemon juice, orange zest, and vanilla and beat until stiff peaks form. Sift the flour-sugar mixture into the egg-white mixture, then gently fold it in.

Place four 3-inch stainless steel rings or ceramic soufflé molds on a baking sheet. Do not spray or grease the rings. Spoon the mixture into the molds about three-quarters of the way up. Bake for 15 to 18 minutes, until the cake tops are golden. Cool the cakes on a wire rack for 5 minutes, then cut them out of the rings with a small knife. Set aside.

Place a cake in the middle of each of 4 plates. Spoon the rhubarb compote around the cakes and top with a scoop of sorbet. Garnish with mint sprigs and serve immediately.

NOTE: *You can make your own strawberry purée by combining 1½ pints fresh strawberries, sliced, with ½ cup sugar in a medium saucepan over medium heat. Bring just to a boil, then remove from the heat, purée in a food processor, and strain.*

NORTH

BEEF CARPACCIO ROLLS
WITH APPLE SYRUP

FROM 1946 TO 1949 CLEVELAND WON
4 STRAIGHT AAFC CHAMPIONSHIPS,
BEFORE JOINING THE NFL IN 1950.

CHEF: Rocco Whalen, Fahrenheit, Cleveland

WINE SUGGESTION: McWilliam's Cabernet Sauvignon

SERVES 6

PREP TIME
00:30+
FREEZE 1 HOUR

BEEF CARPACCIO ROLLS

One 1-pound beef sirloin, well trimmed

7 **tablespoons olive oil**

Salt and coarsely ground black pepper

10 **ounces mushrooms, thinly sliced**

1 **cup bean sprouts**

APPLE SYRUP

2 **tablespoons olive oil**

1 **onion, diced**

2 **garlic cloves, minced**

2 **teaspoons minced fresh ginger**

2 **tart apples, peeled, cored, and minced**

2 **scallions, minced**

1 **quart apple cider**

¼ **cup cider vinegar, or more if needed**

1 **tablespoon soy sauce**

MAKE THE BEEF CARPACCIO: Rub 1 tablespoon of the oil all over the beef, then coat liberally with salt and pepper, pressing the salt and pepper into the beef. Let stand for 20 minutes at room temperature. Heat 2 tablespoons of the remaining oil in a large, heavy skillet over medium-high heat. Add the beef and sear on all sides, turning with tongs about every 2 minutes, about 12 minutes total. Remove from the heat to a plate and cool completely. Cover in plastic wrap and freeze for 1 hour.

In a medium skillet, heat the remaining 2 tablespoons oil over medium heat. Add the mushrooms and sauté until softened, about 5 minutes. Add the sprouts and cook for about 2 minutes, until wilted. Season with salt and pepper to taste. Set aside to cool.

MAKE THE APPLE SYRUP: Meanwhile, heat the remaining oil in a large saucepan over medium heat. Add the onion and sauté until softened and golden brown, about 10 minutes. Add the garlic and ginger and sauté for 1 minute. Add the apples and sauté until softened and the onions are almost caramelized, about 5 minutes. Add the scallions and sauté for 1 minute. Add the apple cider, vinegar, and soy sauce and stir to scrape up any browned bits from the bottom of the pan. Cook until the liquid is reduced by half, about 20 minutes. Taste and add more vinegar if needed. Set aside until ready to serve.

ROLL THE BEEF CARPACCIO: Using a very sharp knife, slice the meat as thinly as possible. Place each slice between two sheets of waxed paper or plastic wrap and pound with a kitchen mallet until paper-thin.

Lay out 1 slice of beef on a flat surface. Place some mushrooms and bean sprouts on the end of the beef slice closest to you and roll up tightly; place seam side down on a serving platter. Repeat with the remaining beef and mushrooms and sprouts. If you're not serving right away, cover with plastic and refrigerate until ready to serve.

Drizzle the beef with the apple syrup and serve immediately.

PROSCIUTTO AND SWISS CHARD–WRAPPED MOZZARELLA

THE PACKERS ARE THE ONLY
COMMUNITY-OWNED MAJOR-LEAGUE
PROFESSIONAL SPORTS TEAM IN THE U.S.

CHEF: Sanford D'Amato, Sanford, Milwaukee

WINE SUGGESTION: DaVinci Chianti

SERVES 6

PREP TIME
00:30+

PROSCIUTTO AND SWISS CHARD–WRAPPED MOZZARELLA

12 large Swiss chard leaves

18 ounces smoked mozzarella cheese, cut into 12 equal pieces

Freshly ground black pepper

6 paper-thin slices prosciutto, cut in half

Extra-virgin olive oil

ANCHOVY SAUCE

2 tablespoons extra-virgin olive oil

6 teaspoons minced shallots

¾ cup dry white wine

¼ cup heavy cream

½ teaspoon minced garlic

¼ cup packed fresh parsley sprigs

¾ ounce anchovy fillets in oil

2 teaspoons fresh lemon juice

¼ teaspoon freshly ground black pepper

Pinch of ground cayenne pepper

4 tablespoons unsalted butter, at room temperature

MAKE THE PROSCIUTTO AND SWISS CHARD–WRAPPED MOZZARELLA:
Blanch the chard for about 10 seconds in a pot of boiling water, until softened. Drain, then immediately plunge the chard into a bowl of ice water to cool. Drain and pat dry with paper towels. Season the mozzarella with pepper. Wrap each piece of mozzarella in a half slice of prosciutto and then wrap one leaf of chard around the prosciutto to make a neat package. Place on a plate seam side down, brush with oil, and set aside until ready to cook.

MAKE THE ANCHOVY SAUCE: In a small saucepan, heat 1 tablespoon of the oil over medium heat. Add 4 teaspoons of the shallots and cook for 20 seconds. Add the wine and cook until reduced to a glaze. Add the cream and remove from the heat. Cover and set aside until ready to serve.

Place the remaining 2 teaspoons shallots and the garlic in a sieve and rinse under hot water. Transfer to a mini food processor, add the remaining 1 tablespoon oil, the parsley, anchovies, lemon juice, black pepper, and cayenne, and blend to a paste. Add the butter and process until smooth. Just before serving, reheat the cream reduction, then whisk in the anchovy butter mixture and heat through but do not bring to a boil.

GRILL THE CHEESE: Heat a stovetop grill pan over medium-high heat. Lightly pat the cheese packages with paper towels to absorb excess oil. Grill for about 1 minute on each side, until just soft but not melting.

Place 2 mozzarella packages on each of 6 serving plates and spoon a small amount of sauce around the cheese.

PEPPERY GLAZED CHICKEN WINGS
WITH GARLIC CHIPS

IN 2006 WILD CARD PITTSBURGH
CAPTURED ITS 5TH SUPER BOWL WIN—
"THE ONE FOR THE THUMB."

CHEF: **Anthony Zello,** Bigelow Grille, Pittsburgh

WINE SUGGESTION: Bridlewood Syrah

SERVES 4

PREP TIME
01:00+

GARLIC CHIPS

- ½ **cup grapeseed oil (see page 178)**
- 15 **garlic cloves, very thinly sliced**
  Salt

CHICKEN WINGS

- 4 **pounds chicken wings**
- ½ **cup sesame oil**
- 2 **tablespoons minced garlic**
  Salt and freshly ground black pepper
- 2 **cups cider vinegar**
- 1½ **cups sugar**
- 3 **tablespoons cracked black pepper**
- 5 **garlic cloves, crushed**
- 1 **tablespoon red pepper flakes**

MAKE THE GARLIC CHIPS: Heat the oil in a medium skillet over medium-low heat. Add the garlic and fry until lightly browned, about 5 minutes. Using a slotted spoon, transfer to paper towels to drain and sprinkle with salt. Set aside.

MAKE THE CHICKEN WINGS: Preheat the oven to 425°F. Line a large baking sheet with aluminum foil.

In a large bowl, combine the oil and minced garlic. Add the chicken wings and turn to coat. Season with salt and pepper to taste. Place the chicken wings on the baking sheet in one layer and bake, turning once, until cooked through and lightly browned, about 30 minutes.

Meanwhile, in a medium saucepan, combine the vinegar, sugar, 1 cup water, the cracked pepper, crushed garlic, and red pepper flakes. Bring to a boil, then reduce the heat and simmer until the mixture becomes syrupy, about 30 minutes. Transfer the cooked chicken wings to a large bowl and toss with the glaze.

Divide the wings among 4 serving plates. Garnish with the garlic chips and serve immediately.

SOFT-SHELL CRAB TEMPURA
WITH TOMATO DIPPING SAUCE

IN 2001 THE RAVENS WON BALTIMORE'S
FIRST SUPER BOWL IN 30 YEARS,
BEATING THE GIANTS 34–7.

PREP TIME 01:00

CHEF: Nancy Longo, Pierpoint, Baltimore

WINE SUGGESTION: Maso Canali

SERVES 4

TOMATO DIPPING SAUCE

- ⅔ **cup mayonnaise**
- ¼ **cup canned crushed roasted tomatoes, drained of juice**
- ½ **teaspoon chipotle chile powder, or to taste**
- 1 **tablespoon fresh lime juice, or to taste**
- 1 **teaspoon brown sugar**
- 1 **teaspoon Tabasco sauce**
- **Salt to taste**

SOFT-SHELL CRAB TEMPURA

- **Vegetable oil for frying**
- 1 **cup ice water**
- 1 **large egg yolk**
- ¼ **cup chopped fresh chives**
- ¼ **teaspoon salt**
- 1 **cup all-purpose flour**
- 4 **soft-shell crabs, cleaned (see Note)**

- **Lemon wedges**

MAKE THE TOMATO DIPPING SAUCE: In a medium bowl, combine all the ingredients. Cover with plastic wrap and refrigerate until ready to serve.

MAKE THE SOFT-SHELL CRAB TEMPURA: In a large saucepan, heat 3 inches of oil over medium-high heat to 375°F.

In a medium bowl, whisk the ice water, egg yolk, chives, and salt until frothy. Add the flour and whisk just until blended and small lumps remain. Dip the crabs in the batter, then carefully add to the oil, 2 at a time, and fry for about 5 minutes, until cooked through and golden brown. Using a slotted spoon, transfer to paper towels to drain.

Place each crab on a serving plate and spoon some tomato dipping sauce onto each plate. Garnish with lemon wedges and serve immediately.

NOTE: *Ask your fish market to clean your crabs if possible. If you're cleaning them yourself, fold back the flaps and remove the gills. Cut off the side aprons and head with kitchen shears. Pull the pointed flap on the underside down and twist it off. Remove the tomalley (liver) and discard.*

CREAMY POLENTA
WITH MASCARPONE AND WHITE TRUFFLE OIL

IN 1948 THE BROWNS BECAME THE FIRST UNBEATEN AND UNTIED TEAM IN PRO FOOTBALL HISTORY.

CHEF: **Paul Minnillo,** Baricelli Inn, Cleveland

WINE SUGGESTION: McWilliam's Chardonnay

SERVES 4

PREP TIME

00:30

2 **cups low-sodium chicken broth**

2 **cups heavy cream**

1 **cup fine white cornmeal**

½ **cup (1 stick) unsalted butter, cut into pieces**

¼ **cup mascarpone cheese, plus more for garnish**

Juice of 1 lemon, or to taste

2 **tablespoons chopped fresh tarragon**

2 **tablespoons chopped fresh thyme**

¼ **cup grated Parmesan cheese**

Salt and freshly ground black pepper

White truffle oil

Fresh tarragon sprigs

Fresh thyme sprigs

In a large saucepan, combine the broth and cream and place over medium heat. Heat just until bubbles begin to form around the edges (watch the pot so it doesn't boil over) and slowly add the cornmeal, whisking constantly until smooth and creamy. Reduce the heat to low and simmer, stirring constantly with a wooden spoon, until the mixture is thick but pourable and leaves the sides of the pan as you stir it, about 20 minutes. Remove from the heat and beat the butter and mascarpone into the polenta. Add the lemon juice, chopped tarragon, chopped thyme, Parmesan, and salt and pepper to taste.

Spoon the polenta onto serving plates and drizzle with truffle oil. Garnish with tarragon and thyme sprigs and a dollop of mascarpone.

MELON GAZPACHO
WITH SHRIMP AND HERB SALAD

FORMER BENGALS RUNNING BACK ICKEY WOODS IS FAMOUS FOR HIS CELEBRATORY TOUCHDOWN DANCE, "THE ICKEY SHUFFLE."

PREP TIME
01:00+
MARINATE OVERNIGHT

CHEF: Jean-Robert de Cavel, Jean-Robert at Pigall's, Cincinnati

WINE SUGGESTION: Bridlewood Viognier

SERVES 6

GAZPACHO

3 slices white bread, crusts removed, cubed

1 tomato, seeded and diced

1 celery stalk, diced

½ red bell pepper, seeded and diced

½ green bell pepper, seeded and diced

½ yellow bell pepper, seeded and diced

¼ cantaloupe, seeded and diced

¼ bulb fennel, diced

¼ cucumber, peeled, seeded, and diced

¼ onion, diced

1 cup seeded and diced watermelon

2 cups tomato juice

3 tablespoons fresh lemon juice

1 teaspoon Tabasco sauce, or to taste

 Salt and freshly ground black pepper to taste

SHRIMP AND HERB SALAD

3 tablespoons ketchup

2 tablespoons mayonnaise

 Splash of brandy

1 cup diced cantaloupe

6 ounces cooked small peeled and deveined shrimp

¼ cup peeled, seeded, and diced cucumber

¼ cup seeded and diced watermelon

1 fresh basil sprig, chopped

1 fresh cilantro sprig, chopped

1 fresh mint sprig, chopped

1 fresh oregano sprig, chopped, plus more for garnish

 Salt and freshly ground black pepper to taste

MAKE THE GAZPACHO: In a large bowl, combine all the ingredients. Cover and refrigerate overnight to marinate. In a blender or food processor, blend a couple of cups at a time until just slightly chunky.

MAKE THE SHRIMP AND HERB SALAD: For the dressing, in a blender, combine the ketchup, mayonnaise, and brandy, and blend until smooth. In a large bowl, combine the remaining ingredients and gently toss with the dressing. Refrigerate until ready to serve.

Divide the gazpacho among 6 bowls. Top with the shrimp and herb salad and garnish with oregano sprigs.

CRIS COLLINSWORTH'S
SMOKED SALMON PIZZA

COLLINSWORTH CAUGHT 417 PASSES FOR 6,698 YARDS AND 36 TDs IN HIS 8-YEAR CAREER AS A BENGALS WIDE RECEIVER.

PREP TIME
00:30

CHEF: Cris Collinsworth, Co-host, Football Night in America

SERVES 4 TO 6

One 12-inch thin-crust Boboli pizza crust

One 8-ounce package cream cheese

1 to 1½ tablespoons bottled horseradish

¼ cup finely chopped red onion

2 tablespoons capers

One 4-ounce package smoked salmon, thinly sliced

½ cup red onion cut into rings

1 tablespoon chopped fresh dill

Chris says, "For watching ballgames at home, we specialize in junk food. One of our favorite family snack foods is, we take cream cheese and spread it in the bottom of a dish, and then put Cincinnati's famous hot Skyline chili on top of it. And you have a dip. It's gobbled up faster than anything else. This smoked salmon pizza is another favorite in our home, and it starts with cream cheese, too."

Preheat the oven to 450°F.

Bake the pizza crust directly on the oven rack for about 5 minutes, until lightly browned and crisp. Cool slightly.

In a medium bowl, combine the cream cheese, horseradish, chopped onion, and capers, using a kitchen fork to fully incorporate the ingredients. Spread the cream cheese mixture evenly over the pizza crust, then top with the smoked salmon and onion rings. Sprinkle the dill on top and cut into slices using kitchen shears. Serve immediately.

CHAD GREENWAY'S
CHICKEN NOODLE SOUP

#52 LINEBACKER
6'2", 242 POUNDS
UNIVERSITY OF IOWA, b. 1-12-83

CHEFS: **Chad Greenway** and his wife, **Jenni Greenway**

SERVES 12

PREP TIME
00:30

2 pounds bone-in chicken breast

12 cups low-sodium chicken broth

2 cups chopped celery

2 cups chopped carrots

8 ounces wide egg noodles, cooked al dente

Salt and freshly ground black pepper

Jenni Greenway makes this soup for Chad throughout the season to get him through those long Minnesota winters. Jenni makes her noodles from scratch, but using packaged noodles makes this a quick but satisfying weeknight meal.

Bring the broth to a boil in a large saucepan. Add the chicken, bring to a simmer, and cook for 15 to 20 minutes, until just cooked through. Using tongs, remove the chicken to a plate and cool. Remove the meat from the bone and shred. Add the celery and carrots to the broth, return to a boil, and simmer for 5 minutes. Add the noodles and chicken and cook to heat through. Season with salt and pepper to taste.

Spoon into soup bowls and serve immediately.

FRAGRANT CURRY SOUP
WITH CRANBERRY AND RADISH CHUTNEY

PREP TIME 01:30	CHEF: **Sanford D'Amato,** Sanford, Milwaukee
	WINE SUGGESTION: MacMurray SC Pinot Noir

CURRY SOUP

1	cinnamon stick, crushed
1	tablespoon peppercorns
1	tablespoon fennel seeds
½	tablespoon yellow mustard seeds
¼	teaspoon ground allspice
¼	teaspoon red pepper flakes
3	tablespoons grapeseed oil (see page 178)
1	onion, diced
1	leek, cleaned and sliced, white and light green parts only
2	carrots, sliced
2	celery stalks, sliced
2	pears, peeled, cored, and diced
2	garlic cloves, sliced
¼	cup sliced ginger
	Salt and freshly ground black pepper
2	tablespoons mild curry powder
1	teaspoon garam masala
8	cups low-sodium chicken broth, plus more if needed

CRANBERRY AND RADISH CHUTNEY

1	teaspoon black mustard seeds
¼	cup packed brown sugar
¼	cup red wine vinegar
1	cup diced radishes
	Pinch of ground cayenne pepper
1	cup dried cranberries
	Salt and freshly ground black pepper

CARDAMOM CREAM

¼	cup heavy cream
½	teaspoon ground cardamom
¼	teaspoon honey
¼	teaspoon fresh lemon juice

THE PACKERS HAVE WON
12 NFL CHAMPIONSHIPS,
MORE THAN ANY OTHER TEAM.

SERVES 8

MAKE THE CURRY SOUP: In a small skillet, combine the cinnamon, peppercorns, fennel seeds, yellow mustard seeds, and allspice. Place over medium heat and toast for 1 to 2 minutes, until the spices are fragrant and starting to color. Add the red pepper flakes, stir, then immediately transfer the spice mixture to a spice grinder and coarsely grind. Place the spice mixture in a double thickness of cheesecloth and tie together with string into a bundle.

In a large saucepan, heat the oil over medium heat. Add the onion, leek, carrots, celery, pears, garlic, and ginger. Season lightly with salt and pepper, then cover the pan and cook for about 10 minutes, stirring occasionally, until the ingredients are softened but not colored. Add the curry powder, garam masala, spice-filled bag, and broth and bring to a boil. Reduce the heat and simmer for 1 hour. Run through a food mill fitted with the medium blade. Strain through a medium strainer, return

the liquid to the pot, and simmer for 10 minutes, adding additional broth or water to thin the soup if necessary. Season with salt and pepper to taste.

MAKE THE CRANBERRY AND RADISH CHUTNEY: In a small skillet, toast the black mustard seeds over medium heat for 1 to 2 minutes, until fragrant and starting to pop. Transfer to a small plate. In a large sauté pan, combine the brown sugar, vinegar, and radishes and place over medium heat. Bring to a boil and cook until the radishes are crisp-tender, about 5 minutes. Strain the radishes, reserving the liquid, and return the liquid to the pan. Put the radishes in a bowl and set aside. Add the cayenne, black mustard seeds, and cranberries to the sauté pan and cook until the liquid is almost all absorbed. Pour the mixture into the bowl with the radishes, season with salt and pepper to taste, and set aside until ready to serve.

MAKE THE CARDAMOM CREAM: In a medium bowl with an electric mixer, whip together all the ingredients until lightly thickened (about the thickness of sour cream). Refrigerate until ready to serve.

Spoon a mound of chutney into each of 8 soup bowls. Ladle the hot soup around the chutney, leaving the top part of the chutney showing. Spoon dollops of the cardamom cream around the soup and serve immediately.

BEET SALAD
WITH GOAT CHEESE
MEDALLIONS

THE 1950 BROWNS WON THE NFC
CHAMPIONSHIP IN THEIR FIRST NFL SEASON,
BEATING THE RAMS 30–28.

PREP TIME
02:00+

CHEF: **Paul Minnillo,** Baricelli Inn, Cleveland

WINE SUGGESTION: Bridlewood Viognier

SERVES 4

ROASTED BEETS

- 1 **cup white balsamic vinegar**
- 1 **cup (2 sticks) unsalted butter, melted**
- 1 **cup white wine**
  Salt and freshly ground black pepper
- 2 **red beets, peeled and halved**
- 2 **golden beets, peeled and halved**

GOAT CHEESE MEDALLIONS

- 3 **tablespoons crushed peppercorns**
- ½ **teaspoon finely chopped fresh tarragon**
  One 8-ounce goat cheese log

VINAIGRETTE

- 1 **large egg yolk**
- 1 **tablespoon Dijon-style mustard**
- ¼ **cup fresh lemon juice**
- 1 **garlic clove, chopped**
- ¼ **cup finely chopped fresh sorrel (see *Note*)**
- ¼ **cup finely chopped fresh spinach**
- 1 **tablespoon minced fresh thyme**
- ½ **cup extra-virgin olive oil**
  Salt and freshly ground black pepper

- 2 **cups baby lettuce**
  Cracked peppercorns

MAKE THE ROASTED BEETS: Preheat the oven to 375°F.

In a roasting pan, combine the vinegar, butter, wine, 1 cup water, and salt and pepper to taste. In separate sides of the pan, toss each color beet in the liquid. Cover with aluminum foil and roast for 1½ hours, or until tender. Cool, then cut the beets into ½-inch cubes. Set aside.

MAKE THE GOAT CHEESE MEDALLIONS: In a small bowl, combine the peppercorns and tarragon. Cut the goat cheese into 4 medallions and dust with the mixture on both sides.

MAKE THE VINAIGRETTE: In a blender, combine the egg yolk, mustard, lemon juice, garlic, sorrel, spinach, and thyme and purée until smooth. With the the motor running, pour in the oil through the hole in the lid and blend until thickened. Season with salt and pepper to taste.

Divide the lettuce among 4 serving plates. Mound the red and golden beets on either side of the plates and place a goat cheese medallion between the beets. Drizzle with the vinaigrette and garnish with cracked peppercorns.

NOTE: *Sorrel is a tangy green herb the shape of spinach. It's available year-round but at its peak in the spring, when it is milder and best for eating raw in salads and dressings.*

ROASTED VEGETABLE TERRINE

SOUL LEGEND MARVIN GAYE
TRIED OUT FOR THE LIONS IN 1970
BUT WAS CUT EARLY ON.

CHEF: Brian Polcyn, Five Lakes Grill, Milford

WINE SUGGESTION: Gallo of Sonoma Merlot

SERVES 8

PREP TIME

00:30+

REFRIGERATE OVERNIGHT

1	**eggplant, peeled and sliced ¼ inch thick**
2	**zucchini, sliced ¼ inch thick**
2	**yellow squash, sliced ¼ inch thick**
1¼	**cups extra-virgin olive oil**
	Salt and freshly ground black pepper
¼	**cup balsamic vinegar**
1	**tablespoon minced garlic**
3	**tomatoes, thinly sliced**
8	**ounces soft goat cheese, at room temperature**
1	**roasted red bell pepper (see page 100), cut lengthwise into 1-inch strips**

Heat a grill pan over medium-high heat. Put the eggplant in a medium bowl and the zucchini and squash together in a separate bowl. Toss each with ¼ cup of the oil and season with salt and pepper to taste. Put the zucchini and squash on the grill pan and cook until completely softened and lightly browned on both sides, about 5 minutes. Transfer to paper towels to drain. Put the eggplant on the grill pan and cook until completely softened and lightly browned on both sides, 5 to 7 minutes. Transfer to paper towels to drain and cool.

In a medium bowl, whisk together the vinegar and garlic. Slowly whisk in the remaining ¾ cup oil until thickened, and season with salt and pepper to taste.

Line a 8½-by-4½-inch loaf pan with plastic wrap, leaving a 3-inch overhang. Arrange a snug layer of eggplant slices over the bottom of the pan and brush with vinaigrette. Repeat with layers of zucchini and yellow squash, brushing each layer with vinaigrette. Lay the tomatoes down the center, connecting them end to end. Spread the softened goat cheese over the top and place the roasted pepper on top of the goat cheese. Drizzle with vinaigrette. Cover the vegetables with the plastic overhang, weight the terrine with a 3- to 4-pound weight, and refrigerate overnight. The terrine may be made up to 2 days in advance.

Run a thin knife around the edges of the terrine; invert onto a cutting board and discard the plastic wrap. Using a sharp knife, slice the terrine into 8 pieces, place on plates, and serve.

BEEF SHORT RIBS
WITH RED WINE VINEGAR SAUCE

THE 1985 SUPER BOWL CHAMPION BEARS
ARE OFTEN CONSIDERED THE MOST
DOMINANT TEAM IN NFL HISTORY.

PREP TIME

CHEF: **Susan Goss,** West Town Tavern, Chicago

WINE SUGGESTION: Frei Brothers Merlot

SERVES 4

SHORT RIBS

	Four 9-ounce square-cut boneless beef short rib pieces
	Salt and freshly ground black pepper
1	tablespoon vegetable oil
½	cup chopped carrots
½	cup chopped celery
1	cup chopped red onion
2	bay leaves
5	sprigs fresh flat-leaf parsley
1	cup Zinfandel or other dry red wine
2	cups low-sodium beef broth

RED WINE VINEGAR SAUCE

4	cups good-quality red wine vinegar, preferably Zinfandel vinegar
1½	cups packed dark brown sugar
¾	cup raisins

The intense sweet-and-sour sauce works brilliantly against the deep meatiness of the ribs. For maximum flavor, make sure to fully brown the ribs before braising.

MAKE THE SHORT RIBS: Preheat the oven to 350°F.

Pat the short ribs dry with paper towels and season with salt and pepper. In a large, heavy pot or Dutch oven, heat the oil over medium-high heat. Brown the short ribs on all sides, turning with tongs, about 8 minutes. Transfer to a plate.

Combine the carrots, celery, onion, bay leaves, and parsley in the bottom of the pot. Top with the short ribs and add the wine and broth. Place over medium-high heat and bring to a boil. Remove the pan from the heat, cover, and braise for 3 to 3½ hours, or until the meat is very tender. Remove from the oven and let the meat stand in the braising liquid until ready to serve. The ribs may be prepared up to this point.2 days ahead; reheat in the braising liquid.

MAKE THE RED WINE VINEGAR SAUCE: In a heavy medium saucepan, combine the vinegar and brown sugar over medium heat. Bring to a boil, then reduce the heat and simmer until the liquid reduces to about 2½ cups. Add the raisins, then bring back to a simmer and reduce to about 2 cups, watching carefully so the sauce doesn't burn. The sauce should be black, syrupy, and glossy. Let cool slightly.

Divide the ribs among 4 serving plates and top with the sauce.

BRAISED LAMB SHOULDER
WITH MASHED POTATOES, CORN CAKES, AND BARBECUE SAUCE

PREP TIME
03:00+
MARINATE OVERNIGHT

CHEF: **Susan Goss,** West Town Tavern, Chicago

WINE SUGGESTION: Mirassou Pinot Noir

LAMB

½	cup packed dark brown sugar
2	tablespoons salt
2	tablespoons freshly ground black pepper
1	teaspoon ground allspice
	One 4-pound boneless lamb shoulder roast
2	tablespoons canola oil
1	carrot, roughly chopped
2	celery stalks, roughly chopped
1	red onion, roughly chopped
2	bay leaves
2	sprigs fresh thyme
½	bunch fresh flat-leaf parsley

BARBECUE SAUCE

1	cup Worcestershire sauce
1	cup cider vinegar
2	tablespoons packed dark brown sugar
2	tablespoons fresh lemon juice
1	tablespoon freshly ground black pepper
½	teaspoon ground allspice

MASHED POTATOES

2	pounds russet potatoes, peeled and cut into quarters
3	tablespoons unsalted butter
¾	cup milk, warmed
	Salt and freshly ground black pepper

CORN CAKES

2	large eggs
1	cup buttermilk
1½	tablespoons unsalted butter, melted and cooled, plus more for brushing the griddle
½	cup yellow cornmeal
⅓	cup all-purpose flour
½	teaspoon baking powder
½	teaspoon baking soda
½	teaspoon salt
¼	teaspoon freshly ground black pepper
1	cup cooked corn kernels
2	tablespoons minced scallion
2	tablespoons chopped fresh parsley
	Shredded cabbage

THE BEARS BORROWED THE
NICKNAME "MONSTERS OF THE MIDWAY"
FROM THE UNIVERSITY OF CHICAGO.

SERVES 6 TO 8

MAKE THE LAMB: In a small bowl, combine the brown sugar, salt, pepper, and allspice. Rub the spice mixture all over the lamb. Place the lamb in a large bowl, cover with plastic wrap, and refrigerate overnight.

Preheat the oven to 300°F.

Heat the oil in a large Dutch oven or ovenproof pot over medium-high heat. Sear the lamb for about 5 minutes on each side. Remove the lamb to a large plate and add the carrot, celery, and onion to the pot. Reduce the heat to medium and sauté for 5 minutes, or until softened. Return the lamb to the pot and add the bay leaves, thyme, and parsley. Add water to cover the lamb halfway, increase the heat, and bring to a boil. Cover and transfer to the oven. Braise the lamb for 2½ to 3 hours, until meltingly tender. Add 1 tablespoon salt to the cooking liquid and let lamb cool in the liquid. When cool enough to handle, remove the lamb from the liquid and shred the meat. Discard the liquid.

MAKE THE BARBECUE SAUCE: Meanwhile, combine all the barbecue sauce ingredients in a small saucepan over medium heat. Bring to a simmer and simmer for 10 minutes, stirring to dissolve the sugar. Reheat just before serving.

MAKE THE MASHED POTATOES: Put the potatoes in a large pot with salted water to cover. Cook until soft, 20 to 30 minutes. Drain, then return to the pot and heat for 1 minute to evaporate excess moisture. Remove from the heat, add the butter, and mash well. Stir in the milk and season with salt and pepper to taste. Reheat just before serving.

MAKE THE CORN CAKES: In a large bowl, whisk the eggs, buttermilk, and melted butter. In a separate bowl, whisk the cornmeal, flour, baking powder, baking soda, salt, and pepper. Quickly mix the wet ingredients into the dry with a few strokes of the whisk. Do not whisk until smooth—leave some lumps. Fold in the corn, scallion, and parsley.

Heat a nonstick griddle over medium-high heat and brush with butter. When the butter is sizzling, drop the batter in ¼-cupfuls onto the griddle. Spread the batter to form 3-inch cakes and cook for 2 to 3 minutes on each side, until golden. You should have 12 corn cakes.

Place 2 corn cakes on each of 6 serving plates. Spoon some mashed potatoes over the corn cakes, top with the lamb, and drizzle with the barbecue sauce. (This sauce is very spicy—use sparingly!) Garnish with the cabbage and serve immediately.

SPICY SAUSAGE AND PEPPER SANDWICH

COACH GEORGE HALAS AND QUARTERBACK SID LUCKMAN ORIGINATED THE MODERN T-FORMATION.

PREP TIME 00:30

CHEF: Susan Goss, West Town Tavern, Chicago

WINE SUGGESTION: McWilliam's Cabernet

SERVES 8

2 tablespoons corn oil

1 large red onion, thinly sliced

2 large yellow bell peppers, seeded and thinly sliced

2 large red bell peppers, seeded and thinly sliced

¼ cup whiskey

¼ cup packed dark brown sugar

1 tablespoon chopped fresh thyme

Salt and freshly ground black pepper

Eight 4-ounce spicy Italian sausages

8 good-quality hot dog buns, split

In a large skillet, heat the oil over medium heat. Add the onion and peppers and sauté until softened and beginning to brown, about 10 minutes. Add the whiskey and stir until almost evaporated. Add the brown sugar and stir until it melts. Add the thyme and salt and pepper to taste.

While the onion and peppers cook, preheat the broiler and prick the sausages all over with a fork. Put the sausages on the rack of a broiler pan and broil 3 to 5 inches from the heat, turning once, until slightly blackened and cooked through, 10 to 12 minutes.

Brush the hot dog buns with a little sausage grease and toast under the broiler.

Nestle 1 sausage in each bun and top with the onion and peppers.

BRADY POPPINGA'S
MOTHER-IN-LAW'S POWER CHILI

#51 LINEBACKER
6'3", 245 POUNDS
BRIGHAM YOUNG, b. 9-21-79

PREP TIME
00:30

CHEF: **Brady Poppinga**

SERVES 4

1	tablespoon olive oil
1	pound ground turkey, preferably organic
½	green bell pepper, seeded and finely chopped
	One 14-ounce can diced tomatoes with juice
	One 1¼-ounce packet hot chili seasoning mix, such as McCormick
	One 15-ounce can kidney beans, drained
1	tablespoon Worcestershire sauce
1½	tablespoons sugar
2	teaspoons chili powder, or to taste
	Cheddar cheese
	Corn chips

This brings a whole new meaning to the mother-in-law punchin' it to you. According to Poppinga, this protein-packed, easy-to-fix dish will help you "blast off" on the field the day after.

In a large saucepan over medium-high heat, heat the oil. Add the turkey, stirring to break it up with the back of a wooden spoon, until no longer pink, about 5 minutes. Add the pepper and cook for 1 minute. Add the remaining ingredients except the cheese and chips, bring to a simmer, then reduce the heat, cover, and simmer for 15 minutes.

Spoon the chili into serving bowls and top with cheese and some corn chips. Serve immediately.

#84 WIDE RECEIVER
6'1", 199 POUNDS
OREGON STATE, b. 9-26-77

T.J. HOUSHMANDZADEH'S
SHRIMP AND CHICKEN WITH GARLIC BUTTER

CHEF: **T.J. Houshmandzadeh**

SERVES 4

PREP TIME
01:00+

1　whole bone-in chicken breast

　　Salt

6　tablespoons unsalted butter, softened

　　3 to 4 garlic cloves, minced

1　tablespoon olive oil

¾　pound large shrimp, peeled and deveined

　　Freshly ground black pepper

2　tablespoons white wine

2　tablespoons chopped fresh parsley (optional)

T.J. says, "I'm definitely a seafood guy, and I like this dish because I can mix it up with chicken or any type of vegetables that I'm craving. A healthy, balanced meal is what I love, since I need the energy to perform on the field."

Bring a large pot of salted water to a boil. Add the chicken, then immediately remove from the heat, cover, and let sit for 45 minutes to 1 hour, until the chicken is cooked through and no longer pink. Remove the chicken to a carving board and pull the meat from the bones, discarding the skin and bones. Set aside.

In a medium bowl, beat the butter with a fork until fluffy. Stir in the garlic; set aside.

In a large skillet, heat the oil over medium-high heat. Season the shrimp with salt and pepper, then add the shrimp to the skillet in a single layer. Cook until the edges turn pink, about 1 minute, then, using tongs, flip each shrimp and cook for 1 minute on the other side. Add the wine and stir until almost evaporated. Add the butter and

cook, stirring, until the butter is melted and the shrimp are cooked through, about 1 minute. Add the chicken and cook just to heat through. Season with salt and pepper to taste and sprinkle with parsley, if using. Serve immediately.

VEAL GOULASH
WITH SPAETZLE

DETROIT ENJOYED ITS GREATEST SUCCESS
IN THE 1950s, WINNING THE LEAGUE
CHAMPIONSHIP IN 1952, 1953, AND 1957.

PREP TIME
02:00+

CHEF: Brian Polcyn, Five Lakes Grill, Milford

WINE SUGGESTION: LMM Napa Cabernet Sauvignon

SERVES 4

VEAL GOULASH

2	tablespoons unsalted butter
1	tablespoon olive oil
3	large onions, diced
3	garlic cloves, minced
2	teaspoons caraway seeds, toasted and ground
2	tablespoons sweet or hot Hungarian paprika
2	teaspoons grated lemon zest
2	tablespoons tomato paste
2	tablespoons red wine vinegar
4	cups low-sodium veal broth or beef broth
2	pounds boneless veal shank, cut into 1-inch cubes
	Salt and freshly ground black pepper
1	pound Yukon gold potatoes, peeled and diced

SPAETZLE

2	cups all-purpose flour
1	teaspoon salt
⅔	cup milk
3	large eggs
2	tablespoons unsalted butter
2	tablespoons olive oil
2	tablespoons chopped fresh parsley
¼	teaspoon freshly grated nutmeg
½	teaspoon freshly ground black pepper

This trademark Hungarian stew loaded with paprika is served with spaetzle, tiny dumplings that are made by pushing batter through a strainer or colander into boiling water and then tossed with butter. Feel free to substitute beef for the veal.

MAKE THE VEAL GOULASH: In a large saucepan, heat the butter and oil over medium heat until the butter is melted. Add the onions and sauté until softened and golden brown, about 10 minutes. Add the garlic and caraway seeds and cook for 1 minute. Add the paprika and lemon zest and cook for about 1 minute, until aromatic. Add the tomato paste, then add the vinegar and broth and stir to scrape up any browned bits from the bottom of the pan. Add the veal, bring just to a boil, season lightly with salt and pepper, then lower the heat, cover, and simmer until very tender, stirring occasionally, about 1½ hours. Add the potatoes and cook an additional 15 minutes, or until the potatoes are tender.

MAKE THE SPAETZLE: Meanwhile, bring a large saucepan of salted water to a boil; keep at a bare simmer. Fill a large bowl with ice water and set aside.

In a medium bowl, whisk together the flour and ½ teaspoon of the salt. In a separate bowl, whisk together the milk and eggs, then whisk into the flour until smooth.

Working over the pot of barely simmering water, using a rubber spatula, force some of the dough through a colander with ¼-inch holes. As the spaetzle float to the surface, about 1 minute, use a skimmer or fine-mesh sieve to transfer to the ice water to cool, then drain. Repeat with the remaining dough. The spaetzle can be prepared a day ahead, covered, and refrigerated.

In a medium skillet, melt the butter with the oil over medium heat. Add the spaetzle and cook, stirring occasionally, until lightly browned, about 10 minutes. Add the parsley, nutmeg, remaining ½ teaspoon salt, and the pepper.

Divide the spaetzle among 4 serving bowls, top with the goulash, and serve immediately.

JEROME BETTIS's
BISON BURGERS

2006 SUPER BOWL CHAMPION BETTIS RETIRED AS THE NFL'S 5TH-BEST RUSHER OF ALL TIME AND A 6-TIME PRO BOWL SELECTION.

PREP TIME
00:30

CHEF: Jerome Bettis, Analyst, Football Night in America, Former Pittsburgh Steeler

SERVES 4

ROASTED GARLIC-MUSTARD SPREAD

2   tablespoons Worcestershire sauce

1   tablespoon Dijon-style mustard

2   teaspoons brown sugar, or to taste

½   head garlic, roasted

1   teaspoon minced fresh sage

BISON BURGERS

1¼   pounds ground bison

     Salt and freshly ground black pepper

4   whole wheat buns, split

     Onion rings (optional)

     Lettuce (optional)

     Tomato slices (optional)

Jerome Bettis prefers his burgers made with bison meat; he loves that it's low in fat but just as flavorful and tender as beef. Serve on whole wheat buns and with a green salad on the side for a healthy twist on America's favorite dish.

MAKE THE ROASTED GARLIC–MUSTARD SPREAD: In a small bowl, combine all the ingredients, breaking up the garlic with the back of a spoon until smooth. Set aside.

MAKE THE BURGERS: In a medium bowl, combine the bison and salt and pepper to taste, mixing lightly with your hands. Shape the meat into 4 burgers.

Preheat a large, heavy skillet, preferably cast-iron, over medium-high heat until very hot. Add the burgers and cook for 3 to 4 minutes on each side, to desired doneness. As bison has very little fat, make sure not to overcook to keep it tender.

Assemble the burgers with the buns and add the toppings of your choice. Serve immediately.

"I wasn't a football junkie as a kid. We were a family of bowlers. We were at tournaments a lot, so I didn't see many pro games. But living in Detroit, the Lions played every Thanksgiving afternoon. We would always go to my grandmother's house, and she made a spread that would rival anyone's: turkey and ham, macaroni and cheese, yams, cakes, pies. I would always have a spot on the floor in front of the television and watch football. That's how I became a huge Dallas Cowboys fan, because Dallas used to play on Thanksgiving all the time."

FRIED CHICKEN SALAD
WITH ROASTED VEGETABLES

CHEF: Nancy Longo, Pierpoint, Baltimore

WINE SUGGESTION: Frei Brothers RR Chardonnay

SERVES 8

PREP TIME
01:00+
MARINATE 2 HOURS

FRIED CHICKEN

Eight 8-ounce boneless, skinless chicken breasts, cut into 1-inch strips

2 **cups buttermilk**

1½ **cups all-purpose flour**

½ **cup medium-grind cornmeal**

1 **tablespoon Old Bay Seasoning**

1 **teaspoon salt**

Vegetable oil for frying

DRESSING

¼ **cup sherry vinegar or cider vinegar**

1 **tablespoon Dijon-style mustard**

1 **shallot, minced**

2 **teaspoons chopped fresh thyme leaves**

½ **teaspoon salt**

½ **teaspoon freshly ground black pepper**

¾ **cup extra-virgin olive oil**

ROASTED VEGETABLE AND MIXED GREENS SALAD

4 **red beets with greens, peeled and diced, greens reserved**

2 **yellow squash, cut into 1-inch cubes**

2 **large red onions, chopped**

1 **red bell pepper, seeded and chopped**

1 **yellow bell pepper, seeded and chopped**

1 **green bell pepper, seeded and chopped**

1 **pound button mushrooms, halved**

1 **bunch scallions, cut into 2-inch pieces**

¼ **cup olive oil**

Salt and freshly ground black pepper

2 **bunches spinach, stems trimmed**

1 **bunch mustard greens, torn into pieces**

1 **head radicchio, cored and julienned**

MARINATE THE CHICKEN: Put the chicken in a large bowl. Pour the buttermilk over the chicken, cover, and refrigerate for 2 hours to marinate.

MAKE THE DRESSING: In a large bowl, whisk together all the ingredients except the oil. Add the oil in a slow stream, whisking until thickened. Set aside until ready to use.

MAKE THE ROASTED VEGETABLES: Preheat the oven to 375°F.

In a large roasting pan, combine the beets, squash, red onions, peppers, mushrooms, and scallions with the oil. Season with salt and pepper to taste. Roast for about 25 minutes, until the vegetables are softened and lightly browned. Set aside.

FRY THE CHICKEN: Preheat the oven to 200°F.

On a large plate, combine the flour, cornmeal, Old Bay, and salt. In a large, deep sauté pan, heat about 3 inches of oil to 375°F. Dredge the chicken strips in the flour mixture, then, working in batches, fry the chicken until golden brown, 3 to 4 minutes per side. Transfer to paper towels to drain, then place on a baking sheet and keep warm in the oven until ready to serve.

FINISH THE SALAD: In a large bowl, combine the beet greens, spinach, mustard greens, and radicchio. Toss with the dressing. Heat a large sauté pan over medium heat and add the roasted vegetables. Heat to warm through. Add the greens and briefly wilt, about 2 minutes, tossing with tongs.

Divide the salad among 8 serving plates, top with the fried chicken, and serve immediately.

CHICKEN BREASTS
STUFFED WITH SPINACH AND SHIITAKE MUSHROOMS

PREP TIME
01:00+

CHEF: Jean-Robert de Cavel, Jean-Robert at Pigall's, Cincinnati

WINE SUGGESTION: Gallo of Sonoma Chardonnay

STUFFED CHICKEN BREASTS

1	bunch spinach, stems trimmed
4	boneless, skinless chicken legs (including thighs)
1	large egg
2	tablespoons heavy cream
6	ounces shiitake mushrooms, diced
	Salt and freshly ground black pepper
8	boneless, skinless chicken breast halves
2	tablespoons olive oil, plus more as needed

SAUCE

3	tablespoons olive oil
1	apple, peeled, cored, and finely chopped
2	onions, finely chopped
1	yellow bell pepper, cored and finely chopped
1	green bell pepper, cored and finely chopped
1	red bell pepper, cored and finely chopped
½	pineapple, peeled, cored, and finely chopped
¼	cup raisins
2	tablespoons mild curry powder
½	teaspoon ground cayenne pepper
2	tablespoons spiced rum
¼	cup pineapple juice
½	cup unsweetened coconut milk
1	cup low-sodium chicken broth
½	cup heavy cream
	Leaves from 1 bunch fresh parsley, chopped
	Leaves from 1 bunch fresh cilantro, chopped
	Salt and freshly ground black pepper
1	tablespoon unsalted butter
4	cups cooked long-grain white rice

ON JANUARY 10, 1982, THE BENGALS BEAT THE CHARGERS IN -9°F TEMPERATURES IN THE AFC CHAMPIONSHIP GAME.

SERVES 8

If you have a full-service butcher nearby, instead of buying separate packages of chicken breasts and legs, you can ask for two 3½-pound whole chickens— the butcher can skin and bone the chickens and cut them up for you.

MAKE THE STUFFED CHICKEN BREASTS: Preheat the oven to 375°F.

Blanch the spinach for 30 seconds in a pot of boiling water. Drain, then immediately plunge the spinach into a bowl of ice water to cool it. Drain in a sieve, pressing on the spinach to remove excess water. In a food processor, process the chicken leg meat until almost smooth. Add the egg, cream, and spinach and process until smooth. Transfer to a large bowl, add the mushrooms, and season with salt and pepper to taste. Pat the chicken breasts dry. Starting at the thicker end of the breast, make a deep 3-inch-long horizontal cut, stopping about 1 inch from the opposite end. Fill each pocket with one-eighth of the spinach mixture, securing the pockets with wooden picks if you like.

In a large skillet, heat the oil over medium-high heat and sear the chicken breasts in batches, about 2 minutes on each side, adding more oil to the skillet as needed. Transfer the chicken breasts to a baking dish as they are browned. Cover and bake until cooked through, about 30 minutes.

MAKE THE SAUCE: Meanwhile, in a large sauté pan, heat 2 tablespoons of the oil over medium heat. Add the apple, 1 of the onions, the peppers, pineapple, and raisins and sauté until softened, about 5 minutes. Transfer to a bowl and set aside. Wipe out the skillet, add the remaining 1 tablespoon of oil to the pan, and heat over medium heat. Add the remaining onion and sauté until softened, about 5 minutes. Add the curry powder and cayenne and cook for 1 minute. Raise the heat to high, add the rum, and stir until almost evaporated. Add the pineapple juice and cook until reduced by half, about 2 minutes. Add the coconut milk and cook until reduced by half, about 5 minutes. Add the broth and cook until reduced by half, about 10 minutes. Add the cream, reduce the

heat, and simmer until thickened, about 5 minutes. Stir in the apple mixture. Add the parsley and cilantro, reserving some for garnish, and season with salt and pepper to taste. Remove from the heat and stir in the butter.

Mound the rice in the center of each of 8 serving plates. Slice the stuffed chicken breasts, fan the slices around the rice, and drizzle with the sauce. Serve garnished with parsley and cilantro.

ONION-CRUSTED WALLEYE
WITH WILD RICE SALAD

IN 1969 THE VIKINGS HAD 12 STRAIGHT WINS, THE LONGEST SINGLE-SEASON WINNING STREAK IN 35 YEARS.

CHEF: **Mark Haugen,** Tejas, Edina

WINE SUGGESTION: Whitehaven Sauvignon Blanc

SERVES 4

PREP TIME
01:00+

WILD RICE SALAD

- 2 cups cooked wild rice
- 1 red bell pepper, roasted (see page 100), peeled, seeded, and thinly sliced
- ½ cup minced celery
- ½ cup thinly sliced scallions
- 1 garlic clove, minced
- 1 teaspoon chopped fresh marjoram
- ⅓ cup extra-virgin olive oil
- ¼ cup sherry vinegar
- 1 tablespoon fresh lemon juice
- ½ cup coarsely chopped pecans, toasted
- ½ cup dried cranberries
  Salt and freshly ground black pepper to taste

WATERCRESS DRESSING

- 2 cups watercress
- 1 teaspoon minced shallot
- 1 tablespoon Dijon-style mustard
- ¼ cup sherry vinegar
- 1 cup extra-virgin olive oil
  Salt and freshly ground black pepper

ONION-CRUSTED WALLEYE

- 1 tablespoon olive oil
- 1 onion, thinly sliced
- 1 cup fresh bread crumbs
- 1 teaspoon salt
  Four 4- to 6-ounce walleye fillets (or sole, snapper, or flounder)
- 4 tablespoons unsalted butter, softened
- 4 tablespoons clarified butter (see page 171)

  Watercress sprigs

MAKE THE WILD RICE SALAD: In a large bowl, toss all the ingredients together. Set aside until ready to serve.

MAKE THE WATERCRESS DRESSING: In a blender, combine the watercress, shallot, mustard, vinegar, and ¼ cup water and purée until almost smooth. With the motor running, slowly add the oil through the hole in the lid and blend until thickened, adding more water if needed. Season with salt and pepper to taste. Transfer to a bowl and refrigerate if not using right away.

MAKE THE ONION-CRUSTED WALLEYE: In a medium skillet, heat the oil over medium heat. Add the onion and sauté until caramelized, about 20 minutes. Remove from the heat and cool. Preheat the oven to 350°F.

In a food processor, grind the bread crumbs with the caramelized onions and ½ teaspoon of the salt. Season the walleye fillets with remaining ½ teaspoon salt and spread a thin layer of butter on top of each fillet. Top each walleye fillet with the bread crumb–onion mixture.

Heat the clarified butter in a large ovenproof sauté pan over medium-high heat. Put the fillets in the pan breaded side down; lower the heat to medium and cook until the breading is lightly browned, about 5 minutes. Flip the fillets, place in the oven, and bake for about 5 minutes, until just cooked through.

Spoon some of the dressing over each of 4 serving plates. Place some wild rice salad in the center of the plates and arrange the walleye fillets, breaded side up, on top. Drizzle with dressing, garnish with watercress sprigs, and serve immediately.

FIERY FILET MIGNON
WITH CORN CAKES

PREP TIME
01:00+

CHEF: **Bob Malone,** Treesdale Golf and Country Club, Gibsonia

WINE SUGGESTION: Bridlewood Syrah

FILET MIGNON

Six 7-ounce center-cut filet beef tenderloin (filet mignon) steaks, preferably Black Angus

1 cup olive oil

1 teaspoon salt

1 teaspoon freshly ground black pepper

1 teaspoon chipotle chile powder

1 teaspoon ground cumin

1 teaspoon chili powder

ROASTED VEGETABLE MAYONNAISE

¼ pound cremini mushroom caps

1 red bell pepper, seeded and chopped

¼ pound asparagus, ends snapped off

1 cup mayonnaise

Salt and freshly ground black pepper

CORN CAKES

2 medium ears white corn, shucked

½ cup yellow cornmeal

½ cup all-purpose flour

½ teaspoon baking soda

½ teaspoon salt

¼ teaspoon freshly ground black pepper

1 cup buttermilk

2 large eggs

2 tablespoons unsalted butter, melted and cooled, plus more for brushing the griddle

Fresh chives

SERVES 6

MAKE THE FILET MIGNON: Preheat the oven to 425°F.

Pat the steaks dry. In a large bowl, combine the oil with the remaining ingredients. Reserve ¼ cup of the marinade and rub the remaining marinade over the steaks. Set aside to marinate at room temperature for 15 minutes. Heat 2 large skillets over medium-high heat. Put the steaks in the skillets and brown on both sides, about 5 minutes total. Transfer to the oven and roast for about 10 minutes, or until a meat thermometer registers 145°F for medium-rare. Lower the oven temperature to 250°F. Transfer the steaks to a cutting board, cover loosely with aluminum foil, and let stand while finishing the recipe.

MAKE THE ROASTED VEGETABLE MAYONNAISE: Heat a stovetop grill pan over medium-high heat. In a large bowl, combine the mushrooms, pepper, and asparagus and toss to coat with 2 tablespoons of the reserved marinade. Put on the grill pan and cook, turning with tongs, until softened and browned, about 5 minutes. Cool, then transfer to a

food processor. Add the mayonnaise and purée until smooth. Season with salt and pepper to taste. Refrigerate until ready to serve.

MAKE THE CORN CAKES: Bring a large saucepan of water to a boil. Add the corn, return to a boil, then cover and remove from the heat. Let stand for 10 minutes, then drain. Let cool slightly, then pat with paper towels to dry.

Heat a large skillet over medium-high heat. Brush the corn with the remaining 2 tablespoons reserved marinade and put on the skillet, turning occasionally with tongs, until blackened in spots, about 5 minutes. Remove from the skillet, cool, then cut the corn from the cobs and put in a large bowl.

In a separate large bowl, whisk together the cornmeal, flour, baking soda, salt, and pepper. In a medium bowl, whisk together the buttermilk, eggs, and butter. Stir in the corn kernels. Add the buttermilk mixture to the cornmeal mixture and whisk just until blended.

Heat a griddle over medium-high heat. Brush with butter, and, working in batches, drop the batter in ¼-cupfuls onto the griddle. Spread the batter to form 3-inch cakes and cook for 2 to 3 minutes on each side, until golden. Place the corn cakes on a baking sheet as you go along and keep warm in the oven. You should have 12 corn cakes.

Cut the steaks into ¼-inch-thick slices. Place 2 corn cakes on each of 6 plates. Fan the steak over the corn cakes, top with a dollop of the mayonnaise, and garnish with chives.

HINES WARD'S
KOREAN-STYLE BRAISED SHORT RIBS

#86 WIDE RECEIVER
6'0", 205 POUNDS
UNIVERSITY OF GEORGIA, b. 3-8-76

PREP TIME
02:00+

CHEF: Hines Ward

SERVES 4

1 tablespoon vegetable oil

Four 3- to 4-inch beef short rib pieces with bones (about 3 pounds)

Salt and freshly ground black pepper

1 white onion, chopped

4 garlic cloves, chopped

One 2-inch piece ginger, chopped

¼ cup rice wine (mirin)

½ cup soy sauce

3 tablespoons rice vinegar

¼ cup packed light brown sugar

1 small apple, peeled and chopped

3 tablespoons toasted sesame oil

3 cups hot cooked white rice

Chopped scallions

Sesame seeds

Hines says, "My mom is Korean, and she would often make a big tub of ribs for special occasions, like my birthday. I still prefer her Korean ribs to anyone else's. She marinates them for two or three days to really let the flavor soak in."

In a large, heavy saucepan or Dutch oven, heat the oil over medium-high heat. Season the short ribs with salt and pepper. Working in batches, sear the ribs, turning, 10 to 12 minutes. Transfer the ribs to a large plate.

Add the onion, garlic, and ginger to the fat in the pan, reduce the heat, and sauté about 5 minutes. Add the rice wine and cook until almost evaporated, stirring. Add the soy sauce, vinegar, brown sugar, and apple and stir to dissolve the sugar. Return the ribs to the pan and add water to cover. Raise the heat, bring to a boil, then reduce the heat to low, cover, and simmer for 1½ to 2 hours, turning occasionally to keep the meat fully covered, until the meat is very tender and falling off the bone.

Remove the ribs from the braising liquid, pat dry with paper towels, and place on a wire rack above a roasting pan covered with aluminum oil.

Preheat the oven to 450°F.

Strain the braising liquid and return half of the liquid to the pan. Cook over medium-high heat until reduced by about half and slightly thickened, 15 to 20 minutes.

Meanwhile, brush the short ribs with the sesame oil. Roast until browned and crisp, 10 to 12 minutes. Let rest for a couple of minutes.

Spoon the rice into shallow serving bowls, place the ribs on top, and drizzle with a small amount of the sauce. Garnish with scallions and sesame seeds and serve immediately.

#88 TIGHT END
6'3", 249 POUNDS
WAKE FOREST UNIVERSITY, b. 4-20-77

DESMOND CLARK'S
GARLICKY BAKED CHICKEN BREAST

CHEF: Desmond Clark

SERVES 4

PREP TIME
01:30

- **2** whole boneless chicken breasts, with skin
- **4** garlic cloves, minced
- **3** tablespoons olive oil
- **¾** teaspoon garlic salt, or to taste
- **¾** teaspoon seasoned salt, or to taste
- **1** onion, finely chopped
- **1** cup low-sodium chicken broth
- **2** tablespoons chopped fresh parsley

Desmond says that the secret to this dish is to really massage the garlic into the chicken, and if you have time, let it marinate overnight so the flavors can develop to the max.

Carefully loosen the skin of the chicken breasts with your finger. Put the garlic under the skin and work it in, massaging with your hands to fully incorporate the garlic. Set aside for 20 minutes at room temperature or cover and refrigerate overnight.

Preheat the oven to 350°F.

Brush the chicken with the oil and sprinkle with both salts.

Place the chicken skin side up in a flameproof baking dish large enough to fit the chicken comfortably. Sprinkle the onion around the chicken and add the broth. Bake, basting occasionally, until golden brown and cooked through, about 45 minutes.

Cut the breasts in half lengthwise and divide among 4 plates. Reheat the pan juices slightly over high heat, scraping up any browned bits from the bottom of the pan and spoon over the chicken. Sprinkle with parsley and serve immediately.

ASIAN-STYLE SALMON
WITH SOBA NOODLES

ARTHUR JOSEPH ROONEY SPENT
$2,500 TO FOUND THE FIFTH-OLDEST
NFL FRANCHISE IN 1933.

PREP TIME
00:30+

CHEF: Bob Malone, Treesdale Golf and Country Club, Gibsonia

WINE SUGGESTION: Martin Codax Albarino

SERVES 4

1   bunch fresh chives

3   tablespoons plus 2 teaspoons sesame oil

2   teaspoons rice vinegar

1   tablespoon fish sauce

1   tablespoon chili-garlic sauce (see page 231)

1   roasted red bell pepper (see *Note*), finely chopped

    One 8-ounce package soba noodles

½   cup chopped salted peanuts

2   tablespoons chopped fresh cilantro

4   tablespoons sesame seeds

    Four 6-ounce salmon fillets

    Salt and freshly ground black pepper to taste

Chop half the chives and save the rest for garnish. In a large bowl, whisk together 3 tablespoons of the oil, the vinegar, fish sauce, chili-garlic sauce, roasted pepper, and chives.

Bring a large pot of salted water to a boil. Add the soba and cook until al dente, about 6 minutes. Drain and toss with the dressing. Add the peanuts and toss again.

In a food processor, combine the cilantro and sesame seeds and process to form a paste, adding a little water if necessary. Pat the salmon dry with paper towels and season with salt and pepper. Coat both sides of the salmon with the cilantro-sesame paste. In a large skillet, heat the remaining 2 teaspoons oil over medium-high heat. Add the salmon, skin side up, to the skillet and cook for 3 minutes. Turn and cook on the other side for 3 minutes, or until just cooked through.

Arrange the noodles in the center of each of 4 serving plates. Top with a salmon fillet and garnish with chives.

NOTE: *To roast peppers: Put the peppers directly over an open flame for about 5 minutes, turning them with tongs, until the skins are blackened. (Alternatively, broil the peppers on a broiler pan under the broiler about 2 inches from the heat, turning every 5 minutes, for 20 to 25 minutes, until the skins are blistered and blackened.) Transfer the peppers to a paper bag or bowl, cover, and let them steam until they are cool enough to handle. Peel the peppers, cut off the tops, and discard the seeds and ribs.*

ROY WILLIAMS's
CREAMY SEAFOOD AND MUSHROOM PASTA

#12 WIDE RECEIVER
6'3", 220 POUNDS
UNIVERSITY OF TEXAS, b. 12-20-81

CHEF: Roy Williams

SERVES 4 TO 6

PREP TIME
00:40+

1	pound penne pasta
¼	cup olive oil
¾	pound peeled and deveined large shrimp
10	ounces white mushrooms, thinly sliced
3	garlic cloves, chopped
¼	cup white wine
8	ounces jumbo lump crabmeat, picked over and slightly flaked
¾	cup heavy cream
2	teaspoons grated lemon zest
1	tablespoon fresh lemon juice
2	teaspoons minced fresh rosemary, plus more for garnish
	Salt and freshly ground black pepper
3	tablespoons unsalted butter
	Grated Parmesan cheese

Roy says he's a penne pasta kind of guy, and what he loves most with his pasta is seafood, lots of it. Add some mushrooms and cook it all in a light cream sauce and he's a happy man.

Cook the pasta in a large pot of salted boiling water until al dente, about 12 minutes. Drain, reserving 1 cup of the cooking water, then toss with a little oil and set aside.

In a large sauté pan, heat the oil over medium-high heat. Add the shrimp and cook, turning once, until they just turn pink, about 2 minutes, then transfer with a slotted spoon to a large bowl.

Add the mushrooms to the oil in the pan and sauté until softened and lightly browned, about 5 minutes. Add the garlic and cook for 1 minute. Add the wine and cook until half absorbed, stirring to scrape up any browned bits from the bottom of the skillet. Return the shrimp to the pan. Add the crab and cream and simmer for about 2 minutes, until the shrimp are fully cooked through and the sauce thickens slightly. Add the lemon zest and juice, rosemary, and salt and pepper to taste.

Stir in the butter until melted. Add the penne and heat through, adding some of the reserved cooking water if needed to keep it moist. Remove from the heat and spoon into bowls. Garnish with cheese and rosemary and serve immediately.

CHICKEN AND WILD RICE BURRITOS
WITH MANGO-HABANERO SAUCE

CHEF: Mark Haugen, Tejas, Edina

WINE SUGGESTION: Whitehaven Sauvignon Blanc

SERVES 4

PREP TIME
01:00+

MANGO-HABANERO SAUCE

1 tablespoon peanut oil

½ onion, diced

1 carrot, diced

1 habanero chile (see *Note*), diced

3 mangos, peeled, pitted, and chopped

½ cup Champagne vinegar

1 tablespoon ketchup

1 tablespoon sugar

Salt

BURRITOS

2 tablespoons unsalted butter

1 tablespoon olive oil

1 onion, diced

2 garlic cloves, minced

8 ounces portobello mushrooms, thinly sliced

3 red bell peppers, roasted (see page 100), peeled, seeded, and diced

3 poblano peppers, roasted (see page 100), peeled, seeded, and diced

1 cup cooked wild rice

3 tablespoons chopped fresh marjoram

3 ounces Asiago cheese, grated

3 ounces Monterey Jack cheese, grated

Salt and freshly ground black pepper to taste

Four 4-ounce hot cooked chicken breasts, cut into ½-inch-thick strips

Four 12-inch flour tortillas

MAKE THE MANGO-HABANERO SAUCE: In a medium saucepan, heat the oil over medium heat. Add the onion, carrot, and chile and sauté until the onion is softened, about 5 minutes. Add the mangos, vinegar, ketchup, and sugar. Bring to a simmer and simmer for 10 minutes. Transfer to a blender, add ¼ cup water, and purée until smooth, adding a little more water if needed to thin out the sauce. Season with salt to taste. Gently rewarm just before serving.

MAKE THE BURRITOS: In a large skillet, heat the butter and oil over medium heat until the butter melts. Add the onion and sauté until softened, about 5 minutes. Add the garlic and mushrooms and sauté until softened, about 5 minutes. Add the roasted peppers, wild rice, marjoram, and cheeses. Season with salt and pepper to taste.

Working with one tortilla at a time, heat the tortillas over an open flame or electric burner until they soften and brown in spots, 15 to 20 seconds per side. Spoon the wild rice mixture along the center of each tortilla; top with the chicken. Fold in the sides of the tortillas over the filling; then roll them up, enclosing the filling.

Place the burritos on serving plates and top with the sauce. Serve immediately.

NOTE: *Usually orange or red in color, the lantern-shaped habanero chile is extremely hot, with a fruity flavor that pairs well with tropical fruits such as mangos. To tone down the heat of habaneros, remove the seeds and membrane before using.*

LIMAS SWEED'S
CHICKEN AND SHRIMP FETTUCCINE

#14 WIDE RECEIVER
6'4", 220 POUNDS
UNIVERSITY OF TEXAS, b. 12-25-1984

PREP TIME
00:45

CHEF: Limas Sweed

SERVES 6

- ¾ pound chicken breast cutlets
- 4 teaspoons olive oil
- Salt and freshly ground black pepper
- ¾ pound peeled and deveined large shrimp
- ½ cup (1 stick) unsalted butter
- 1 cup heavy cream
- 1 pound dried fettuccine
- ¾ cup freshly grated Parmesan cheese, plus more for garnish

Limas says, "This is one of the things that I like to eat day in and day out. I'd eat pasta with shrimp and chicken seven days a week. I feel like we work out enough where we can eat what we want at least a couple days out of the week."

Lightly oil a grill pan and heat over medium-high heat until hot but not smoking. Pat the chicken dry with paper towels and coat with 2 teaspoons of the oil, then season with salt and pepper. Grill the chicken, turning once, until just cooked through, 5 to 7 minutes total. Transfer the chicken to a cutting board, cool, and chop. Clean the grill pan and heat over medium-high heat again. Pat the shrimp dry with paper towels and coat with the remaining 2 teaspoons oil, then season with salt and pepper. Grill the shrimp, turning once, until just cooked through, about 5 minutes.

Meanwhile, in a large sauté pan, combine the butter and cream over low heat. Cook until the butter is melted and the cream comes to a bare simmer. Turn off the heat and set aside.

Cook the fettuccine in a pot of salted boiling water according to the package directions for al dente. Reserve ⅓ cup of the cooking water and drain. Add the fettuccine and cooking water to the sauté pan, along with the cheese. Stir to incorporate the cheese, then add the chicken and season with salt and pepper to taste. Cook over very low heat, stirring to fully coat the pasta and chicken with sauce, until the sauce is slightly thickened, 1 to 2 minutes. Spoon into pasta bowls and top with the grilled shrimp. Garnish with cheese and serve immediately.

**#55 LINEBACKER
6'5", 268 POUNDS
USC, b. 12-11-72**

WILLIE MCGINEST'S
LEMON-HERB CHICKEN
WITH ASPARAGUS

CHEF: Willie McGinest

SERVES 4

PREP TIME
00:30+
MARINATE 30 MINUTES

2	pounds boneless, skinless chicken breasts
⅔	cup olive oil
3	tablespoons fresh lemon juice
1	tablespoon grated lemon zest
1	tablespoon minced fresh thyme
2	teaspoons minced fresh sage
1	teaspoon salt
½	teaspoon freshly ground black pepper
1	teaspoon sugar
4	garlic cloves, pressed through a garlic press
1	pound thin asparagus spears, ends trimmed
1	tablespoon unsalted butter, plus more if needed
	Lemon wedges

Trim the chicken breasts of excess fat and lay the breasts flat on a cutting board, smooth side facing up. Using a sharp knife, slice the chicken in half horizontally to make 2 cutlets. Place the cutlets on a cutting board covered with a large sheet of plastic wrap. Cover with another sheet of plastic and pound with a meat mallet so the cutlets are the same thickness in all places.

In a large bowl, whisk together the oil, lemon juice and zest, thyme, sage, salt, pepper, sugar, and garlic. Put the chicken in a large zip-top bag, pour in all but 1 tablespoon of the marinade, and seal the bag. Refrigerate for 30 minutes to 1 hour.

Meanwhile, bring a large pot of salted water to a boil. Add the asparagus and cook for 1 minute. Drain, rinse with cold water, then pat dry with paper towels.

In a large skillet, melt the butter over medium heat. Remove the chicken from the bag, allowing most of the marinade to drip off. Add half the chicken to the skillet and cook for about 5 minutes, turning once, until

lightly browned and no longer pink inside. Repeat with the remaining chicken, adding more butter if needed.

Wipe the skillet with a paper towel and add the reserved marinade. Add the asparagus and cook until tender, about 2 minutes.

Divide the chicken and asparagus among serving plates and serve immediately with lemon wedges on the side.

POTATO GNOCCHI
WITH GORGONZOLA
CREAM SAUCE

ON JANUARY 7, 1961, THE LIONS
DEFEATED THE BROWNS 17–16 IN THE
FIRST-EVER PLAYOFF BOWL.

PREP TIME

00:45+

CHEF: **Brian Polcyn,** Five Lakes Grill, Milford

WINE SUGGESTION: Frei Brothers RR Chardonnay

SERVES 4

GNOCCHI

2   pounds russet potatoes

1¾ cups all-purpose flour

1   large egg yolk

1   teaspoon salt

½   teaspoon freshly ground
     black pepper

SAUCE

2   cups heavy cream

8   ounces crumbled Gorgonzola
     cheese

     Chopped fresh chives

Gnocchi, little potato dumplings, are fairly easy to make, and the sauce is even easier. The gnocchi can be made up to two days ahead, so when you're ready to sit down to eat you can put the meal together in just a few minutes.

MAKE THE GNOCCHI: Put the potatoes in a large saucepan with cold water to cover. Bring to a boil and cook until tender and easily pierced with a skewer, about 30 minutes. Drain and peel when just cool enough to handle. Press the potatoes through a ricer or food mill fitted with the fine disc. Add the egg yolk, salt, and pepper. Mix in enough flour to make a firm, slightly elastic dough, adding more if the dough is too wet. Turn the dough onto a lightly floured surface and divide into 4 equal pieces. Roll each piece out to form a ½-inch-thick rope about 16 inches long and cut into ½-inch pieces. Roll each piece over the tines of a dinner fork to make grooves. Arrange the gnocchi on a lightly floured baking sheet and repeat with the remaining dough.

Bring a large pot of salted water to a boil. Add the gnocchi, in 2 batches, and cook until they are tender and rise to the top, about 5 minutes. Remove with a slotted spoon and transfer the cooked gnocchi to a serving bowl.

MAKE THE SAUCE: Put the cream in a medium saucepan over medium-high heat and bring to a boil. Lower the heat and cook until reduced by half, about 10 minutes. Add the cheese and stir until melted.

Divide the gnocchi among 4 serving plates, spoon the sauce over the top, and garnish with chives. Serve immediately.

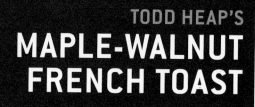

TODD HEAP'S
MAPLE-WALNUT FRENCH TOAST

#86 TIGHT END
6'5", 252 POUNDS
ARIZONA STATE UNIVERSITY, b. 3-16-80

CHEF: **Todd Heap**

SERVES 6

PREP TIME
00:45

¼ cup (½ stick) unsalted butter

1 cup walnut halves, toasted

6 tablespoons plus 2 teaspoons brown sugar

4 tablespoons maple syrup, plus more for serving

1 cup half-and-half

3 large eggs

1 teaspoon maple extract

¼ teaspoon salt

Six ½-inch-slices day-old or stale challah bread or brioche

Vanilla ice cream

Berries (optional)

Todd says, "Breakfast foods are my favorite. I'd eat breakfast for dinner, or for dessert. With French toast, I'd always been a big fan of just butter and syrup, but some friends of mine, they got me into using sour cream and fruits—blueberries, strawberries, raspberries."

In a medium skillet, melt 1 tablespoon of the butter over medium heat. Add the walnuts, 2 teaspoons of the brown sugar, and 2 tablespoons of the maple syrup and cook, stirring constantly, until the walnuts are fully coated with the syrup, about 5 minutes. Transfer to a plate lined with parchment paper and cool, then break up any walnuts that stick together. Set aside.

In a large bowl, whisk together the half-and-half, eggs, the remaining 2 tablespoons maple syrup, the maple extract, and salt. Transfer the mixture to a baking dish and soak the bread slices for 30 seconds, then turn and soak for 30 seconds on the other side. Remove to a wire rack placed over a baking sheet. Let sit until you're ready to cook each slice.

In a large nonstick skillet, melt 1 tablespoon of the butter over medium-low heat. Place 2 slices of bread in the pan and cook until golden brown on the bottom, 2 to 3 minutes. Sprinkle 1 tablespoon brown sugar over the top of each slice, turn the slices over, and cook until golden brown on the bottom. Repeat with

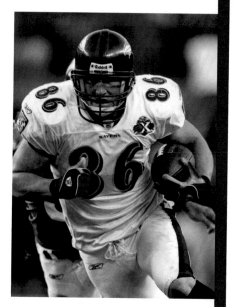

the remaining bread slices, using 1 tablespoon butter for each batch and sprinkling 1 tablespoon brown sugar over each slice.

Place 1 slice of French toast on each of 6 rimmed dessert plates. Top with a scoop of ice cream, drizzle with maple syrup, and sprinkle with the walnuts and berries. Serve immediately.

CHOCOLATE-CHERRY TAMALES

IN 1998 THE VIKINGS SET A THEN–
NFL RECORD BY SCORING A TOTAL OF
556 POINTS IN A SINGLE SEASON.

CHEF: Mark Haugen, Tejas, Edina

WINE SUGGESTION: Barefoot Bubbly

SERVES 6

PREP TIME
02:00+

CHOCOLATE-CHERRY TAMALES

15 dried corn husks (see *Notes*)

5 ounces bittersweet dark chocolate, chopped

1 cup milk

2 cups masa harina for tamales (see *Notes*)

¼ teaspoon baking powder

½ cup (1 stick) softened unsalted butter, lard, or shortening

¼ cup sugar

⅓ cup dried cherries

CAJETA SAUCE

1½ cups cajeta (see *Notes*)

½ cup milk

1 tablespoon unsalted butter

Ice cream

MAKE THE CHOCOLATE-CHERRY TAMALES: Soak the corn husks in a large bowl of hot water for about 1 hour to soften, turning them a couple of times. Tear 3 of the husks into ¼-inch strips to use to tie the tamales.

Put the chocolate in a medium heatproof bowl. In a small saucepan over medium-high heat, bring the milk to a boil. Pour over the chocolate and stir until the chocolate melts. Set aside to cool.

In a large bowl, combine the masa harina and baking powder. Using an electric mixer, slowly beat in the chocolate at low speed. Continue beating for 10 minutes. In a separate bowl, cream the butter and sugar until fluffy. Add the chocolate-masa mixture, one-third at a time, beating well after each addition until the mixture is fluffy. Fold in the cherries.

Arrange a steamer rack in a very large tall stockpot and add water to just below the bottom of the rack. Cover and bring the water to a boil.

Spread about 4 tablespoons of tamale dough in the center of a corn husk. Fold the long sides over the filling, then fold the other sides to make a package. Tie the ends closed with husk strips. Repeat to make 12 tamales. Place the tamales upright in the steamer. Cover and steam for about 1 hour, until the dough is firm to the touch and separates from the husk easily.

MAKE THE CAJETA SAUCE: Meanwhile, in a medium saucepan, combine the cajeta, milk, and butter over medium heat and bring to a boil. Cook for 5 minutes, or until thickened but still pourable. Set aside until ready to serve.

Make a slit in the middle of each tamale and squeeze a little so part of the tamale comes to the top. Place 2 tamales in each of 6 shallow dessert bowls, top with a scoop of ice cream, and drizzle with the sauce.

NOTES: *Dried corn husks are available at Latino markets. Masa is the Spanish word for dough; masa harina is corn that has been treated with lime and water and ground and dried. It is available in Latino markets. Make sure you buy the masa specified for making tamales rather than tortillas. Cajeta is a thick, intensely sweet syrup traditionally made from sugar and goat's milk, popular in Mexico, where it's used as a topping for desserts or made into candies.*

ORANGE PHYLLO NAPOLEONS

THE BENGALS' MASCOT IS WHO DEY, WHOSE NAME ORIGINATES FROM A POPULAR BENGALS CHEER.

PREP TIME
02:00

CHEF: Jean-Robert de Cavel, Jean-Robert at Pigall's, Cincinnati

WINE SUGGESTION: Barefoot Bubbly

SERVES 6

PHYLLO ROUNDS

3 sheets phyllo, defrosted

6 tablespoons clarified butter (see page 171)

3 tablespoons sugar

ORANGE-GRAND MARNIER SAUCE

2 cups orange juice

3 tablespoons honey

1 tablespoon Grand Marnier

PASTRY CREAM FILLING

2 cups milk

1 vanilla bean

6 large egg yolks

⅔ cup sugar

¼ cup all-purpose flour

1 tablespoon Grand Marnier

¾ cup heavy cream

3 oranges, sectioned (see *Note*)

Fresh mint leaves

Candied orange peel (optional)

Confectioners' sugar

MAKE THE PHYLLO ROUNDS: Preheat the oven to 350°F.

Line 2 baking sheets with parchment paper. Unroll the phyllo sheets, stack them, and cover with plastic wrap followed by a damp kitchen towel. Keep the phyllo covered while you work to prevent it from drying out. Place one phyllo sheet on a work surface; brush with clarified butter and sprinkle with 1 tablespoon of the sugar. Place a second sheet on top; brush with clarified butter and sprinkle with 1 tablespoon of the remaining sugar. Repeat with the third sheet. Using a 4-inch cookie cutter, cut out 18 rounds. Place the rounds on the baking sheets and bake until light golden, 10 to 15 minutes. Place the baking sheets on a wire rack and cool completely.

MAKE THE ORANGE-GRAND MARNIER SAUCE: Meanwhile, combine the orange juice, honey, and Grand Marnier in a medium saucepan over medium-high heat. Bring to a boil and cook until reduced to a syrup, 20 to 30 minutes. Remove from the heat and cool.

MAKE THE PASTRY CREAM FILLING: Put the milk in a large saucepan. Using a small paring knife, scrape the seeds from the vanilla bean. Add the bean and seeds to the pan. Bring the milk just to a boil over medium-high heat. Remove from the heat and discard the vanilla bean. In a large bowl, beat the egg yolks and sugar until pale yellow. Beat in the flour. Gradually whisk half of the hot milk into the egg mixture. Add the mixture to the pan and whisk over medium heat until it reaches a boil and thickens, about 5 minutes. Add the Grand Marnier, cover with plastic wrap, and refrigerate until cold. Just before serving, whip the cream until stiff peaks form, then fold in the pastry cream.

ASSEMBLE THE NAPOLEONS: Place 1 phyllo round in the center of each of 6 dessert plates. Spread a generous tablespoon of the pastry cream over each. Arrange 2 orange segments over the cream. Top with another phyllo round, 1 more tablespoon pastry cream, and 2 orange segments. Top with a third phyllo round. Drizzle with the sauce, garnish with mint and candied orange peel, if using, and sprinkle with confectioners' sugar. Serve immediately.

NOTE: *To section oranges: Peel the oranges. Cut between the membranes, separating the sections.*

LEMON SEMOLINA CAKE

THE SUPER BOWL TROPHY WAS RENAMED
THE VINCE LOMBARDI TROPHY AFTER
THE LEGENDARY PACKERS COACH.

CHEF: Sanford D'Amato, Sanford, Milwaukee

WINE SUGGESTION: Barefoot Bubbly

SERVES 10 TO 12

PREP TIME
01:00+

LEMON CREAM

1 cup heavy cream

3 tablespoons confectioners' sugar

⅓ cup sour cream

1 tablespoon grated lemon zest

LEMON SEMOLINA CAKE

2½ cups fine semolina (see *Note*)

1 teaspoon ground cardamom

1 teaspoon baking powder

¼ teaspoon salt

¾ cup (1½ sticks) unsalted butter, melted and cooled

¾ cup sugar

1 cup plain yogurt

1 teaspoon baking soda

2 teaspoons vanilla extract

Grated zest of 2 lemons, plus some for garnish

LEMON SYRUP

2 cups sugar

Zest and juice of 1 lemon

Also called basboosa, this Middle Eastern cake drenched in sugar syrup is a sinfully sweet way to end a meal. The syrup keeps the cake moist for several days, so it's a great make-ahead dessert.

MAKE THE LEMON CREAM: In a medium bowl using an electric mixer, beat the cream with the sugar until soft peaks form. Fold in the sour cream and lemon zest. Cover and refrigerate until ready to serve. Whisk lightly before serving.

MAKE THE LEMON SEMOLINA CAKE: Preheat the oven to 350°F. Butter a 9-by-13-inch baking pan.

In a large bowl, combine the semolina, cardamom, baking powder, salt, butter, and sugar. In a separate bowl, combine the yogurt and baking soda and set aside for 15 minutes, then add the vanilla and lemon zest. Add the yogurt to the semolina mixture. Transfer the batter to the baking dish, smoothing with a rubber spatula to evenly distribute. Bake for about 30 minutes, or until lightly browned and a cake tester comes out clean when inserted into the cake. Remove to a wire rack.

MAKE THE LEMON SYRUP: While the cake is baking, in a medium saucepan, combine the sugar, 2 cups water, and the lemon zest and juice over medium heat and stir until the sugar dissolves. Bring to a boil without stirring, washing down any sugar crystals from the sides of the pan with a pastry brush dipped in cold water, until the mixture is a runny, thin syrup consistency, about 10 minutes.

FINISH THE CAKE: While the cake is still warm, with a very sharp knife, cut into squares directly in the pan, then cut each square in half diagonally to form triangles. Pour the warm syrup over the cake, ideally while the cake is still hot so it absorbs the syrup completely.

Arrange 2 triangles of cake on dessert plates. Top with some lemon cream, garnish with lemon zest, and serve.

NOTE: *Semolina, a coarse grind of wheat, is widely used in Middle Eastern and Indian cakes and puddings and can be found in international markets.*

APPETIZERS

 Lamb Sliders with Tzatziki // 116

 Barbecue Duck Spring Rolls with Chow-Chow // 118

 Duck Confit with Warm White Bean Salad // 120

 Sea Trout Crudo // 122

 Asian Salmon Spread with Curried Apple Slaw // 124

 Creole Boiled Shrimp with Dipping Sauce // 125

 Sautéed Calamari in Yuzu Soy Glaze with Edamame // 126

 Caprese Salad // 128

 Faith Hill's Greek Salad // 129

 Clam and Corn Chowder // 130

MAIN COURSES

 Chipotle Beef Tenderloin with Red and Green Chimichurri // 132

 Asian Barbecue Baby Back Pork Ribs with Pineapple Napa Slaw // 134

 Crawfish Curry // 136

 Paella with Blackened Shrimp and Red Snapper // 138

 Country Gumbo // 140

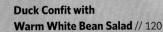 Fred Taylor's Shrimp Creole // 141

 Poached Chicken and Zucchini-Parmesan Salad // 142

 Pork Belly with Collard Green Risotto, Feta, and Pickled Okra // 144

 Sam Baker's Calzones with Ricotta, Mozzarella, Mushrooms, and Pepperoni // 146

 Craig Hentrich's Chicken Marbella // 147

 Bobby McCray's Tomato and Onion Braised Chicken // 148

 Chester Pitts's Potato Casserole // 149

 Prosciutto-Wrapped Tuna Muffuletta // 150

 Bob Sanders's Lemon Pepper Tilapia // 152

 Baked Eggplant with Mozzarella and Parmesan // 153

 Dwight Freeney's Brown Stew Chicken // 154

 Jon Beason's Hoppin' John // 155

 Lobster and Brie Mac and Cheese // 156

DESSERT

 White Chocolate Banana Cream Pie // 158

 Warm Chocolate Hazelnut Pudding // 160

Citrus Rice Pudding // 162

Ronde Barber's Peanut Crunch Cake // 163

Buttermilk Panna Cotta with Balsamic Macerated Strawberries // 164

SOUTH

LAMB SLIDERS WITH TZATZIKI

FORMER RUNNING BACK JAMAL ANDERSON
COINED THE FALCONS' NICKNAME,
THE "DIRTY BIRDS," IN 1998.

PREP TIME
00:30

CHEF: **Kevin Rathbun,** Rathbun's, Atlanta

WINE SUGGESTION: Frei Brothers Merlot

SERVES 8 TO 10

TZATZIKI

½ cup plain Greek-style yogurt

½ tablespoon minced garlic

3 tablespoons grated cucumber

1 tablespoon olive oil

2 teaspoons fresh lemon juice

1 tablespoon chopped fresh parsley

1 teaspoon salt

½ teaspoon freshly ground
   black pepper

LAMB BURGERS

1 pound lean ground lamb

5 ounces ground pork fat (see *Note*)

2 tablespoons minced garlic

1 tablespoon fennel seeds, toasted
   and ground

2 tablespoons chopped fresh parsley

1 tablespoon salt

2 teaspoons cracked black pepper

1 tablespoon olive oil

8 to 10 small rolls of any kind,
preferably brioche, split

These little burgers, studded with garlic, fennel seeds, and black pepper and slathered with a bright, creamy cucumber-yogurt sauce, pack a punch. They're good simply cooked on a griddle on the stove-top, as here, but are even better grilled over hot coals. Pile them on a large platter and set them out for snacking during the game.

MAKE THE TZATZIKI: In a small bowl, combine all the ingredients. Set aside.

MAKE THE LAMB BURGERS: In a large bowl, combine all the ingredients except the oil. Form the mixture into 8 to 10 small, thin patties.

Heat a large cast-iron griddle over high heat and brush with oil. Add the lamb burgers and cook for about 2 minutes on each side for medium.

Lightly toast the rolls on the griddle, then sandwich a lamb burger in each and spread with tzatziki. Serve immediately.

NOTE: *Your butcher should be able to supply you with ground pork fat (especially if the shop also sells house-made sausage). If not, omit the fat and use 1⅓ pounds ground lamb.*

BARBECUE DUCK SPRING ROLLS
WITH CHOW-CHOW

AT 7–9, THE 1995 PANTHERS HAD
THE BEST RECORD EVER FOR AN
NFL EXPANSION TEAM.

PREP TIME
00:30+
CURE 4 TO 6 HOURS

CHEF: Blake Hartwick, Bonterra Dining & Wine Room, Charlotte

WINE SUGGESTION: MacMurray SC Pinot Noir

SERVES 8

CHOW-CHOW

- 1 head green cabbage, shredded
- ½ cup diced sweet onion
- ½ cup chopped green or red bell peppers
- 2 tablespoons salt
- 2 cups apple cider vinegar
- 1½ cups sugar
- 2 teaspoons dry mustard
- 2 teaspoons celery seeds
- 2 teaspoons mustard seeds
- 1 teaspoon ground turmeric
- ½ teaspoon ground ginger

SPRING ROLLS

- 6 duck legs confit (see *Notes*)
- 1 carrot, grated
- 1 red onion, grated
- Barbecue sauce to taste, plus more for garnish
- Salt and freshly ground black pepper
- 8 spring roll wrappers (see *Notes*)
- 1 large egg
- Vegetable oil for frying

Chow-chow, a sweet and sometimes spicy cabbage-based vegetable relish, is a staple of home canners' pantries in the South, where it's usually served at room temperature.

MAKE THE CHOW-CHOW: In a large bowl, toss together the cabbage, onion, peppers, and salt. Cover and refrigerate for 4 to 6 hours; the vegetables will release some of their liquid. Drain well in a colander.

In a large nonreactive saucepan, combine the remaining ingredients and bring to a simmer over medium heat. Add the cabbage mixture and simmer for 5 minutes. Set aside.

MAKE THE SPRING ROLLS: Pull the meat from the duck legs and shred it coarsely in a large bowl. Toss with the carrot, onion, and just enough barbecue sauce to coat the ingredients; season the filling with salt and pepper to taste.

Soak the spring roll wrappers in warm water for about 2 minutes, until pliable. In a small bowl, beat the egg. Lay the wrappers flat on a work surface and brush all over with the egg. Arrange a row of the duck filling (about the size and shape of a cigar) down the center of each wrapper. Fold the edges of each wrapper over the ends of the row of filling, then roll up tightly to enclose the filling.

In a large, heavy pot, heat 2 to 3 inches of oil to 350°F. Fry the spring rolls in batches, being careful not to crowd the pot, for 2 to 3 minutes, until golden brown on all sides. Remove to paper towels to drain.

Divide the chow-chow among 8 serving plates. Cut each spring roll in half on the diagonal and set 2 halves on the chow-chow on each plate. Drizzle barbecue sauce around the chow-chow and serve immediately.

NOTES: *You can make your own duck confit (see page 121 for a classic version) or purchase prepared confit at specialty grocery stores or by mail order. Spring roll wrappers can be found in the frozen foods section at Asian grocery stores. The Thai or Chinese wrappers made with wheat flour stand up to frying better than the Vietnamese rice and tapioca flour versions.*

DUCK CONFIT
WITH WARM
WHITE BEAN SALAD

THE JACKSONVILLE JAGUARS ADVANCED TO THE AFC CHAMPIONSHIP GAME IN 1995, JUST THEIR SECOND SEASON IN THE LEAGUE.

CHEF: Charles Charbonneau, North Beach Bistro, Jacksonville

WINE SUGGESTION: McWilliam's Shiraz

SERVES 6

PREP TIME
02:00+
REFRIGERATE OVERNIGHT

DUCK CONFIT

- ¾ cup kosher salt
- 6 duck legs (including thighs)
- 1 teaspoon peppercorns
- 8 garlic cloves, crushed
- 3 bay leaves, crumbled
- 8 fresh thyme sprigs
- 4 cups melted duck fat (see *Note*)

WHITE BEAN SALAD

- 8 ounces dried white beans (soaked overnight in cold water)
- 4 ounces bacon, chopped
- 1 cup diced onion
- 4 garlic cloves, chopped
- ½ cup diced carrot
- 1 bay leaf
- 2 fresh thyme sprigs, stemmed

  Salt and freshly ground black pepper
- 2 tablespoons chopped fresh parsley
- 2 tablespoons Champagne vinegar

Begin preparations for this dish a day in advance. The duck legs for the confit (meat that is cooked slowly, covered in fat) need to cure in the refrigerator for 8 hours, and the beans need to be soaked overnight.

MAKE THE DUCK CONFIT: Put the salt on a large plate. Press the flesh side of each duck leg into the salt, and lightly sprinkle the skin side with salt. Arrange 3 legs, skin side down, in a nonreactive container deep enough to hold the duck legs in 2 layers. Sprinkle with the peppercorns, garlic, and bay leaves, and arrange the thyme sprigs on top. Arrange the remaining 3 legs on top of the thyme, flesh side down, pressing them down firmly into the thyme. Cover and refrigerate for 8 hours or overnight.

Remove the legs from the container and rinse under cold running water to remove the salt and seasonings. Pat dry. Put the legs in a heavy, deep saucepan or Dutch oven large enough to hold the legs in 1 layer. Pour in the fat and bring to a simmer over medium heat; immediately reduce the heat to very low and cook until the meat can be very easily pulled from the bones, 2 to 3 hours. Let cool in the fat. The legs can be stored, covered with fat, in an airtight container in the refrigerator for up to 2 weeks.

MAKE THE WHITE BEAN SALAD: Drain the beans; set aside. In a medium heavy pot, cook the bacon over medium heat, stirring frequently, until almost crisp, then add the onion and garlic and sauté until tender, about 4 minutes. Add the beans, carrot, bay leaf, thyme, 4 cups water, and a pinch of salt. Bring to a boil, then lower the heat and simmer for 1½ to 2 hours, until the beans are tender but still hold their shape. Transfer to a shallow dish and let cool to warm or room temperature. Season with salt and pepper to taste, and gently fold in the parsley and vinegar.

Pull the duck meat from the bones in large chunks. Put it in a large skillet or sauté pan over low heat and sauté until warmed through, then raise the heat to high and sauté for about 5 minutes, until crisp and lightly browned.

Divide the beans among 6 serving plates and top with the duck meat. Serve immediately.

NOTE: *You can buy duck fat at good butcher shops, or you can substitute clarified butter (see page 171) or goose, chicken, or pork fat.*

SEA TROUT CRUDO

THE COLTS WERE THE FIRST
NFL FRANCHISE TO HAVE
PROFESSIONAL CHEERLEADERS.

PREP TIME

00:30+

STEEP OVERNIGHT

CHEF: Greg Hardesty, Elements, Indianapolis

WINE SUGGESTION: Whitehaven Sauvignon Blanc

SERVES 6

DRESSING

- 2 teaspoons rice vinegar
- ¼ cup extra-virgin olive oil
- 2 garlic cloves, crushed

SEA TROUT CRUDO

- 6 medium fingerling potatoes, boiled until tender and thinly sliced

 Salt and freshly ground black pepper

- 1 fennel bulb, shaved paper-thin with a mandoline or sharp knife
- 1 tablespoon capers, rinsed and drained
- 12 large basil leaves, torn into small pieces
- ¼ cup thinly sliced celery hearts (white part only)

 Thai chiles, very thinly sliced, to taste

- 1 teaspoon minced shallot
- 12 ounces very fresh sea trout fillet, very thinly sliced into ribbons
- 1 russet potato, julienned with a mandoline and fried in oil until crisp (optional)

Crudo (Italian for "raw") is a dish that features raw fish or meat. For this dish, ask your fishmonger for the very freshest fish he has— "sashimi-grade." Salmon or tuna fillets can be used in place of the sea trout.

MAKE THE DRESSING: Put the vinegar in a blender. With the motor running, slowly add the oil through the hole in the lid until thickened. Add the garlic and let sit overnight in the refrigerator. Bring the dressing to room temperature, then pour through a fine-mesh sieve and discard the garlic. Reblend if necessary. Set aside.

MAKE THE SEA TROUT CRUDO: Put the boiled fingerling potatoes in a medium bowl and toss with just enough vinaigrette to coat them. Season with salt and pepper to taste. Arrange the slices on 6 chilled serving plates, spreading them out into a thin layer in a circle 3 to 4 inches in diameter.

Toss the remaining ingredients, except the potatoes, together in the same bowl, with just enough vinaigrette to lightly coat them, and season with salt and pepper. Divide the mixture equally among the plates, gently mounding it in the center of each potato circle. Garnish with the fried potato, if using. Serve immediately.

ASIAN SALMON SPREAD
WITH CURRIED APPLE SLAW

IN 2002 THE BUCS WON
SUPER BOWL XXXVII, DEFEATING
THE RAIDERS 48–21.

PREP TIME
00:30+

CHEF: Marty Blitz, Mise en Place, Tampa

WINE SUGGESTION: Bridlewood Chardonnay

SERVES 4

APPLE SLAW

- ½ cup rice vinegar
- ¼ cup sugar
- 2 cups shredded green cabbage
- 1 cup julienned Fuji or other sweet, crisp apples
- ¼ cup finely julienned red bell pepper
- 1 teaspoon thinly sliced scallion
- 1 teaspoon curry powder
- Pinch of salt

SALMON SPREAD

- One 8-ounce boneless, skinless salmon fillet
- 3 tablespoons olive oil
- 1 serrano chile, diced
- 1 tablespoon chopped fresh cilantro
- 2 teaspoons Dijon-style mustard
- 2 teaspoons thinly sliced scallion
- 1 teaspoon sesame oil
- 1 teaspoon grated fresh ginger
- 1 teaspoon soy sauce
- Salt and freshly ground black pepper
- Fresh cilantro leaves
- Sesame seeds, toasted
- Sesame crackers

MAKE THE APPLE SLAW: In a large bowl, combine the vinegar and sugar and stir to dissolve the sugar. Add all the remaining ingredients and toss to combine. Let sit while you make the salmon spread.

MAKE THE SALMON SPREAD: Preheat the oven to 400°F.

Rub the salmon with ½ teaspoon of the oil and put it on a baking sheet. Roast for about 10 minutes, until just opaque in the center. Put the salmon in a medium bowl and let it cool for about 5 minutes. Add the chile, chopped cilantro, mustard, scallion, remaining sesame oil, ginger, and soy sauce and mix to combine well, breaking up the salmon into small pieces. Season with salt and pepper to taste. Garnish with cilantro leaves and sesame seeds. Serve with the slaw and crackers on the side.

CREOLE BOILED SHRIMP
WITH DIPPING SAUCE

THE NFL AWARDED NEW ORLEANS ITS EXPANSION FRANCHISE ON NOVEMBER 1, 1966—ALL SAINTS' DAY.

CHEF: Neal Swidler, Emeril's Delmonico, New Orleans

WINE SUGGESTION: Maso Canali

SERVES 4 TO 6

PREP TIME
00:30

DIPPING SAUCE

- ¼ cup fresh lemon juice
- ¾ cup vegetable oil
- ½ cup chopped onion
- ½ cup chopped scallions
- ¼ cup chopped celery
- 2 tablespoons chopped garlic
- 2 tablespoons prepared horseradish
- 3 tablespoons prepared Creole or other whole-grain mustard
- 3 tablespoons prepared yellow mustard
- 3 tablespoons ketchup
- 3 tablespoons chopped fresh parsley
- 1 teaspoon salt
- ¼ teaspoon ground cayenne
- ⅛ teaspoon freshly ground black pepper

SHRIMP

- 2 lemons, halved
- 4 bay leaves
- 3 teaspoons salt
- ½ teaspoon ground cayenne
- 2 tablespoons concentrated shrimp and crab boil such as Zatarain's (see *Note*)
- 3 pounds large shrimp with shells and heads on, or 2½ pounds headless shrimp

For a more substantial dish, serve the shrimp with boiled potatoes or another vegetable on the side, along with buttered French bread and a green salad. Remember to put out bowls for the shrimp shells.

MAKE THE DIPPING SAUCE: Put all the ingredients in a food processor and process for 30 seconds.

MAKE THE SHRIMP: Squeeze the juice from the lemons into a large pot and drop in the lemons. Add 4 quarts water, the bay leaves, salt, cayenne, and liquid boil. Bring to a boil and cook for 5 minutes. Add the shrimp. Return the pot to a boil, then immediately remove from the heat, cover the pot, and let stand for 4 to 5 minutes, until the shrimp are just cooked through. Drain and let the shrimp cool for 5 minutes.

Arrange the shrimp around the edge of a large platter, or divide them among individual serving plates. Put the dipping sauce in a small dish in the center of the platter. Serve immediately.

NOTE: *Concentrated shrimp and crab boil is a potent bottled mixture of essential oils and spices. Look for it in the spice aisle at the grocery store, or near the seafood counter. Substitute Cajun spice blend to taste if necessary.*

SAUTÉED CALAMARI IN YUZU SOY GLAZE
WITH EDAMAME

A 103-FOOT-LONG REPLICA OF A PIRATE SHIP SITS IN THE NORTH END ZONE OF RAYMOND JAMES STADIUM.

CHEF: Marty Blitz, Mise en Place, Tampa

WINE SUGGESTION: Whitehaven Sauvignon Blanc

SERVES 4

PREP TIME
00:30

YUZU SOY GLAZE

- ¼ cup yuzu juice (see *Notes*)
- ¼ cup soy sauce
- ¼ cup rice vinegar
- ¼ cup sugar
- ½ teaspoon grated ginger

CALAMARI

- 1 tablespoon vegetable oil
- ¼ teaspoon minced garlic
- 10 thin slices Thai chiles
- 8 shiitake mushrooms, stemmed and sliced
- 4 ounces shelled edamame, fresh or thawed frozen (see *Notes*)
- 20 ounces cleaned calamari bodies, cut into ¼-inch rings
- 8 fresh Thai or regular basil leaves, cut into chiffonade
- 4 fresh mint leaves, cut into chiffonade
- 2 teaspoons chopped fresh cilantro
- 1 tablespoon unsalted butter, softened

MAKE THE YUZU SOY GLAZE: In a medium bowl, whisk all the ingredients together with 1 cup water.

MAKE THE CALAMARI: In a medium sauté pan, heat the oil over high heat. Add the garlic, chiles, mushrooms, and edamame and sauté for about 1 minute, until just starting to brown. Add the calamari and sauté for 1 minute. Add the glaze and cook until the liquid is reduced by half, 2 to 4 minutes. Add the Thai basil, mint, cilantro, and butter and stir to combine.

Divide among 4 small serving dishes and serve immediately.

NOTES: *Yuzu is a Japanese citrus about the size of an orange. Fresh yuzu is difficult to find in markets, but bottled yuzu juice is readily available in Asian groceries. Its juice is very sour and distinctive, but you can substitute fresh lime juice to good effect.*

Look for fresh edamame—baby soybeans—in Asian markets in the warmer months, when they're in season. Frozen edamame, either in the pods or shelled, is available in most supermarkets and health food stores. Edamame in the pods can be blanched in boiling water for a few minutes, drained, and tossed with pepper and toasted fine sea salt and served as a game-day snack—set out an empty bowl for the pods.

CAPRESE SALAD

IN THE NFL'S FIRST SUDDEN-DEATH
OVERTIME GAME, THE COLTS BEAT
THE GIANTS 23–17 IN 1958.

PREP TIME
00:30+

CHEF: Tony Hanslits, Malibu on Maryland, Indianapolis

WINE SUGGESTION: Maso Canali

SERVES 4

6   canned whole plum tomatoes

12   slices fresh mozzarella cheese

12   fresh basil leaves, stems removed

¼   cup olive oil

Freshly ground black pepper

Use the best-quality canned tomatoes you can find—those from San Marzano, Italy, are a good bet—and the milky white, baby-fist–sized balls of fresh mozzarella that come packed in water.

Preheat the oven to 375°F.

Cut the tomatoes in half lengthwise and gently squeeze out the juice and most of the seeds. Put the tomato halves on a lightly oiled baking sheet and roast for about 30 minutes, turning them over with tongs once or twice, until nicely browned at the edges. Let cool.

Layer a slice of cheese, a basil leaf, and a tomato half on each of 4 serving plates. Repeat with the remaining cheese, basil, and tomatoes on a serving platter. Drizzle with the oil and season with pepper to taste.

FAITH HILL'S
GREEK SALAD

FIVE-TIME GRAMMY WINNER FAITH HILL
SINGS THE SNF OPENING SONG,
"WAITING ALL DAY FOR SUNDAY NIGHT."

CHEF: Faith Hill

SERVES 6

PREP TIME
00:30

4	romaine lettuce hearts, leaves torn into bite-size pieces
2	cups crumbled feta cheese
2	Japanese seedless cucumbers, chopped
2	tomatoes, preferably heirloom, chopped
1	green bell pepper, seeded and cut into strips
1	red bell pepper, seeded and cut into strips
1	yellow bell pepper, seeded and cut into strips
1	red onion, sliced
½	cup pitted kalamata olives
½	cup pitted green olives
⅔	cup extra-virgin olive oil
⅓	cup balsamic vinegar
	Salt and freshly ground black pepper

The key here is to use good-quality ingredients—perfectly ripe tomatoes, good feta and olives, and a high-quality cold-pressed olive oil. You can arrange this spectacular-looking salad on the platter up to an hour in advance, then dress it right before serving; just be sure to tear the lettuce rather than cut it with a metal knife so the edges don't turn brown.

Put the lettuce on a large, deep oval serving platter. Arrange the cheese, cucumbers, tomatoes, peppers, onion, and olives in rows on top of the lettuce.

In a small bowl, whisk together the oil and vinegar; season with salt and pepper to taste, then drizzle the vinaigrette over the salad. Serve immediately.

CLAM AND CORN CHOWDER

THE HALL OF FAME IN CANTON, OHIO, INDUCTED ITS INAUGURAL CLASS OF 17 MEMBERS ON SEPTEMBER 7, 1963.

PREP TIME
00:30+

CHEF: Michael Meffe, Peter Shear's Downtown, Canton

SERVES 4

4	ears of corn
4	cups heavy cream
½	cup (1 stick) unsalted butter, at room temperature
2	cups chopped fresh or jarred clams
1	teaspoon brown sugar
1	teaspoon Old Bay Seasoning
	Salt
1	lemon
	Tabasco sauce

Using a sharp knife, cut the corn kernels from the cobs and set aside. Break the corn cobs in half. Put the cream, half of the corn kernels, and the cobs in a medium saucepan. Bring to a boil, then lower the heat and simmer for 30 minutes. Remove and discard the corn cobs and transfer the cream and corn to a blender. Purée until smooth, then push the cream mixture through a fine-mesh sieve into a bowl and discard the solids.

In a large sauté pan over medium-high heat, melt 4 tablespoons of butter and add the reserved corn kernels. Sauté for 2 to 4 minutes, until just tender, then add the clams and sauté for 1 minute. Add the cream mixture and heat through. Stir in the remaining 4 tablespoons of butter, the sugar, and Old Bay and season to taste with salt, a squeeze of lemon, and a dash of Tabasco sauce. Serve immediately.

NOTE: *Serve this luxurious chowder in small bowls. You can replace half of the heavy cream with whole milk, if you'd like, and reduce the amount of butter, but the chowder won't be quite as silky and rich.*

CHIPOTLE BEEF TENDERLOIN
WITH RED AND GREEN CHIMICHURRI

PREP TIME
01:30+
MARINATE FOR 1 HOUR

CHEF: Bruce Molzan, Ruggles Grill, Houston

WINE SUGGESTION: Don Miguel Gascon Malbec

CHIPOTLE SAUCE AND TENDERLOIN

¼	cup olive oil
1	onion, diced
1	yellow bell pepper, seeded and diced
½	cup minced chipotle chiles in adobo
3	jalapeño chiles, chopped
8	garlic cloves, chopped
8	plum tomatoes, chopped
1½	cups packed brown sugar
1	cup red wine
1	cup fresh orange juice
1	cup red wine vinegar
	One 6-ounce can tomato paste
½	cup chopped fresh basil
½	bunch fresh cilantro, chopped
2	tablespoons freshly ground black pepper
2	tablespoons dried thyme
	One 6- to 7-pound whole beef tenderloin

GREEN CHIMICHURRI

¼	cup chopped garlic
¼	cup fresh lemon juice
¼	cup white wine vinegar
2	tablespoons dried oregano
1	teaspoon freshly ground black pepper
1	teaspoon salt
1	bunch fresh parsley, stemmed
1½	cups olive oil

RED CHIMICHURRI

1	cup red wine vinegar
½	cup sun-dried tomatoes, soaked in warm water to soften
¼	cup chopped shallots
¼	cup chopped garlic
	1 or 2 dried guajillo chiles, soaked in warm water to soften, then seeded and chopped (¼ cup)
3	tablespoons honey
1	tablespoon dried oregano
2	teaspoons salt
1	teaspoon freshly ground black pepper
1	roasted red bell pepper, seeded
1	bunch fresh parsley, stemmed
1	bunch fresh cilantro, stemmed
1½	cups olive oil

TENDERLOIN RUB

1	tablespoon chopped fresh basil
1	tablespoon chopped fresh thyme
1	tablespoon chopped fresh cilantro
	Coarse salt and cracked black pepper
	Basil sprigs

ON OCTOBER 6, 1999, THE NFL VOTED TO
AWARD THE 32ND FRANCHISE AND THE
2004 SUPER BOWL TO HOUSTON.

SERVES 15

If you're short on time, make only one of the chimichurri sauces—red or green—as an accompaniment.

MAKE THE CHIPOTLE SAUCE AND MARINATE THE TENDERLOIN:
Heat the oil in a medium saucepan over medium heat. Add the onion, bell pepper, chiles, and garlic and sauté for about 8 minutes, or until the vegetables are soft and the onions are transparent. Add the remaining ingredients, except the tenderloin, and simmer for 1 hour. Purée in a food processor, then transfer to a nonreactive baking dish and let cool to room temperature. Add the tenderloin. Let the tenderloin marinate in the sauce for 1 hour at room temperature.

MAKE THE GREEN CHIMICHURRI:
In a food processor, combine ½ cup water with the remaining ingredients, except the oil, and purée until smooth. With the motor running, slowly add the oil through the feed tube and process until thickened. Set aside.

MAKE THE RED CHIMICHURRI:
In a food processor, combine 1 cup water with all the remaining ingredients except the oil, and purée until smooth. With the motor running, slowly add the oil through the feed tube and process until thickened. Set aside.

MAKE THE TENDERLOIN RUB: In a small bowl, combine the herbs and salt and cracked pepper to taste.

COOK THE TENDERLOIN: Preheat the oven to 375°F.

Remove the tenderloin from the sauce and rub it all over with the herb mixture. Reserve the chipotle sauce.

Heat a heavy skillet over high heat. Add the tenderloin and cook until well browned on all sides, 10 to 14 minutes total. Transfer the tenderloin to a roasting pan and bake for about 30 minutes, or until the internal temperature registers 145°F on a meat thermometer, brushing with the chipotle sauce once after 10 minutes and once after 20 minutes. Discard any leftover sauce.

Thinly slice the tenderloin into medallions and serve with the red and green chimichurri, garnished with basil sprigs.

ASIAN BARBECUE BABY BACK PORK RIBS
WITH PINEAPPLE NAPA SLAW

IN 1998 THE JAGUARS BECAME THE FIRST EXPANSION TEAM TO MAKE THE PLAYOFFS 3 TIMES IN ITS FIRST 4 SEASONS OF PLAY.

PREP TIME

CHEF: **Charles Charbonneau,** Augustine Grille, Ponte Vedra Beach

WINE SUGGESTION: MacMurray SC Pinot Noir

SERVES 4

DRY RUB

- 2 tablespoons Chinese five-spice powder (see page 47)
- 2 tablespoons salt
- 2 teaspoons Sichuan peppercorns (see *Note*)
- 1 tablespoon ground ginger
- 1 tablespoon garlic powder
- 2 tablespoons packed dark brown sugar
- 2 tablespoons barbecue spice mix

RIBS

- 2 slabs baby back pork ribs
- ½ cup soy sauce
- 1 tablespoon minced fresh ginger
- 4 scallions, chopped
- 1 bunch fresh cilantro, chopped
- 1 head of garlic, cloves peeled and chopped
- 4 cups low-sodium chicken broth
- 1 cup hoisin sauce

SLAW

- 6 tablespoons vegetable oil
- 2 tablespoons rice vinegar

  Sambal oelek (see page 35)

  Salt and freshly ground black pepper
- ½ head napa cabbage, cored and shredded
- 1 small carrot, peeled and cut into julienne strips
- ¼ fresh pineapple, peeled and diced
- 1 bunch fresh cilantro, stemmed and minced
- 4 scallions, minced
- ½ cup diced red bell pepper

MAKE THE DRY RUB: Preheat the oven to 425°F. In a small bowl, combine all the ingredients.

MAKE THE RIBS: Rub the dry rub all over the ribs and put them in a roasting pan. Roast for about 1 hour, or until well browned. Lower the oven temperature to 325°F.

In a medium saucepan, combine the soy sauce, ginger, scallions, cilantro, garlic, broth, and hoisin sauce, bring to a simmer, then pour the mixture over the ribs in the pan. Cover the pan with aluminum foil and braise for 1½ to 2 hours, until the ribs are very tender. Remove the ribs to a large platter.

Pour the braising liquid through a fine-mesh sieve into a medium saucepan and bring to a boil. Lower the heat and simmer until the liquid is reduced by half and is the consistency of a thick glaze, 30 to 40 minutes. Set aside.

MAKE THE SLAW: Meanwhile, in a large bowl, whisk together the oil, vinegar, sambal oelek to taste, and salt and pepper to taste. Add the cabbage, carrot, pineapple, cilantro, scallions, and bell pepper and toss to combine. Add more sambal oelek, salt, and pepper if necessary.

FINISH THE RIBS: Preheat the oven to 450°F. Brush the ribs with the glaze and put them in a clean roasting pan. Roast until browned and heated through, about 5 minutes. Cut between the bones and arrange on individual plates with small bowls of the slaw.

NOTE: *Sichuan peppercorns are not peppercorns at all, but part of the dried fruit of the prickly ash tree. They can be found in Chinese markets. You can use freshly ground black pepper as a subtitute here, though the flavor will not be the same.*

CRAWFISH CURRY

AFTER HURRICANE KATRINA, THE SAINTS PLAYED 2005 HOME GAMES IN TIGER STADIUM, THE ALAMODOME, AND GIANTS STADIUM.

PREP TIME
00:45+

CHEF: **Susan Spicer,** Bayona, New Orleans

WINE SUGGESTION: Whitehaven Sauvignon Blanc

SERVES 4

3   tablespoons peanut oil

1   yellow onion, chopped

1   red bell pepper, seeded and chopped

1   green bell pepper, seeded and chopped

1   teaspoon minced garlic

3   tablespoons all-purpose flour

4   cups shrimp stock (see page 139) or low-sodium chicken or vegetable broth

One 6-ounce can pineapple juice

2   tablespoons mild or hot curry paste (see *Notes*), or more to taste

1   pound crawfish tails or peeled and deveined large shrimp

1   green apple, peeled, cored, and diced

2   zucchini, diced

Salt

Ground cayenne (optional)

4   cups hot cooked basmati rice

TOPPINGS

Sliced onions, fried until crisp

Chopped nuts

Chutney

Chopped hard-cooked egg

Toasted coconut

Lime pickle (see *Notes*)

Pappadum, deep-fried or crisped on a dry griddle (see *Notes*)

In a 2- to 3-quart saucepan, heat 1 tablespoon of the oil over medium heat. Add the onion, peppers, and garlic and sauté for 5 to 10 minutes, stirring frequently, until lightly browned. Sprinkle the flour over the vegetables, stir, and cook for 2 minutes, then whisk in the stock, pineapple juice, and curry paste. Bring to a boil, whisking, then lower the heat and simmer for about 20 minutes, or until the sauce is slightly thickened.

Meanwhile, in a large sauté pan, heat the remaining 2 tablespoons oil. Add the crawfish, apple, and zucchini and sauté for about 3 minutes, until the zucchini is just starting to soften, then transfer the mixture to the sauce and simmer for about 5 more minutes, until the crawfish are bright pink and opaque. Season with salt and cayenne, or add a bit more curry paste if necessary. Serve with the rice and any or all of the toppings.

NOTES: *Indian curry paste is available in jars in Indian markets—one popular brand is Patak's—but you can also make your own by puréeing curry spices (cumin, coriander, and turmeric especially) or premixed mild or hot curry powder with chopped onion, garlic, and a bit of red bell pepper.*

Jars of tangy, usually spicy lime pickle are also available in Indian markets. Try it as a topping for dal or hard-cooked eggs.

Pappadum are very thin pancakes that can be found in Indian markets and in the international foods section of good supermarkets. Premade pappadum come in dozens of flavors—spiced with cumin, cracked pepper, green chiles, garlic, fennel, and combinations. To prepare pappadum, heat a heavy griddle or skillet until it is very hot; add a pappadum and cook for about 1 minute, pushing down on it gently with a metal spoon or spatula, until bubbles form in the pappadum and it's browned in spots, then flip it over and briefly brown the other side. You can also deep-fry them in hot oil until bubbly and crisp.

PAELLA WITH BLACKENED SHRIMP AND RED SNAPPER

PREP TIME
01:00+

CHEF: **Bruce Molzan,** Ruggles Grill, Houston

WINE SUGGESTION: Martin Codax Albarino

PAELLA

2½ cups diced chicken breast

1 cup diced pork

 Salt and freshly ground black pepper

¼ cup olive oil

1 onion, diced

2 garlic cloves, chopped

2 jalapeño chiles, seeded and chopped

1 yellow bell pepper, seeded and diced

1 red bell pepper, seeded and diced

1 poblano pepper, seeded and diced

1 cup diced chicken or pork sausage

2 cups converted rice such as Uncle Ben's

½ cup white wine

½ teaspoon saffron threads

2 cups shrimp stock (see *Note*) or low-sodium chicken broth

1¼ cups pineapple juice

½ cup coconut milk

1 cup stemmed fresh cilantro

½ pound large shrimp, peeled and deveined

1 pound small clams in the shells

BLACKENED SHRIMP AND FISH

12 large shrimp, peeled and deveined

6 red snapper fillets

2 teaspoons chopped fresh cilantro

1½ tablespoons Creole seasoning salt

 Freshly ground black pepper

6 tablespoons unsalted butter

KRIS BROWN WAS THE FIRST KICKER IN NFL HISTORY TO MAKE 3 FIELD GOALS OF 54 YARDS OR LONGER IN A SINGLE GAME.

SERVES 6

Paella, with its profusion of meat and seafood, is a communal food, perfect for gatherings of friends and family. This version uses converted rice instead of the usual Spanish or Arborio. Use whatever seafood looks best at your market—scallops, mussels, crabmeat, fish fillets—and add it with the clams toward the end of the cooking time.

MAKE THE PAELLA: Sprinkle the chicken and pork lightly with salt and pepper. In a very large sauté pan, heat the oil over medium heat. Add the chicken and pork and sauté until lightly browned, about 5 minutes. Add the onion, garlic, jalapeños, peppers, and sausage. Cook, stirring frequently, until the onion is lightly browned, 6 to 8 minutes. Transfer the mixture to a large bowl. Return the pan to the heat and add the rice; sauté for 3 minutes, or until just starting to turn golden. Return sausage mixture to the pan on top of the rice. Add the wine, saffron, stock, pineapple juice, and coconut milk and stir to combine. Cover and simmer for 35 minutes. Fold in the cilantro, then arrange the shrimp and clams on top of the rice, cover, and steam until the shrimp is opaque and the clams open, about 5 minutes.

MAKE THE BLACKENED SHRIMP AND FISH: While the paella simmers, sprinkle the shrimp and fish with the cilantro, seasoning salt, and pepper. Heat two large cast-iron skillets over medium-high heat and add 3 tablespoons butter to each. When the butter is melted, add the shrimp to one skillet and the fish to another and cook, turning once or twice, until the shrimp is opaque and the fish is just cooked through, 4 to 6 minutes.

Spoon the paella into serving plates and divide the blackened shrimp and fish evenly among the plates. Serve immediately.

NOTE: *Use the shells from the shrimp in this dish to make a flavorful stock. Put them in a large saucepan with 1 roughly chopped onion and cover with water or low-sodium chicken broth. Bring to a boil, then lower the heat and simmer for 30 minutes. Pour through a fine-mesh sieve set over a bowl.*

COUNTRY GUMBO

IN 2000 THE SAINTS DEFEATED
THE ST. LOUIS RAMS FOR THE TEAM'S
FIRST EVER PLAYOFF WIN.

PREP TIME
03:00+

CHEF: Emeril Lagasse, Emeril's, New Orleans

WINE SUGGESTION: McWilliam's Cabernet Sauvignon

SERVES 12

One 4- to 5-pound duck, well trimmed of fat

Salt and cracked black pepper

¼ cup vegetable oil

1 cup all-purpose flour

1½ pounds wild mushrooms, stemmed and diced

1½ cups diced onions

¾ cup diced celery

¾ cup diced green, red, or yellow bell peppers, or a mixture

2 tablespoons minced garlic

One 12-ounce bottle stout beer

6 cups dark low-sodium chicken broth or water

1 teaspoon dried thyme

2 bay leaves

4 teaspoons Original Essence Seasoning, or more to taste

¼ teaspoon ground cayenne

Hot cooked white rice

1 cup chopped scallions

½ cup chopped fresh parsley

This recipe makes classic use of the ingredients known in Cajun and Creole cooking as the holy trinity: chopped onions, celery, and green bell peppers. Just as many traditional French dishes would be nearly impossible to make without a mirepoix (chopped onions, celery, and carrots), a gumbo, étouffée, or any braised dish lacking the trinity would be considered by most Louisianans to be downright sacrilegious.

Rinse the duck under cold running water inside and out. Use a sharp knife to cut down through the back on either side of the backbone. Remove the backbone and reserve for stock. Cut the duck in half through the breastbone. Cut the legs and wings from each half (cut off the wing tips and reserve for stock). Cut the breasts in half horizontally. (Alternatively, have your butcher do this for you.)

Season the duck pieces with 1 teaspoon salt and ½ teaspoon pepper. Heat a large Dutch oven over medium-high heat until hot. Place the duck, skin side down, in the pan and sear, turning once, until well browned on both sides, 14 to 16 minutes. Remove the duck to a platter and set aside.

Add the oil and flour to the pot. Cook over medium heat, stirring slowly and constantly, for 20 to 25 minutes, until it is dark brown, the color of chocolate. Add the mushrooms, onions, celery, peppers, and garlic and cook, stirring, for 4 to 5 minutes, until the vegetables have softened. Add the beer and stir to incorporate. Add the broth, thyme, bay leaves, Essence, cayenne, and 3 teaspoons salt, stirring well. Raise the heat to medium-high and bring to a boil. Return the duck pieces to the pot and lower the heat to maintain a simmer. Cook, uncovered, stirring occasionally, for 1½ hours, skimming off any fat or foam that rises to the surface. Remove the duck pieces from the gumbo, cool slightly, then remove the skin and meat from the bones and return the meat to the gumbo. Season with more salt, pepper, and Essence if necessary.

Spoon the gumbo into 12 deep serving bowls and top each with a scoop of rice. Garnish with the scallions and parsley and serve immediately.

FRED TAYLOR'S
SHRIMP CREOLE

#28 RUNNING BACK
6'1", 226 POUNDS
UNIVERSITY OF FLORIDA, b. 1-27-76

CHEFS: Fred Taylor and his wife, **Andrea Taylor**

SERVES 4

PREP TIME
00:45+

2	tablespoons vegetable oil
1	cup diced onion
1	cup diced celery
1	garlic clove, chopped
	Three 14-ounce cans whole peeled tomatoes, roughly chopped, with their juices
	One 14-ounce can tomato sauce
1	teaspoon chili powder, or more to taste
1	teaspoon sugar
1	teaspoon salt
1½	tablespoons Worcestershire sauce
	Red pepper flakes
1	cup diced green bell pepper
2	pounds frozen cooked and peeled small or medium-sized shrimp
4	cups hot cooked long-grain white rice

In a large pot, heat the oil over medium heat. Add the onion, celery, and garlic and cook, stirring frequently, until softened but not browned, about 5 minutes. Add the tomatoes and their juices, the tomato sauce, chili powder, sugar, salt, Worcestershire sauce, and red pepper flakes to taste. Bring to a boil, then lower the heat and simmer, uncovered, for 30 minutes.

Add the pepper and simmer for 5 minutes. Add the shrimp, bring to a simmer, and cook for 5 minutes more, or until thawed and heated through. Add more chili powder or red pepper flakes, if necessary.

Put a mound of rice in each of 4 large serving dishes and spoon the Shrimp Creole over the rice. Serve immediately.

POACHED CHICKEN
AND ZUCCHINI-PARMESAN SALAD

FORMER FALCONS QUARTERBACK JUNE JONES (1977–1981) RETURNED TO COACH THE TEAM FROM 1994–1996.

PREP TIME
01:30+

CHEF: Kevin Rathbun, Rathbun's, Atlanta

WINE SUGGESTION: Whitehaven Sauvignon Blanc

SERVES 4

POACHED CHICKEN

One 3½-pound whole chicken

1-inch piece ginger, peeled and roughly chopped

2 scallions, chopped

3 tablespoons salt

ZUCCHINI-PARMESAN SALAD

6 zucchini, quartered lengthwise

3 ounces Parmigiano-Reggiano cheese, shaved with a vegetable peeler

¼ cup extra-virgin olive oil

1 tablespoon fresh lemon juice

1 tablespoon basil cut into thin strips

Salt and cracked black pepper

This method of poaching a whole chicken—covering it with cold water, bringing it to a boil, then turning off the heat and letting it sit, covered, until it's cooked through—helps the chicken retain its juices as it cooks and cools it a bit at the same time. Make sure your bird is not too large, and use a good-quality local hen if possible.

MAKE THE POACHED CHICKEN: Put the chicken, ginger, scallions, and salt in a large pot and cover completely with cold water. Bring to a rolling boil, then immediately remove from the heat, cover, and let sit for 1 hour to 1 hour and 15 minutes, or until the chicken is cooked through and no longer pink. Remove the chicken to a cutting board and pull the meat from the bones, discarding the skin and bones. Set aside.

MAKE THE ZUCCHINI-PARMESAN SALAD: Use a vegetable peeler to shave thin lengthwise ribbons of the zucchini, starting from the skin side of each quarter and stopping when you get to the seeds; discard the seeds.

In a medium bowl, toss the zucchini, cheese, oil, lemon juice, and basil together and season with salt and cracked pepper to taste. Add the chicken and toss gently to combine. Divide among 4 serving plates and serve immediately.

PORK BELLY
WITH COLLARD GREEN RISOTTO, FETA, AND PICKLED OKRA

PREP TIME
04:30+
CURE FOR 2 DAYS

CHEF: **Dustin Pritchett**, Sunset Grill, Nashville

WINE SUGGESTION: MacMurray SC Pinot Noir

CURE

2	tablespoons salt
1	tablespoon sugar
4	garlic cloves, crushed
4	shallots, chopped
2	tablespoons red pepper flakes
½	teaspoon ground cinnamon

PORK

1½	pounds pork belly, skin trimmed off
1	tablespoon olive oil
1	carrot, coarsely chopped
½	onion, coarsely chopped
2	celery stalks, coarsely chopped
1	fennel bulb, coarsely chopped
1	cup white wine
½	cup fresh orange juice
	Low-sodium chicken broth

COLLARD GREENS

1	tablespoon olive oil
1	cup thinly sliced onion
2	pounds collard greens, tough stems removed, cut into 2-inch squares
3	cups low-sodium chicken broth
5	teaspoons apple cider vinegar
1	teaspoon salt, or more to taste

RISOTTO

2	tablespoons unsalted butter
1½	cups Arborio rice
1½	quarts low-sodium chicken broth, simmering, plus more if needed
1	teaspoon salt
2	ounces smoked feta cheese (or good-quality feta cheese)
4	spicy pickled okra pods

Pork belly is the cut that bacon is made from (bacon is cured and smoked) and is popular in Korean and Chinese cooking. The layers of meat and fat take beautifully to long, slow braising at low temperatures, as in this recipe: The meat becomes very tender, and the fat becomes silky. Pork belly can be found at Asian markets or at good butcher shops, which should be able to supply it with some advance notice. Look for pork belly with about equal parts fat and lean—the cuts from the front of the animal offer more lean than those from the back.

SERVES 4

MAKE THE PORK: Rub the cure all over the pork and put in a glass dish. Cover with plastic wrap and refrigerate for 2 days, turning pork over after the first day.

Preheat the oven to 300°F.

Rinse the pork and pat dry. In a large sauté pan over high heat, heat the oil. Add the pork and cook until well browned on both sides, about 8 minutes total. Remove the pork to a roasting pan or casserole dish. Add the carrot, onion, celery, and fennel to the pan and cook, stirring until lightly browned, about 8 minutes. Pour in the wine and orange juice and bring to a boil, stirring up any browned bits on the bottom of the pan. Pour the vegetables and liquid over the pork and add enough broth to come up just to the top of the pork (do not cover it). Cover the pan tightly with aluminum foil and cook for 3 hours. Remove the foil and cook for an additional 1½ hours, basting every 10 minutes with the braising liquid. Remove from the oven and drain off the braising liquid. (The pork can be prepared to this point a day or so in advance; set a dish

on top of the pork to press it down flat, cover the pan, and refrigerate.)

Transfer the pork to a cutting board and let rest for 10 minutes. Cut the pork into 2-by-½-inch rectangles and set aside.

MAKE THE COLLARD GREENS:
In a large pot, heat the oil over medium heat. Add the onion and sauté until softened and lightly browned, about 4 minutes. Add the greens and cook, tossing to coat in the oil, until wilted, 2 to 3 minutes. Add the broth, vinegar, and 1 teaspoon salt, then lower the heat and cook, covered, for 45 minutes, or until the greens are tender but there is still liquid in the pan. Adjust the seasoning if necessary. Drain the greens in a colander set over a bowl, reserving the cooking liquid (pot liquor) for serving. Cover the pot liquor to keep warm, or put it in a saucepan and rewarm just before serving.

MAKE THE RISOTTO: In a small saucepan, melt the butter over medium heat. Add the rice, stir, and cook for 2 minutes, or until lightly toasted. Add enough broth to just cover the rice. Add the salt. Cook, stirring constantly, for 20 to 25 minutes, adding broth a little at a time, until the rice is al dente (firm to the bite) and is a creamy consistency. Stir the collard greens into the risotto and cook for 2 minutes. Remove from the heat and gently fold in the cheese.

Meanwhile, put the pork slices in a small baking dish, cover with foil, and heat in a 350°F oven for 3 to 5 minutes before serving.

Place a mound of the risotto in the center of each of 4 serving bowls. Pour the warm pot liquor over the top. Arrange 2 pieces of pork belly and 1 pickled okra on top of each serving. Serve immediately.

SAM BAKER'S
CALZONES
WITH RICOTTA, MOZZARELLA, MUSHROOMS, AND PEPPERONI

#72 OFFENSIVE TACKLE
6'5", 305 POUNDS
USC, b. 5-30-85

PREP TIME
01:00

CHEF: Sam Baker

SERVES 6

1 tablespoon olive oil

8 ounces mushrooms, sliced

½ onion, diced

Salt and freshly ground black pepper

15 ounces ricotta cheese

One 8-ounce ball of fresh mozzarella cheese, shredded

¼ cup chopped fresh basil

Cornmeal for the baking sheet

2 pounds prepared pizza dough

4 ounces pepperoni, diced or sliced

1 large egg, beaten with 1 teaspoon water

2 cups hot marinara sauce

Grated Parmesan cheese

6 fresh basil sprigs

Sam says, "When I went to USC, I used to go home pretty much every Thursday night, and this is what we would always have."

In a medium sauté pan, heat the oil over high heat. Add the mushrooms, onion, and salt and pepper to taste and sauté until the mushrooms have released their liquid and the liquid has evaporated, about 8 minutes. Transfer to a bowl to cool.

In a medium bowl, combine the ricotta and mozzarella cheeses, the basil, and salt and pepper to taste.

Preheat the oven to 450°F. Sprinkle a baking sheet with cornmeal.

Divide fresh pizza dough into 6 balls. Working with 1 ball at a time, roll the ball out into a thin circle about 8 inches in diameter. Spread one-sixth of the ricotta mixture on half of the circle, leaving a ½-inch border around the edge. Top with some of the mushroom-onion mixture and some pepperoni. Fold the empty half of the dough circle over the filling and pinch the edges to seal. Fold the bottom of the edge over the top and pinch it into a rope shape around the curved edge

of the calzone, making sure to seal the edges tightly. Transfer the calzone to a baking sheet. Repeat with the remaining dough and filling. Brush the tops of the calzones with the egg wash and bake for 15 to 20 minutes, until well browned.

Put a calzone on each plate, spoon the marinara sauce over the top, sprinkle with Parmesan cheese, and garnish with basil sprigs. Serve immediately.

CHICKEN MARBELLA

#15 PUNTER
6'3", 213 POUNDS
NOTRE DAME UNIVERSITY, b. 5-18-71

CHEF: Craig Hentrich

SERVES 6

PREP TIME
01:00
MARINATE 8 HOURS

½ cup red wine vinegar

½ cup olive oil

1 head of garlic, cloves peeled and puréed

¼ cup dried oregano

Salt and freshly ground black pepper to taste

1 cup pitted prunes

½ cup Spanish green olives

½ cup capers, partially drained

6 bay leaves

6 boneless, skinless chicken breasts

1 cup packed brown sugar

1 cup white wine

¼ cup chopped fresh parsley or cilantro

Craig Hentrich's version of a classic recipe from The Silver Palate Cookbook *is a great party dish: It's easily doubled, and nearly all the preparation can be done a day in advance.*

In a large, nonreactive bowl, combine the vinegar, oil, garlic, oregano, a pinch each of salt and pepper, the prunes, olives, capers, and bay leaves. Add the chicken and turn to coat it with the marinade. Cover with plastic wrap and put in the refrigerator to marinate for 8 hours or overnight.

Preheat the oven to 350°F.

Transfer the chicken and marinade to a baking dish large enough to hold the breasts in a single layer and sprinkle with the brown sugar and wine. Bake for 50 to 60 minutes, until the chicken is cooked through. Serve immediately, garnished with the parsley.

BOBBY MCCRAY'S
TOMATO AND ONION BRAISED CHICKEN

#93 DEFENSIVE END
6'6", 261 POUNDS
UNIVERSITY OF FLORIDA, b. 8-8-81

PREP TIME
01:00+

CHEF: Bobby McCray

SERVES 4

8   boneless, skinless chicken thighs (about 2 pounds)

    Salt and freshly ground black pepper

1   tablespoon extra-virgin olive oil

1   large onion, sliced

4   garlic cloves, minced

½   teaspoon red pepper flakes

½   cup white wine

½   cup low-sodium chicken broth

    One 28-ounce can whole tomatoes, crushed with your hands

1   tablespoon chopped fresh oregano

1   tablespoon chopped fresh thyme

    One 1-pound package Spanish yellow rice with seasonings (such as Vigo)

Trim the excess fat from the chicken thighs and season them with salt and pepper. In a deep sauté pan, heat the oil over high heat; add the chicken and cook until browned on both sides, 8 to 10 minutes total. Remove the chicken to a plate.

Return the pan to medium-high heat, add the onion, cook until just softened, about 4 minutes, then add the garlic and red pepper flakes and cook, stirring frequently, until the onion is lightly browned and the garlic is soft, about 5 minutes. Add the wine, stirring to scrape up any browned bits in the bottom of the pan, and simmer until reduced by half, about 5 minutes. Add the broth, tomatoes, oregano, thyme, and chicken. Bring to a boil, then lower the heat and simmer for 30 to 40 minutes, until the chicken is tender and the sauce has thickened slightly. Season with salt and pepper to taste.

Meanwhile, cook the rice according to the package directions. Divide the rice among 4 serving plates and top with the chicken. Spoon the sauce over and serve immediately.

POTATO CASSEROLE

#69 OFFENSIVE TACKLE
6'3", 320 POUNDS
SAN DIEGO STATE UNIVERSITY, b. 6-26-79

CHEF: Chester Pitts

SERVES 6

PREP TIME
01:00+

CASSEROLE

One 2-pound bag frozen diced potatoes (Southern-style hash browns)

One 10¾-ounce can cream of chicken soup

8 ounces shredded cheddar cheese

½ cup (1 stick) unsalted butter, melted

1 cup light sour cream

Salt and freshly ground black pepper to taste

TOPPING

1 tube Ritz crackers, crushed (about 1½ cups)

¼ cup (½ stick) unsalted butter, melted

Chester says, "This recipe has been in my household for about five years—I learned to make it from my fiancé, Latoyah. I only cook it for my family and it's always a hit, especially with the little ones. It's easy and delicious."

MAKE THE CASSEROLE: Preheat the oven to 350°F.

In a large bowl, combine all the ingredients. Spread in an 8-by-11½-inch baking dish.

MAKE THE TOPPING: Combine the crackers and ¼ cup butter. Top the casserole with the cracker mixture and bake for 50 to 60 minutes, until very bubbly and deep golden brown on top. Serve immediately.

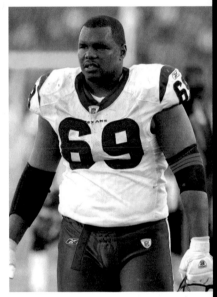

PROSCIUTTO-WRAPPED TUNA MUFFULETTA

THE SAINTS' COLORS, BLACK AND GOLD, SYMBOLIZE NEW ORLEANS' STRONG TIES TO THE OIL INDUSTRY.

CHEF: Susan Spicer, Herbsaint, New Orleans

WINE SUGGESTION: McWilliam's Shiraz

SERVES 4

PREP TIME
00:30
LET SIT 1 HOUR

OLIVE SALAD

- 1 cup pitted kalamata olives
- 1 cup mixed pickled Italian vegetables (giardiniera), chopped
- ½ cup chopped celery heart
- ½ cup pimiento-stuffed green olives
- ½ cup extra-virgin olive oil
- 8 pepperoncini, stemmed and chopped
- 2 tablespoons capers, drained
- 2 tablespoons chopped fresh flat-leaf parsley
- 2 tablespoons red wine vinegar
- 2 teaspoons minced garlic

TUNA

- 1 teaspoon fennel seeds, toasted and crushed
- 1 teaspoon grated lemon zest
- ½ teaspoon red pepper flakes
- ½ teaspoon minced garlic
- ¼ cup olive oil
- 1 pound fresh tuna loin, cut into four 4-ounce pieces
- 4 thin slices prosciutto
- 8 slices ciabatta or seeded Italian bread
- 8 slices provolone cheese

This nontraditional muffuletta is good as it is, but even better (and less traditional) if you put the assembled sandwiches on a baking sheet and warm them in a 400°F oven for a few minutes to melt the cheese. To save time, use one jar of prepared Italian olive salad instead of making the olive salad.

MAKE THE OLIVE SALAD: In a medium bowl, combine all the ingredients and let sit at room temperature for 1 hour.

MAKE THE TUNA: Meanwhile, in a small bowl, combine the fennel seeds, lemon zest, red pepper flakes, garlic, and oil and brush the mixture on both sides of the tuna. Wrap each piece of tuna around its center with 1 slice of prosciutto. Refrigerate for at least 30 minutes.

Heat a cast-iron grill pan over high heat. Lightly oil the pan and grill the wrapped tuna, turning it over once, until medium-rare, about 4 minutes on each side.

Lay out 4 slices of bread. Put 2 slices of provolone on each slice of bread, and top with a piece of tuna, some olive salad, and another slice of bread.

BOB SANDERS's
LEMON PEPPER TILAPIA

#21 SAFETY
5'8", 206 LBS.
UNIVERSITY OF IOWA, b. 2-24-81

PREP TIME
00:1:30

CHEF: Bob Sanders

SERVES 2

2   tablespoons unsalted butter, softened

     Grated zest and juice of ½ lemon

2   tablespoons chopped fresh parsley (optional)

¼   cup all-purpose flour

     Salt and freshly ground black pepper

2   tilapia fillets

     Lemon pepper

1   tablespoon olive oil

Bob says, "I love tilapia. It's something that I try to eat a couple times a week. It's so easy, and it's really light. I don't like a lot of heavy foods. You don't want to put too much flour on here. You want to just coat the top of the fish, a very thin coating." Feel free to increase the amount of lemon zest and lemon juice if you like it extra lemony.

In a small bowl, combine the butter, lemon juice and zest, and parsley, if using.

Spread the flour on a large plate and season it with salt and pepper to taste. Season the fish on both sides with lemon pepper and dredge the fillets in the flour, shaking off the excess. Heat the oil in a large sauté pan over medium-high heat and add the fish. Cook until golden brown on the bottom, about 3 minutes, then turn and cook until the other side is lightly browned and the fish is almost cooked through, about 3 more minutes. Add the butter mixture and cook, shaking the pan a bit, until the butter starts to brown at the edges of the pan.

Remove the fillets to serving plates and spoon the butter and lemon sauce over them. Serve immediately.

BAKED EGGPLANT WITH MOZZARELLA AND PARMESAN

IN 2006 THE COLTS BECAME THE FIRST NFL TEAM TO OPEN BACK-TO-BACK SEASONS WITH 9 STRAIGHT WINS.

CHEF: Tony Hanslits, Tavola di Tosa, Indianapolis

WINE SUGGESTION: Frei Brothers RR Chardonnay

SERVES 4

PREP TIME
01:00

1 Sicilian eggplant (see *Note*)

2 large eggs

¾ cup fresh bread crumbs

Salt and freshly ground black pepper

2 tablespoons olive oil, or more if necessary

2 cups prepared tomato sauce

8 ounces fresh mozzarella, thinly sliced

1 cup grated Parmesan cheese

3 tablespoons chopped fresh flat-leaf parsley

Preheat the oven to 400°F. Butter an 8-inch square baking dish.

Cut the eggplant crosswise into ¼-inch-thick slices. In a shallow bowl, lightly beat the eggs. Put the bread crumbs in another shallow bowl and season with salt and pepper to taste. Dip the eggplant slices in the eggs, then coat with bread crumbs. When all the slices are coated, heat the oil in a large skillet over medium heat. Working in batches if necessary to avoid crowding the pan, and adding a little more oil if necessary, add the eggplant slices and cook, turning once, until browned on both sides, about 4 minutes per side. As each slice browns, remove it to paper towels to drain until all the slices are browned.

Spread a thin layer of tomato sauce over the bottom of the baking dish. Arrange a layer of eggplant slices over the sauce, then top with some of the mozzarella and Parmesan. Continue layering sauce, eggplant, and cheeses until you have three layers, finishing with cheese. Bake for 35 to 45 minutes, until bubbling and lightly browned on top. Serve hot, garnished with the parsley.

NOTE: *Sicilian eggplants are fat and globe-shaped rather than oblong, but you can substitute a long, thin Italian eggplant or a small regular eggplant in this dish, as the flavor of each variety is nearly identical. Choose a male eggplant if you can, one that does not have a deep indentation in the flower end (the end opposite the stem)— it will have fewer seeds than a female eggplant.*

DWIGHT FREENEY'S
BROWN STEW CHICKEN

#93 DEFENSIVE END
6'1", 268 POUNDS
SYRACUSE UNIVERSITY, b. 2-19-80

PREP TIME
00:45+
MARINATE 1 HOUR

CHEF: Dwight Freeney

SERVES 4

2½ pounds bone-in chicken pieces (see *Note*)

Salt

½ teaspoon black pepper

¼ teaspoon dried thyme

1 teaspoon all-purpose adobo seasoning

1 teaspoon plus 2 tablespoons brown gravy mix

1 large onion, diced

2 garlic cloves, chopped

½ green bell pepper, diced

½ red bell pepper, diced

1 tomato, diced

1 scallion, chopped

Vegetable oil for frying

Dwight says, "My family is from Jamaica—I've got to thank my mom for this recipe. I usually cook this stew for my boys, and serve it with rice and beans."

Put the chicken in a large bowl and sprinkle with ½ teaspoon salt, the pepper, thyme, adobo seasoning, and 1 teaspoon gravy mix. Add onion, garlic, peppers, tomato, and scallion and toss to combine. Cover and marinate in the refrigerator for 1 to 2 hours.

Remove the chicken from the marinade and brush off the vegetables; reserve the vegetables.

In a deep, heavy pot, heat 2 to 3 inches of oil to 375°F. Working in batches to avoid crowding the pot, fry the chicken until golden brown, about 2 minutes; let the oil come back up to temperature between batches. Remove the chicken to a deep skillet large enough to hold the pieces snugly in one layer.

Add the reserved vegetables and 1½ cups water and bring to a boil over high heat. Lower the heat and simmer for about 30 minutes, or

until the chicken is cooked through and tender. Using tongs, remove the chicken to a serving dish. In a small bowl or measuring cup, stir together the remaining 2 tablespoons gravy mix and 1 cup cold water. Whisking constantly, gradually add the mixture to the sauce and vegetables in the skillet and simmer for 5 minutes longer, until thickened. Season with salt to taste and pour the sauce over the chicken. Serve immediately.

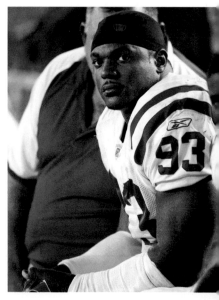

JON BEASON'S
HOPPIN' JOHN

#42 LINEBACKER
6'0", 237 POUNDS
UNIVERSITY OF MIAMI, b. 1-14-85

CHEF: **Jon Beason**

SERVES 4 TO 6

PREP TIME
01:00+

In the South and in other parts of the country, Hoppin' John is eaten on New Year's Day for good luck. Some say the black-eyed peas are supposed to bring good luck in the form of coins. Others say it's wise to eat "poor" on New Year's—the main ingredients here being fairly cheap and plentiful—so you'll eat "rich" the rest of the year. Jon Beason serves the dish as part of a meal that includes fried pork chops, corn bread, and banana pudding (see page 55).

Wash the neck bones and put them in a medium saucepan with enough water to just cover. Bring to a boil, skim the foam from the surface, then reduce the heat and simmer until the meat can be easily pulled from the bones, about 1 hour, skimming occasionally. Using tongs or a slotted spoon, remove the neck bones to a plate, cover to keep warm, and set aside.

Skim the foam from the cooking liquid; you should have about 3 cups—add more water or pour off some if necessary to make 3 cups. Add the garlic salt, thyme, black-eyed peas, onion, and peppers. Bring to a boil, then stir in the rice. Cover the pan and lower the heat to very low. Cook for about 30 minutes, until the liquid is absorbed and the rice and peas are cooked through. Season generously with salt and pepper. Transfer the rice mixture to a serving bowl and top with the neck bones. (Alternatively, pull the meat from the bones while the rice and peas cook and fold it in at the end.) Serve immediately.

NOTE: *Fresh pork neck bones may be scarce in grocery stores outside the South, but you can substitute the readily available smoked pork neck bones, ham hocks, or smoked pork chops for even more flavor. Look in the corners of supermarket meat cases, or in the frozen meats section, or ask the meat counterperson for help finding the smoked pork products.*

1½ **pounds fresh or smoked pork neck bones, in at least 4 pieces (see *Note*)**

1 **teaspoon garlic salt**

½ **teaspoon dried thyme**

Two 1-pound bags frozen black-eyed peas

1 **cup chopped onion**

½ **cup diced red and orange bell peppers**

1 **cup raw long-grain white rice**

Salt and freshly ground black pepper

LOBSTER AND BRIE MAC AND CHEESE

THE TITANS WERE THE ONLY TEAM TO BEAT THE JAGUARS IN 1999, TWICE IN THE REGULAR SEASON AND IN THE AFC CHAMPIONSHIP GAME.

PREP TIME
00:30+

CHEF: Brian Uhl, Sunset Grill, Nashville

WINE SUGGESTION: McWilliam's Chardonnay

SERVES 4

8	paper-thin slices country ham or prosciutto
1	teaspoon olive oil
2	cups heavy cream
4	cups cooked ditalini pasta, or any small macaroni
	Salt and cracked black pepper
5	ounces Brie, cut into small cubes
⅓	cup grated Parmesan cheese
8	ounces cooked lobster meat
2	tablespoons minced fresh chives
	Micro greens (optional)

Preheat the oven to 350°F.

Brush the ham or prosciutto slices with the oil and arrange them on a baking sheet in a single layer. Bake for 6 to 8 minutes, until crisp. Set aside.

In a large sauté pan over high heat, bring the cream to a boil. Add the pasta and cook until the cream is reduced and thickened slightly. Season with salt and cracked pepper to taste, then stir in the cheeses and lobster meat. Cook until the cheeses are melted and the lobster is just warmed through, about 4 minutes. Divide the mac and cheese among 4 serving plates. Top with the ham slices and sprinkle with the chives and greens, if using. Serve immediately.

WHITE CHOCOLATE BANANA CREAM PIE

ENTERING 2008 THE FALCONS WERE 44–34 ALL-TIME AGAINST THEIR NFC SOUTH RIVAL, THE SAINTS.

CHEF: Kevin Rathbun, NAVA, Atlanta

WINE SUGGESTION: Barefoot Bubbly

SERVES 8

PREP TIME

00:30

CHILL 1 HOUR

PASTRY CREAM

- 1 large egg
- 2 tablespoons sugar
- 1 tablespoon cornstarch
- ¾ cup half-and-half
- 2 ounces white chocolate, finely chopped

FILLING

- 2 cups heavy cream
- ½ cup sugar
- 6 bananas, cut into ½-inch-thick rounds
- ½ ounce banana liqueur
- 1 tablespoon crème de cacao

- One 10-inch prebaked pie crust
- 8 ounces white chocolate, shaved
- Unsweetened cocoa powder
- Whipped cream

MAKE THE PASTRY CREAM: In a medium bowl, whisk together the egg, sugar, and cornstarch.

In a small saucepan, bring the half-and-half to a boil. Remove from the heat and slowly add one-third of the half-and-half to the egg mixture, whisking constantly. Pour the mixture back into the saucepan and cook over low heat, whisking constantly, until almost boiling; do not overheat or the eggs will scramble. Remove from the heat and whisk in the white chocolate. Transfer the pastry cream to a clean bowl and set aside to cool completely, about 1 hour.

MAKE THE FILLING: In a large bowl with an electric mixer, whip the cream and sugar until soft peaks form. Gently fold in the cooled pastry cream, then fold in the bananas and the liqueurs, folding just until combined; do not overmix.

Fill the pie crust with the mixture. Top with the white chocolate shavings and sprinkle lightly with cocoa powder.

Place a slice of pie on each of 8 serving plates and top with whipped cream.

WARM CHOCOLATE HAZELNUT PUDDING

THE 1995 PANTHERS BECAME THE FIRST
EXPANSION TEAM TO BEAT AN NFL
DEFENDING CHAMPION, THE 49ERS.

CHEF: **Tobin McAfee,** Sir Edmond Halley's, Charlotte

WINE SUGGESTION: Barefoot Bubbly

SERVES 6

PREP TIME

00:45+

1½ cups unsalted butter,
plus more for the molds

½ cup granulated sugar,
plus more for the molds

½ cup confectioners' sugar,
plus more for dusting

10 large egg yolks

10 large egg whites

3½ ounces semisweet chocolate,
grated

½ cup ground hazelnuts

½ cup ground walnuts

½ cup graham cracker crumbs

Fresh red currants on the stem
(optional)

6 fresh mint sprigs (optional)

Preheat the oven to 350°F. Butter the insides of six 6-ounce ramekins or round cake molds and dust with granulated sugar.

In a large bowl, using an electric mixer, beat the butter, confectioners' sugar, and egg yolks until thick. Set aside.

In a separate bowl using clean beaters, beat the egg whites and granulated sugar until stiff peaks form. Fold the whites into the yolk mixture. Fold in the chocolate, hazelnuts, walnuts, and graham cracker crumbs. Pour the batter into the prepared ramekins and set them in a larger baking dish. Pour hot water into the dish to come halfway up the sides of the ramekins. Bake for 35 minutes. Remove the ramekins from the water bath and let cool slightly on wire racks.

Place the ramekins on larger serving plates and dust lightly with confectioners' sugar. Garnish with currants and mint, if desired, and serve warm.

CITRUS RICE PUDDING

THE SAINTS'
OFFICIAL FIGHT SONG IS
"WHEN THE SAINTS GO MARCHING IN."

PREP TIME

CHILL 1 HOUR

CHEF: Megan Roen, Bayona, New Orleans

WINE SUGGESTION: Barefoot Bubbly

SERVES 4

½ cup short- or medium-grain white rice

2 cups whole milk

Grated zest of ½ lemon

Grated zest of ½ orange

½ cup sugar

2 large egg yolks

2 tablespoons honey

2 oranges

½ cup any combination of chopped candied kumquats, candied Meyer lemon peel, candied tangerine peel, or satsuma orange peel

Nut brittle, broken into shards

Put the rice with water to cover in a heavy saucepan. Bring just to a boil, then drain in a sieve. Rinse the rice thoroughly under cold running water. Rinse out the saucepan and return the rice to the pan, along with the milk, fresh lemon and orange zests, and sugar. Bring to a boil over high heat, then reduce the heat and simmer, uncovered, stirring occasionally as the rice absorbs the liquid, for 25 minutes.

In a small bowl, stir the egg yolks and honey together. Stir about ¼ cup of the hot rice mixture into the yolk mixture, then pour the yolk mixture back into the saucepan, stirring constantly until the mixture comes to a boil. Remove the saucepan from the heat and transfer the rice mixture to a bowl. Cover with plastic wrap and put in the refrigerator for about 1 hour, until the pudding is thoroughly chilled.

Peel the oranges and separate them into segments by cutting between the membranes. Cut the segments in half crosswise and gently fold them into the chilled pudding, along with the candied citrus. Spoon the pudding into martini glasses or small serving bowls, garnish with the brittle, and serve immediately.

RONDE BARBER'S
PEANUT CRUNCH CAKE

#20 CORNERBACK
5'10", 184 POUNDS
UNIVERSITY OF VIRGINIA, b. 4-7-75

CHEF: Ronde Barber

SERVES 8 TO 10

PREP TIME
01:00

1	box yellow cake mix
1	cup creamy peanut butter
½	cup packed brown sugar
3	large eggs
¼	cup vegetable oil
½	cup semisweet chocolate chips
½	cup peanut butter chips
½	cup roasted salted chopped peanuts

Preheat the oven to 350°F. Butter a 9-by-13-inch cake pan.

In a large bowl using an electric mixer, beat the cake mix, peanut butter, and brown sugar on low speed until thoroughly combined and crumbly. Reserve ½ cup of the crumb mixture for the topping. To the remainder, add 1 cup water, the eggs, and oil, and mix on low speed until the ingredients are evenly moistened, then increase the speed to high and beat for 2 minutes, until lighter in color and smooth. Stir in ¼ cup of the chocolate chips and ¼ cup of the peanut butter chips. Pour into the prepared pan.

Combine the peanuts, reserved crumb mixture, and the remaining chips, and sprinkle the topping over the batter. Bake for 40 to 45 minutes, until a toothpick inserted near the center comes out clean. Cool completely on a wire rack, then cut into squares and serve.

BUTTERMILK PANNA COTTA
WITH BALSAMIC MACERATED STRAWBERRIES

AS THE HOUSTON OILERS, THE FRANCHISE WON THE FIRST AFL CHAMPIONSHIP, BEATING THE L.A. CHARGERS IN 1961.

PREP TIME	CHEF: **Brian Uhl,** Sunset Grill, Nashville	
01:00+ CHILL 12 HOURS	WINE SUGGESTION: Barefoot Bubbly	SERVES 6

PANNA COTTA

- 2 teaspoons unflavored gelatin
- 1 cup heavy cream
- 7 teaspoons sugar
- 2 cups buttermilk
- ¾ teaspoon vanilla extract

MACERATED STRAWBERRIES

- 1 cup quartered strawberries
- ½ cup packed brown sugar
- ¼ cup balsamic vinegar
- ¼ cup strawberry preserves

Panna cotta ("cooked cream" in Italian) is a classic, simple dessert of cream that has been heated to just below boiling and then mixed with gelatin and chilled until firm. The best panna cotta is creamy and smooth, not too firm, and not too heavy or rich. Here the cream is set off by the tartness of the buttermilk and the sweet-sour balsamic vinegar in the strawberries.

MAKE THE PANNA COTTA: In a small cup, combine the gelatin and 2 tablespoons water. Let stand until the gelatin is softened, about 10 minutes.

In a small saucepan, combine the cream and sugar and cook over medium heat until the sugar is dissolved and the mixture is hot but not boiling. Remove from the heat and add the gelatin mixture. Stir until the gelatin is completely dissolved and the mixture is smooth. Cool to room temperature, about 45 minutes.

Stir in the buttermilk and vanilla. Pour through a fine-mesh sieve into a 4-cup measuring cup. Divide the mixture among six 5- to 6-ounce ramekins and refrigerate for 12 hours, or until set.

MAKE THE MACERATED STRAWBERRIES: Put the strawberries in a nonreactive bowl. Purée the sugar, vinegar, preserves, and ¼ cup water in a blender. Pour the mixture over the strawberries and let sit for 1 hour.

Top the panna cotta with a spoonful of macerated strawberries and serve immediately.

WEST

LAMB MEATBALLS
WITH MARINATED WINTER VEGETABLES

TWO OF THE QUARTERBACKS WITH THE BEST PASSER RATINGS EVER ARE 49ERS: STEVE YOUNG (96.8) AND JOE MONTANA (92.3).

PREP TIME
01:00+
CHILL 10 HOURS

CHEF: Dennis Leary, Rubicon, San Francisco

WINE SUGGESTION: McWilliam's Cabernet

SERVES 8 TO 10

LAMB MEATBALLS

2	pounds ground lamb shoulder
½	pound bacon, diced
2	small white onions, diced
1	bunch fresh thyme, stemmed
4	garlic cloves, finely chopped
3	tablespoons Dijon-style mustard
¼	pound shiitake mushrooms, diced and sautéed in a little oil
1	tablespoon salt

VINAIGRETTE

	Juice of 2 lemons
	Juice of 1 orange
1	shallot, finely diced
1	cup grapeseed oil (see page 178) or vegetable oil
	Salt and freshly ground black pepper to taste

VEGETABLES

1	celery root (see *Note*)
4	carrots
2	turnips
2	russet potatoes
1	parsnip

MAKE THE LAMB MEATBALLS: In a large bowl, combine all the ingredients and refrigerate, covered, for at least 8 hours or overnight. Form the mixture into small balls or ovals about the size of a large grape. Put the balls on a baking sheet and refrigerate for 2 hours.

When ready to serve, preheat the oven to 450°F.

Take the balls out of the refrigerator and put the baking sheet straight into the oven; bake for 10 minutes, or until nicely browned. Set aside.

MAKE THE VINAIGRETTE: In a medium bowl, whisk all the ingredients together.

MAKE THE VEGETABLES: Peel the vegetables and cut them into ¼-inch dice. One at a time, cook the vegetables in a large pot of rapidly boiling water until just tender, then remove them to a large bowl. Add the vinaigrette while the vegetables are still hot and toss to combine.

Place 3 warm meatballs on each serving plate and pile some of the vegetables alongside. Serve immediately.

NOTE: *Celery root, also called celeriac, is the knobby brown root of a type of celery grown especially for its root (the stalks and leaves are inedible). It tastes like celery but more herbal, and its texture is similar to that of a turnip. Celery root is in season from fall through early spring; look for firm, heavy roots with no soft spots. Put the peeled root in water and lemon juice to prevent discoloration if you don't plan to cook it within a few minutes of chopping it.*

SIZZLING DUNGENESS CRAB CAKES

PREP TIME
01:00+

CHEF: John Howie, Seastar Restaurant and Raw Bar, Bellevue

WINE SUGGESTION: Frei Brothers RR Chardonnay

CRAB CAKES

- 4 tablespoons (½ stick) unsalted butter
- 3 tablespoons minced onion
- 3 tablespoons minced carrot
- 3 tablespoons minced celery
- 6 tablespoons minced yellow, red, and green bell peppers
- ¼ cup heavy cream
- 1 pound Dungeness crabmeat, picked over to remove cartilage
- 1 large egg yolk
- 1 teaspoon salt
- ¼ teaspoon freshly ground black pepper
- 1½ cups all-purpose flour
- 3 large whole eggs
- 1 cup milk
- 4 cups panko bread crumbs (see Notes)

THAI WHITE SAUCE

- 1½ teaspoons cornstarch
- ½ cup sugar
- ¼ cup Thai sweet chile sauce (see Notes)
- 3 tablespoons rice vinegar
- 1½ teaspoons Thai fish sauce
- 1½ teaspoons fresh lime juice
- ½ teaspoon minced ginger
- ¼ teaspoon minced garlic
- 1 cup white wine
- 2 tablespoons white wine vinegar
- 1 tablespoon minced shallot
- ½ cup heavy cream
- 1½ cups (3 sticks) unsalted butter, cut into 2-inch pieces
  Salt
- ¾ cup (1 ½ sticks) unsalted butter, clarified (see Notes)
  Pickled ginger

Here the sweet meat of the Dungeness crab is highlighted by sautéed vegetables, a touch of cream, a crunchy crust of panko bread crumbs, and a classic white sauce made bright and piquant by the inspired addition of Thai sweet-and-sour flavors.

MAKE THE CRAB CAKES: In a small saucepan, melt the butter over medium-low heat. Add the onion, carrot, celery, and bell peppers and cook, stirring, until tender but not browned, about 5 minutes. Add the cream and bring to a boil; cook until the cream is reduced slightly, 1 to 2 minutes. Transfer to a large mixing bowl and let cool for 5 minutes. Add the crabmeat, egg yolk, salt, and pepper and stir gently to combine. Form the mixture into 24 balls. Put the flour in a wide, shallow dish. In a second dish, whisk together the whole eggs and milk. Put the bread crumbs in a third dish.

One at a time, dredge the balls in the flour, then dip them in the egg mixture, then put them in the bread crumbs; gently press the bread crumbs onto each ball and flatten it into a ½-inch–thick round patty. Set the crab cakes aside on a waxed paper–lined baking sheet while you make the sauce.

MAKE THE THAI WHITE SAUCE: In a small bowl, stir together the cornstarch and ¼ cup water; set aside.

In a small saucepan, combine the sugar, chile sauce, rice vinegar, fish sauce, lime juice, ginger, and garlic. Bring to a boil over high heat and cook until the mixture registers 180°F on a candy thermometer. Stir in the cornstarch mixture and cook for 5 minutes, until the sweet-and-sour sauce is thick. Set aside.

A HAWK NAMED TAIMA LEADS THE
SEAHAWKS OUT OF THE TUNNEL AT THE
TEAM'S HOME GAMES.

SERVES 8

In a medium saucepan, combine the wine, white wine vinegar, and shallot and cook over high heat until the liquid is reduced to a syrupy consistency and is almost completely evaporated. Add the cream and cook over medium-high heat until the sauce is reduced by about half. Whisking constantly, add the butter pieces one at a time, whisking each until it is melted before adding the next. Pour the sauce through a fine-mesh sieve into a bowl and stir in the sweet-and-sour sauce and salt to taste. Set aside.

When ready to serve, heat the clarified butter in a large sauté pan over medium heat. Fry the crab cakes in the butter until golden brown on both sides, 4 to 5 minutes per side. Transfer to a plate lined with paper towels to drain.

Spoon some of the sauce onto each of 8 serving plates and arrange 3 crab cakes on each plate. Garnish with pickled ginger and serve immediately.

NOTES: *Panko or Japanese bread crumbs are available in better supermarkets and in Asian markets, but coarse homemade bread crumbs are a fine substitute.*

Thai sweet chile sauce (usually spelled "chilli" on Thai labels) might be most familiar as a sauce served with spring rolls. The spicy, sweet condiment can be found in glass bottles in Asian markets. If you can't find sweet chile sauce, substitute about 2 tablespoons chile-garlic sauce and add sugar to taste, if necessary.

To clarify butter, melt it in a saucepan over low heat, then skim off and discard the foam. Slowly pour the clear melted butter into a bowl or glass measuring cup, leaving the cloudy solids behind; discard the solids. The clarified butter can be heated to higher temperatures than plain melted butter because it won't burn as easily.

DECONSTRUCTED SUSHI

AT CHARGERS HOME GAMES, A CANNON IS FIRED EVERY TIME A TOUCHDOWN IS SCORED.

PREP TIME
01:00+

CHEF: Jonathan Hale, Blue Point Coastal Cuisine, San Diego

WINE SUGGESTION: MacMurray SC Pinot Noir

SERVES 6

SUSHI RICE

- ½ cup short- or medium-grain white rice
- 1½ teaspoons rice vinegar
- 1½ teaspoons sugar
- 1 teaspoon salt

TUNA AND JELLIES

- 3 ounces sashimi-grade ahi tuna

  Two ¼-ounce envelopes unflavored gelatin, or 8 gelatin sheets
- ½ cup soy sauce
- ½ cup cucumber juice (see *Notes*)
- ⅓ cup wasabi powder (see *Notes*)
- ½ teaspoon sesame seeds

MAKE THE SUSHI RICE: Rinse the rice well, then drain. In a small saucepan, combine the rice with 1 cup cold water and bring to a boil, uncovered. Cover the pan, reduce the heat to the lowest setting, and cook for 14 to 15 minutes, until tender. Remove from the heat and let stand, covered, for 10 minutes. In another small saucepan or in a microwave oven, heat the vinegar, sugar, and salt until the sugar and salt are dissolved. Transfer the rice to a bowl and gently fold in the vinegar mixture until all the rice is coated. Press the rice into a flat pan and let cool completely, then cut into 6 ½-inch cubes.

MAKE THE TUNA AND JELLIES: Cut the tuna into 6 equal cubes and put in the refrigerator. Meanwhile, in a small saucepan, combine 1 envelope (or 4 sheets) of the gelatin with the soy sauce and heat over low heat until the gelatin is dissolved. Pour into a flat, shallow pan so that the liquid is ⅛ inch deep and chill in the refrigerator for about 30 minutes, or until set.

Meanwhile, in a small saucepan, combine 1 envelope (or 4 sheets) of the gelatin with the cucumber juice and heat over low heat until the gelatin is dissolved. Pour into a flat, shallow pan so that the liquid is ⅛ inch deep and put in the refrigerator for about 30 minutes, or until set.

Cut the soy sauce and cucumber juice jellies into ½-inch squares and set aside.

Put the wasabi powder in a small bowl and stir in just enough cold water to make a thick paste.

Skewer a piece of the tuna with a sharp-pointed chopstick. Spread a bit of the wasabi paste on the tuna, then skewer a rice cube, then a soy sauce square, then a cucumber juice square. Sprinkle with the sesame seeds. Repeat to make 6 skewers. Serve immediately.

NOTES: *To make cucumber juice: Peel and chop 1 seedless (English) cucumber and put it in a blender with ½ cup water. Purée until very smooth, then pour through a fine-mesh sieve into a glass measuring cup. Chill any leftover juice and enjoy it as a cooling drink over ice with a squeeze of lime and, if you like, a few drops of simple syrup or agave nectar.*

Wasabi powder is available in the Japanese or international food section of most supermarkets, although most of the wasabi sold in both America and Japan is actually made of horseradish with green coloring—it's not real wasabi root, which is much more expensive than imitation.

SMOKED TROUT SALAD SANDWICHES
WITH CREAMY HORSERADISH DRESSING

THE RAMS PLAYED IN LOS ANGELES FROM 1946–1994 BEFORE RELOCATING TO ST. LOUIS.

CHEF: **Bill Cardwell,** Cardwell's at the Plaza, St. Louis

WINE SUGGESTION: Whitehaven Sauvignon Blanc

SERVES 12

PREP TIME
00:30

1	pound skinned and boned smoked trout fillet
1	cup diced celery
½	cup finely chopped scallions
2	tablespoons minced fresh parsley
1	tablespoon minced fresh dill
8	ounces cream cheese, softened
½	cup sour cream
¼	cup prepared horseradish
1	tablespoon honey
1	teaspoon dry mustard
1	tablespoon grated lemon zest
2	tablespoons fresh lemon juice
¼	teaspoon celery salt
¼	teaspoon Tabasco sauce
12	soft small rolls of any kind, preferably brioche, split, toasted and buttered
2	cups baby arugula, washed, patted dry, and torn into small pieces

Flake the trout into a medium bowl. Add the celery, scallions, parsley, and dill.

In a separate bowl, beat the cream cheese until soft, then beat in the sour cream, horseradish, and honey. In a small bowl, combine the dry mustard, lemon zest and juice, celery salt, and Tabasco sauce. Add to the cream cheese mixture and blend well.

Gently fold the cream cheese mixture into the trout, being careful not to overmix and break up the fish. Top the bottom half of each roll with some of the trout salad and arugula. Cover with the top half of the bun. Serve immediately.

CRAB AND SWEET CORN BISQUE

THE SEAHAWKS ARE THE ONLY NFL TEAM TO SWITCH CONFERENCES TWICE IN THE POST-MERGER ERA.

PREP TIME

01:00+

MARINATE OVERNIGHT

CHEF: John Howie, Seastar Restaurant and Raw Bar, Bellevue

WINE SUGGESTION: Frei Brothers RR Chardonnay

SERVES 6

BISQUE

- 1 cup (2 sticks) salted butter
- ½ cup minced white onion
- 2 tablespoons minced shallot
- ¼ cup all-purpose flour
- ½ cup dry sherry
- 8 cups half-and-half
- ¾ cup fresh sweet corn kernels
- 1 cup clam juice
- ½ teaspoon dried ground thyme
- ½ teaspoon ground white pepper
- 2 teaspoons salt

MADEIRA-PORT REDUCTION

- ½ cup Madeira
- ½ cup Tawny Port
- 2 tablespoons balsamic vinegar
- 2 tablespoons sugar

- 18 ounces Dungeness crabmeat, picked over to remove cartilage
- 1½ tablespoons fresh chives cut on the diagonal into ¾-inch lengths

This bisque can be made a day in advance. Cool it quickly by transferring it to a large bowl set in a larger bowl of ice water and stirring until cool; cover and refrigerate. When ready to serve, bring the bisque to a boil over high heat, add the crabmeat, and ladle into bowls. The Madeira-Port reduction can also be made in advance and refrigerated; bring it to room temperature or warm it before serving.

MAKE THE BISQUE: In a large pot over medium heat, melt the butter. Add the onion and shallot and sauté until translucent, about 8 minutes. Sprinkle in the flour and cook, stirring constantly, until golden but not browned, about 5 minutes, lowering the heat if necessary to keep the roux from coloring too quickly. Stirring constantly, add the sherry, then the half-and-half. Bring to a simmer, stirring.

As the half-and-half mixture is heating, put the corn and clam juice in a blender and purée until very smooth. When the bisque reaches a simmer, add the corn mixture and return to a simmer. Add the thyme, white pepper, and salt and simmer until thickened, 15 to 20 minutes.

MAKE THE MADEIRA-PORT REDUCTION: In a small saucepan, combine all the ingredients and bring to a boil over high heat. Boil until the mixture is reduced to ¼ cup, 10 to 12 minutes.

Bring the bisque to a boil, add the crabmeat, then immediately ladle it into 6 soup bowls. Drizzle with a bit of the reduction (you won't use all of it) and garnish with the chives. Serve immediately.

GOLDEN BEET SOUP
WITH SMOKED SALMON

THE 49ERS, ALONG WITH THE STEELERS
AND COWBOYS, HAVE WON 5 SUPER BOWLS,
THE MOST OF ANY TEAMS.

PREP TIME
01:00+

CHEF: **Dennis Leary,** Rubicon, San Francisco

WINE SUGGESTION: MacMurray SC Pinot Noir

SERVES 8

BEET SOUP

2	pints mineral water (not sparkling)
	Salt
4	large yellow beets, peeled (see *Notes*)
2	stalks celery, peeled and diced
½	carrot, diced
1	small onion, diced
2	cups heavy cream
	White wine vinegar

CHIVE PURÉE

3	bunches fresh chives
¼	cup grapeseed oil (see *Notes*) or vegetable oil

SALMON

1	red onion, diced
18	fresh flat-leaf parsley leaves
8	sprigs fresh dill
8	ounces smoked salmon, finely diced
	Juice of 1 lemon
2	tablespoons sour cream
	Olive oil
	Salt and freshly ground black pepper

MAKE THE BEET SOUP: In a nonreactive saucepan, bring the mineral water to a boil. Add a large pinch of salt. Add the beets, celery, carrot, and onion. The water should just cover the vegetables. Reduce the heat and boil gently until all the vegetables are very soft, about 45 minutes. Pour the mixture into a blender and purée until smooth. Add the cream, a few drops of vinegar, and more salt, if necessary, and blend again. Pour through a fine-mesh sieve set over a bowl, cover with plastic wrap, and chill in the refrigerator.

MAKE THE CHIVE PURÉE: Blanch the chives for 5 seconds in a pot of boiling water. Drain, then immediately plunge the chives into a bowl of ice water to cool them. Drain, then put the chives in a blender with 1 ice cube and blend until smooth, adding the oil through the hole in the lid in a slow, steady stream. Set aside.

MAKE THE SALMON: Blanch the onion in a pot of boiling water for 30 seconds. Drain and set aside. Chop the parsley and dill. In a medium bowl, gently fold the parsley and dill together with the salmon, lemon juice, sour cream, blanched onion, and a few drops of oil. Season to taste with salt and pepper.

Place a spoonful of the salmon mixture in the center of each of 8 chilled soup bowls. Pour the chilled soup carefully around the salmon—do not cover it completely—and drizzle with the chive purée. Serve immediately.

NOTES: *If yellow beets are unavailable, substitute medium-sized red beets—the soup will be just as striking.*

Grapeseed oil is extracted from the pits of some varieties of grapes used in winemaking. It's a clean, light-tasting oil, and a good choice here because it won't overpower the flavor of the chives in the purée. Grapeseed oil has a high smoke point, which makes it excellent for sautéing and searing at high temperatures.

WILD MUSHROOM SOUP

WHEN THE RAIDERS AND 49ERS PLAY EACH OTHER, THE GAME IS CALLED THE "BATTLE OF THE BAY."

CHEF: **Michael Mina,** Aqua, San Francisco

WINE SUGGESTION: Frei Brothers RR Chardonnay

SERVES 8

PREP TIME
01:00+

---

2   tablespoons olive oil

1   pound white mushrooms

10 shiitake mushrooms, stemmed

10 oyster mushrooms, stemmed

1   sprig fresh thyme

1   sprig fresh basil

    Salt

4   cups low-sodium chicken broth

2   yellow creamer (golf-ball-sized) potatoes, peeled

1   cup heavy cream

    Freshly ground black pepper

16 bay scallops

2   tablespoons clarified butter (see page 171)

In a large pot, heat the oil over high heat, then add the mushrooms, thyme, basil, and 1 teaspoon salt. Lower the heat to medium-low and cook, stirring occasionally, for 15 minutes, until the mushrooms are soft but not browned. Add the broth and potatoes and bring to a boil over high heat, then lower the heat and simmer for about 20 minutes, until the potatoes are tender. Remove and discard the thyme and basil sprigs.

Add the cream. Working in batches, transfer the soup to a blender and purée until smooth. Return to the pot, bring back to a simmer, and add salt and pepper to taste.

Season the scallops lightly with salt and pepper. In a medium sauté pan, heat the clarified butter over high heat and add the scallops in one layer. Cook, without turning, until browned on the bottom, about 2 minutes, then turn and brown the other side.

Ladle the soup into 8 small serving bowls and top with the scallops. Serve immediately.

GOAT CHEESE AND TOMATO NAPOLEONS
WITH BALSAMIC SYRUP

DENVER'S BACK-TO-BACK SUPER BOWL WINS
IN 1998 AND 1999 CAME AT THE END
OF QUARTERBACK JOHN ELWAY'S CAREER.

CHEF: **Kevin Taylor,** Restaurant Kevin Taylor, Denver

WINE SUGGESTION: Martin Codax Albarino

SERVES 4

PREP TIME
01:00+
MARINATE 6 HOURS

4	**large plum tomatoes, peeled (see *Note*)**
4	**garlic cloves, peeled and crushed**
4	**sprigs fresh thyme**
1	**tablespoon extra-virgin olive oil**
	Salt and freshly ground black pepper
1	**cup balsamic vinegar**
¼	**cup sugar**
	One 1-pound log of goat cheese
1	**bunch arugula, washed and stemmed**
8	**green olives**
4	**ounces Parmesan cheese, in one piece**

Gently squeeze the tomatoes to remove the seeds, leaving the tomatoes whole. Put the tomatoes in a casserole dish and sprinkle with the garlic, thyme, oil, and salt and pepper to taste. Cover with plastic wrap and set aside at room temperature for 6 hours.

In a small saucepan over medium heat, combine the vinegar and sugar with ¼ cup water and bring to a boil, stirring to dissolve the sugar. Cook until the syrup is reduced by half, then let cool to room temperature.

Cut the tomatoes into ¼-inch-thick rounds. Cut the goat cheese into ½-inch-thick rounds and flatten them gently with your palm so that they're ¼ inch thick and about the same size as the tomato slices. On each of 4 serving plates, place a tomato slice; layer the goat cheese and tomato slices on top. Divide the arugula among the plates and drizzle with the balsamic syrup. Garnish with the olives and use a vegetable peeler to shave the Parmesan over the top. Serve immediately.

NOTE: *To peel tomatoes: Cut a shallow X in the bottom of each tomato. Bring a large pot of water to a boil and add the tomatoes. Return to a boil and cook for 1 to 2 minutes, just until the skins are loosened. Using a slotted spoon, remove the tomatoes to a bowl of ice water. When cool enough to handle, slip off the skins.*

ANDREA KREMER'S
CAESAR SALAD CLARE

EMMY AWARD–WINNING KREMER HAS COVERED EVERY SUPER BOWL SINCE 1985.

PREP TIME

00:30

STEEP 2 HOURS

CHEF: Andrea Kremer, NFL Reporter, Sunday Night Football

SERVES 6

½   cup olive oil

4   garlic cloves, halved

¼   cup white wine vinegar

2   tablespoons Dijon-style mustard

2   tablespoons Worcestershire sauce

One 2-ounce can anchovy fillets packed in oil, finely minced

2   large egg yolks

¼   cup grated Parmesan cheese

Salt and freshly ground black pepper

2   heads romaine lettuce

Croutons

This salad is named for Andrea Kremer's mother, the cook of the family. The classic dressing includes raw egg yolks, which give it a rich flavor and mouthfeel. If you're serving the salad to young children or anyone with a weakened immune system, omit the egg yolks and add 2 tablespoons prepared mayonnaise.

Put the oil in a medium bowl and add the garlic. Let steep for 2 hours at room temperature, or longer in the refrigerator. Remove and discard the garlic.

Add the vinegar, mustard, Worcestershire sauce, anchovies, egg yolks, and cheese and whisk until thickened slightly and lighter in color. Season with salt and pepper to taste.

Rinse the lettuce and pat or spin it dry. Tear the leaves into bite-size pieces and put them in a large bowl with enough dressing to just coat the leaves; toss to evenly coat. Divide the lettuce among 6 serving plates and top with croutons. Serve immediately.

"I was a huge football fan as a little girl. My parents were extremely supportive of that interest. We'd had season tickets for the Eagles since Veterans Stadium opened in 1971. I remember what we always had to eat as much as watching the games. If it was a day game, we'd bring our hoagies and, obviously, big vats of hot chocolate. And if it was a late game, well, what else can you have when you're in Philadelphia? Cheese steaks! Plus, soft pretzels and brown mustard, and Tastykakes."

BEACH BOY "CAVIAR"

IN 1979 CHARGERS QUARTERBACK
DAN FOUTS SET AN NFL RECORD WITH
4 CONSECUTIVE 300-YARD PASSING GAMES.

CHEF: Bob Brody, Trellises Garden Grill at the Town and Country Hotel, San Diego

WINE SUGGESTION: Red Rock Merlot

SERVES 6 TO 8

PREP TIME
00:30

"CAVIAR"

- **2** tablespoons red wine vinegar
- **1** teaspoon hot sauce
- **½** teaspoon vegetable oil
- **1** garlic clove, minced

   One 15-ounce can black-eyed peas, drained and rinsed

   One 15-ounce can corn kernels, drained and rinsed

- **1** cup sliced scallions
- **½** bunch fresh cilantro, stemmed and chopped
- **3** small plum tomatoes (8 ounces), seeded and diced

   Salt and freshly ground black pepper to taste

GUACAMOLE

- **1** avocado

   Juice of 1 lime

   Salt (optional)

   Tortilla chips

   One 14-ounce jar nopalito strips, drained (see *Note*)

MAKE THE "CAVIAR": In a large bowl, whisk together the vinegar, hot sauce, oil, and garlic. Add the remaining ingredients and toss to combine. Set aside.

MAKE THE GUACAMOLE: Peel the avocado and remove the pit. In a medium bowl, mash the avocado with a fork until broken up but still somewhat chunky and stir in the lime juice. Add salt to taste, if desired.

Arrange tortilla chips in one layer on a large serving platter and top each with a spoonful of the "caviar," a dollop of the guacamole, and a nopalito strip. Serve immediately.

NOTE: *Nopalitos are prickly pear cactus pads. They're sold in small jars in the Mexican foods section of most supermarkets and Hispanic food markets.*

TONY GONZALEZ'S
TOM KHA TOFU
(THAI GALANGAL AND TOFU SOUP)

**#88 TIGHT END
6'5", 251 POUNDS
UNIVERSITY OF CALIFORNIA, b. 2-27-76**

PREP TIME
00:30

CHEF: Tony Gonzalez

SERVES 4

- 8 ounces firm tofu, drained
- ½ red bell pepper, seeded
- ½ bunch fresh cilantro, stemmed
- 4 cups vegetable stock
- One 13.5-ounce can light coconut milk
- 1 tablespoon palm sugar (see page 35), brown sugar, or white cane sugar, or more if necessary
- 2 teaspoons soy sauce, or more if necessary
- One 2-inch piece of galangal, peeled
- 2 Kaffir lime leaves (see page 20)
- 1 lemongrass stalk, bottom 4 inches
- 2 fresh Thai chiles
- Juice of 1 lime, or more if necessary
- Salt (optional)
- Sriracha hot sauce

Tony Gonzalez is a vegan, and he loves this adaptation of tom kha gai, *or Thai chicken and galangal soup. Here tofu is used in place of chicken, vegetable stock instead of chicken broth, and soy sauce and salt instead of fish sauce.*

Cut the tofu into ½-inch slices, then cut the slices into 1-inch squares. Use a sharp knife to trim the light-colored ribs from the inside of the bell pepper, then cut it into thin strips. Divide the tofu, bell pepper, and cilantro among 4 serving bowls and set aside.

In a large saucepan, combine the stock, coconut milk, palm sugar, and soy sauce. Thinly slice the galangal and add it to the pan. Make several short horizontal tears in the Kaffir lime leaves and add them to the pan. Remove the green outer leaves from the lemongrass. Chop the lemongrass into 1-inch lengths, then use the back of a knife to bruise the pieces and release the flavor; add to the pan. Wearing gloves to protect your hands, thinly slice the chiles, then add them to the pan. Bring just to a simmer over

medium-high heat, stirring frequently, then lower the heat and simmer for 5 to 8 minutes, until the broth is flavorful. Remove from the heat and add the lime juice. Taste and add more sugar, soy sauce, lime juice, or salt if necessary.

Leaving the lemongrass and Kaffir leaves in the pan, ladle the broth into the bowls over the tofu and serve immediately, with the hot sauce on the side.

MATT HASSELBECK'S
COMEBACK CHICKEN CHILI

#8 QUARTERBACK
6'4", 225 POUNDS
BOSTON COLLEGE, b. 9-25-75

CHEF: Matt Hasselbeck

PREP TIME
01:30+

SERVES 6 TO 8

One 15½-ounce can cannellini beans

6 cups low-sodium chicken broth

2 onions, chopped

2 garlic cloves, minced

1 tablespoon vegetable oil

Two 4-ounce cans chopped green chiles

2 teaspoons ground cumin

1½ teaspoons dried oregano

¼ teaspoon ground cloves

¼ teaspoon ground cayenne

4 cups shredded cooked chicken breast (2 large breasts)

Salt and freshly ground black pepper

3 cups grated Monterey Jack cheese

Matt Hasselbeck suggests serving this green chili with bowls of chopped tomatoes, parsley or cilantro, scallions, and black olives, and guacamole, sour cream, crumbled tortilla chips, and salsa on the side. It's also great with corn bread, or spooned over rice.

In a large pot, combine the beans, broth, half of the onions, and the garlic and bring to a boil over high heat.

Meanwhile, in a medium sauté pan, heat the oil over medium-high heat; add the remaining onion and sauté until tender and lightly browned, about 5 minutes. Add the chiles, cumin, oregano, cloves, and cayenne and stir to combine. Scrape the mixture into the broth, add the chicken, and simmer for 1 hour. Season with salt and pepper to taste. Ladle into soup bowls and top with the cheese. Serve immediately.

"SHOW ME STATE" ANTIPASTO

IN 1948 THE RAMS BECAME THE
FIRST PROFESSIONAL FOOTBALL TEAM TO
HAVE A LOGO ON THEIR HELMETS.

PREP TIME
00:30+

CHEF: Bill Cardwell and **Dave Owens**, Cardwell's at the Plaza, St. Louis

WINE SUGGESTION: Mirassou Chardonnay

SERVES 8

ARBORIO RICE SALAD

- 1½ cups Arborio rice
- ¼ cup extra-virgin olive oil
- 1 onion, chopped
- 3 garlic cloves, chopped
- Pinch of saffron threads
- ½ teaspoon red pepper flakes
- Salt
- ½ cup low-sodium vegetable broth
- ¼ cup white balsamic vinegar
- ¼ cup dried currants
- ½ cup Marsala wine
- ¾ cup diced roasted red peppers
- ¾ cup green olives, cut into rounds
- ¼ cup chopped fresh mint
- ¼ cup chopped fresh parsley
- Radicchio leaves

CROSTINI

- ¼ cup olive oil
- 2 teaspoons chopped garlic
- 1 teaspoon dried basil
- 1 teaspoon dried oregano
- Salt and freshly ground black pepper
- 1 tablespoon chopped fresh parsley
- 24 slices Italian bread

ANTIPASTO

- ½ pound prosciutto, thinly sliced
- ½ pound salami, thinly sliced
- ½ pound mortadella, thinly sliced
- ½ pound coppa, thinly sliced

This classic antipasto is a great dish to make for a party, as both the rice salad and the crostini can be made several hours in advance and served at room temperature.

MAKE THE ARBORIO RICE SALAD: Put the rice in a large pot of salted water and bring to a boil. Lower the heat and simmer, covered, until tender, about 15 minutes. Drain well and transfer to a bowl.

In a sauté pan, heat the oil over medium heat. Add the onion, garlic, saffron, red pepper flakes, and a pinch of salt. Cook until the onion is tender, about 5 minutes. Add the broth and vinegar and simmer for 1 minute. Add the mixture to the rice and toss to combine. In the same skillet, combine the currants and wine and simmer until the currants are plump, 2 to 4 minutes. Add to the rice mixture and toss to combine. Add the peppers, olives, mint, parsley, and salt to taste. Using the radicchio leaves as cups, fill the leaves with the salad and arrange them on a large serving platter. Set aside.

MAKE THE CROSTINI: Preheat the oven to 325°F.

In a sauté pan, combine the oil, garlic, basil, and oregano and cook over medium heat until the garlic is aromatic, about 3 minutes. Season with salt and pepper to taste. Remove from the heat and add the parsley. Brush the slices of bread with the oil mixture and arrange them on a baking sheet. Bake until the bread is crisp and lightly browned, 8 to 10 minutes.

ARRANGE THE ANTIPASTO: Arrange the sliced meats and the crostini on the platter and serve.

STEAK WITH FRIED POTATOES
AND TARRAGON AÏOLI

OWNER AL DAVIS'S TEAM MOVED TO
LOS ANGELES IN 1982, THEN
RETURNED TO OAKLAND IN 1995.

PREP TIME
01:00+
MARINATE 6–8 HOURS

CHEF: Chris Rossi, Citron, Oakland

WINE SUGGESTION: LMM Napa Cabernet Sauvignon

SERVES 4

STEAK

- 4 large shallots, thinly sliced
- 2 garlic cloves, crushed
- 1 cup red wine
- ¼ cup olive oil
- Salt and freshly ground black pepper
- 2 tablespoons chopped fresh flat-leaf parsley
- 1 pound hanger or skirt steak

AÏOLI

- 4 large shallots, finely diced
- ½ cup red wine vinegar
- 1 tablespoon dried tarragon
- 2 large egg yolks
- 1 garlic clove, minced
- ¼ cup fresh lemon juice
- 1½ cups vegetable oil
- 2 tablespoons chopped fresh tarragon
- Salt and freshly ground black pepper

FRIED POTATOES

- Peanut oil for frying
- 6 large white baking potatoes, peeled and put in a bowl of water to cover
- Salt

MARINATE THE STEAK: In a nonreactive dish, combine the shallots, garlic, wine, oil, and salt and pepper to taste. Add the steak and turn to coat it with the marinade. Cover and put in the refrigerator to marinate for 6 to 8 hours, turning occasionally.

MAKE THE AÏOLI: In a small nonreactive saucepan, combine the shallots, vinegar, and dried tarragon and bring to a boil over high heat. Cook until the mixture is almost dry, 5 to 7 minutes, then add 1 tablespoon water. Pour through a fine-mesh sieve set over a medium bowl.

Add the egg yolks, garlic, and lemon juice and whisk until frothy. Whisking constantly, add the oil in a thin stream. Whisk in the fresh tarragon and salt and pepper to taste. The aïoli can be made up to 2 days in advance, covered, and refrigerated. Whisk again and add a little more water if necessary.

MAKE THE FRIED POTATOES: In a large, heavy pot, heat 3 inches of oil to 275°F.

Working with 2 potatoes at a time, remove them from the water. Use a mandoline or a sharp knife to cut even ¼-inch-thick slices, then use a knife to cut them into ¼-inch strips, then crosswise into cubes. Pat the cubes with paper towels to dry them completely. Carefully put the cubes in the oil and cook for 1 minute; remove with a slotted spoon to a baking sheet in a single layer. Repeat with the remaining potatoes. Let cool completely.

Increase the heat and bring the oil to 375°F. Working in batches, cook the potato cubes until well browned, 2 to 4 minutes. Remove to paper towels to drain, and season with salt to taste.

COOK THE STEAK: Bring the steak to room temperature when ready to cook. Heat a large cast-iron stovetop grill pan over medium-high heat. Remove the steak from the marinade and pat it dry. Place it in the grill pan and cook to desired degree of doneness, turning once. Transfer to a carving board and let rest for 5 minutes. Slice across the grain as thinly as possible.

Divide the steak among 4 serving plates, pile the fried potatoes on the plates, and drizzle the aïoli over the steak and potatoes. Serve immediately.

SPICY PORK SAUSAGE SANDWICHES
WITH MUSTARD AND HORSERADISH

THE BRONCOS HAVE SOLD OUT
EVERY HOME GAME SINCE THE
NFL MERGER IN 1970.

PREP TIME
00:30
CURE 24 HOURS

CHEF: **Lachlan Mackinnon-Patterson,** Frasca Food and Wine, Denver

WINE SUGGESTION: McWilliam's Shiraz

SERVES 6 TO 8

2½ pounds ground pork loin

12 ounces prosciutto or speck scraps (see *Note*) or a combination, minced

¼ cup white wine

2 tablespoons salt

1 tablespoon cracked black pepper

1 tablespoon red pepper flakes

¼ cup grated Parmesan cheese

6 to 8 Kaiser rolls, split and toasted

Dijon-style mustard

Prepared horseradish

This easy homemade sausage can be simply formed into patties and baked—it doesn't need to be formed into links, so there's no need for a sausage stuffer. However, traditional links make for a more classic presentation.

In a large bowl, combine the pork, prosciutto, wine, salt, cracked pepper, red pepper flakes, and cheese. Cover and refrigerate for 24 hours.

Preheat the oven to 350°F. Line a rimmed baking sheet with parchment paper.

Form the pork mixture into 6 to 8 patties and arrange them on the prepared baking sheet. Bake for about 20 minutes, or until cooked through. Serve hot on the rolls, with mustard and horseradish.

NOTE: *Speck, a staple of the Alto Adige province of northern Italy, is a boned ham (the hind leg of the pig) that is cured with salt and spices (usually including juniper), cold-smoked (usually over beech wood), and matured for several months. It's often served very thinly sliced, like its unsmoked cousin, prosciutto, with German-style dark brown bread, mustard, and pickles, or with fresh fruit such as melon.*

JOHN MADDEN IS A MEMBER OF THE PRO FOOTBALL HALL OF FAME AND THE MOST HONORED NFL BROADCASTER OF ALL TIME.

JOHN MADDEN'S
LOS BAÑOS LAMB STEW

CHEF: John Madden, Analyst, Sunday Night Football

SERVES 12 TO 15

PREP TIME
02:00

7	pounds stewing lamb, cubed
1	cup water
1	pound carrots, peeled, cut into 1-inch sections
2	yellow onions, diced
1	quart tomato sauce
1	quart beer
2	cups white wine
1	garlic clove, chopped
½	cup fresh parsley
	Garlic powder to taste
	Seasoning salt to taste
	Salt and freshly ground black pepper

John says, "This recipe comes from Dave Sagouspe, who is in the hay business, but whose family were herders. You might think seven pounds of stew is a fair potful. No way. When we made this, Danny Fialho, another rancher friend and world-class barbecuer, brought the big stewpot that had been on his family's ranch for three generations. It is all cast iron, stands three feet tall, measures three feet across, and is about four inches thick. You need some heavy machinery or well-fed oxen to move it. Danny says the secret to a good pot is to use it only for a few things. On the ranch this pot was used to make stew, lard, and soap!"

Place lamb in large covered pot or Dutch oven on high heat. Brown meat slightly to render fat. Add water. Bring to a boil. Stir. Keep heat high until meat is browned.

Drain excess fat leaving small amount for flavor.

Add the remaining ingredients, except for seasoning. Stir well.

Add seasonings in small amounts. Cover, bring to a boil. Stir. Boil 15 more minutes. Reduce heat to low. Stir completely. Season to taste. Simmer 1½ hours, stirring every 15 minutes. Check carrot tenderness. Continue seasoning to taste.

Stew is done when carrots are properly tender. Remove from heat. Let stand 10 minutes. Skim fat.

ROAST BEEF SANDWICHES

WITH KANSAS CITY BARBECUE SAUCE

THE CHIEFS' 104–40
HOME RECORD FROM 1990 TO 2007
IS THE NFL'S BEST.

PREP TIME
03:00+

CHEF: **Steve Cole,** Café Allegro, Kansas City

WINE SUGGESTION: Bridlewood Syrah

SERVES 10 TO 12

BARBECUE SAUCE

- ½ cup (1 stick) unsalted butter
- 2 tablespoons minced garlic
- 1 cup minced onion
- Grated zest and juice of 1 lemon
- Grated zest of ½ orange
- Juice of 1 orange
- One 32-ounce bottle ketchup
- 2 cups canned crushed tomatoes
- 1 cup packed brown sugar
- ½ cup molasses
- ½ cup Worcestershire sauce
- ¼ cup chili powder
- 1 tablespoon ground cayenne pepper
- ¼ cup white vinegar
- 2 tablespoons freshly ground black pepper
- 1 teaspoon salt

DRY RUB

- ½ cup packed brown sugar
- 2 tablespoons chili powder
- 1 tablespoon ground cumin
- 1 tablespoon salt
- 1 teaspoon garlic powder
- 1 teaspoon curry powder
- 1 tablespoon dry mustard
- 1 tablespoon paprika
- 2 teaspoons ground cayenne
- 2 tablespoons freshly ground black pepper

RIB-EYE ROAST

- One 10- to 12-pound boneless rib-eye roast, trimmed of excess fat and tied
- ½ cup minced garlic
- 10 to 12 pumpernickel rolls or egg buns, split

For a deeper and more layered barbecue flavor, cold-smoke the beef over pecan wood at 90° to 110°F for 4 hours, then grill it over direct heat—also with pecan—until the meat is medium-rare. If you prefer to cook indoors, the spice-rubbed beef can be roasted in the oven, as directed here.

MAKE THE BARBECUE SAUCE: In a nonreactive saucepan over medium heat, melt the butter. Add the garlic and onions and sauté until the onions are soft but not browned, about 4 minutes. Add all the remaining ingredients, bring to a boil, then reduce the heat to maintain a simmer. Cook, stirring occasionally, for 1 to 1½ hours, until the sauce is thick.

MAKE THE DRY RUB: In a small bowl, combine all the ingredients.

MAKE THE RIB-EYE ROAST: Preheat the oven to 350°F.

Coat the roast all over with the dry rub and the garlic and put it on a rack in a large, shallow roasting pan.

Roast for about 2 hours and 20 minutes (or 14 minutes per pound), until the meat registers 140° to 145°F on a meat thermometer for medium-rare. Transfer the meat to a carving board; cover loosely with aluminum foil and let rest for 15 minutes. Cut into slices and serve on the rolls, with barbecue sauce to taste.

iVillage

BECKY WELBORN'S
GOT BACK BURGERS

CHEF: Becky Welborn, Fort Hood, Texas

SERVES 4

PREP TIME
01:30+

2   tablespoons olive oil

8   ounces mushrooms, trimmed
     and sliced

1   onion, diced

     **Salt and freshly ground
     black pepper**

4   strips bacon

4   ounces cream cheese, softened

1   tablespoon of your favorite
     barbecue spice rub

2   pounds ground sirloin

     **Four ¼-inch-thick slices fresh
     mozzarella cheese**

¼   cup sliced pickled or fresh
     jalapeño chiles

8   slices crusty bread

4   teaspoons hot pepper jelly

1   tomato, sliced (optional)

4   lettuce leaves (optional)

*Becky Welborn, a mother of a combined family of five and a member
of the iVillage online community, contributed her best game-day
creation. "The idea behind these mammoth burgers is to keep all
the trimmings and goodies from falling off the burger when you bite
into it," she says.*

In a medium sauté pan, heat 1 tablespoon of the oil and add the mushrooms and
onion. Season with salt and pepper to taste and cook, stirring, 8 to 10 minutes.
Remove to a bowl and let cool completely.

Return the pan to medium heat and add the bacon. Cook until crisp and
browned on both sides, about 5 minutes. Remove to paper towels to drain; break
into small pieces. Pour off all but about 1 teaspoon of the fat from the pan.

In a small bowl, combine the cream cheese and spice rub and set aside.

Divide the meat into 8 equal-sized balls and flatten them into ¼- to ½-inch-
thick patties. Put a slice of cheese on top of 4 of the patties and top with cooled
mushrooms, onion, bacon, and chiles, leaving ½ inch of space around the edge
of the patty. Lay a second patty on top of the filling and pinch the top and
bottom patty edges together to completely seal and enclose the filling. Press
down gently to flatten the burger slightly. Season the burgers on both sides
with salt and pepper.

Divide the remaining 1 tablespoon oil between two heavy skillets and heat over
high heat. Put 2 stuffed burgers in each pan, then lower the heat to medium and
cook, turning once or twice, for about 15 minutes, until well browned on
the outside and the internal temperature registers 170°F.

Meanwhile, toast the bread slices and spread with the cream cheese.

Just before removing the burgers from the pans, spread 1 teaspoon of the jelly
over each. Transfer the burgers to the bread slices, and serve immediately, with
tomatoes and lettuce, if desired.

BOUDIN BLANC
WITH LENTIL SALAD
AND MUSTARD SAUCE

PREP TIME
02:00+

CHEF: **Chris Rossi,** Citron, Oakland

WINE SUGGESTION: Frei Brothers RR Chardonnay

LENTILS

1   pound French green lentils

1   onion, peeled but left whole

1   carrot, peeled

1   celery stalk

2   bay leaves

6   whole cloves

·   Generous pinch of salt

BOUDIN

1   tablespoon olive oil

1   onion, minced

1   teaspoon ground cloves

1   teaspoon ground allspice

1   teaspoon ground dried thyme

¼   teaspoon ground white pepper

½   cup milk

2   garlic cloves, minced

3   slices stale white bread,
    cut into cubes

1   pound boneless, skinless
    chicken breast

8   ounces pork belly (see page 144)

2   large eggs

1½ teaspoons salt

1   cup heavy cream

    Natural (hog) sausage casings
    (see *Note*), soaked in cold water
    and well rinsed inside and out

MUSTARD SAUCE

½   cup Dijon-style mustard

2   tablespoons fresh lemon juice

1   tablespoon honey

¼   cup olive oil

    Pinch of salt

    Pinch of freshly ground black pepper

1   head frisée (curly endive) leaves
    torn into pieces, rinsed, and spun dry

Boudin blanc ("white pudding" in French) is a delicate, pale-colored sausage, usually made with chicken or pork or a combination of meats, with milk. The assertively spiced version here is paired with peppery French green lentils (also called Le Puy lentils), which hold their shape well enough to be tossed in a salad. Your stand mixer might have come with a sausage stuffer attachment; this is the time to dig it out of your utensil drawer. If you don't have the attachment, inexpensive manual cast-iron stuffers are available at kitchenwares stores.

HALL-OF-FAME COACH JOHN MADDEN'S
RAIDERS WON THEIR FIRST
SUPER BOWL IN 1975.

SERVES 6 TO 8

MAKE THE LENTILS: Place all the ingredients in a medium pot with enough water to cover by 3 inches. Bring to a simmer and cook until lentils are tender but not mushy, about 1 hour. Remove from the heat and remove and discard the onion, carrot, celery, bay leaves, and cloves. Let cool to room temperature. The lentils can be made up to 3 days in advance, covered, and refrigerated. Bring back to room temperature before serving.

MAKE THE BOUDIN: In a medium sauté pan, heat the oil over medium heat. Add the onion, cloves, allspice, thyme, and white pepper. Cook, stirring, until the onion is very soft, about 8 minutes. Transfer to a small bowl and chill in the refrigerator until cold.

In a small saucepan, bring the milk and garlic to a simmer and add the bread. Remove from the heat and stir until the bread absorbs the milk and breaks down. Transfer to a small bowl and put in the refrigerator until cold.

Roughly chop the chicken and pork belly and put in a large bowl. Add the onion mixture, bread mixture, eggs, and the salt and mix well.

Put one-third of the meat mixture in a food processor and process until smooth, about 15 seconds. With the motor running, pour one-third of the cream through the feed tube in a slow, steady stream. Transfer the mixture to a stainless-steel bowl. Repeat in two more batches with the remaining two-thirds of the meat mixture and cream. Fry a small portion of the meat mixture in a skillet and taste for seasoning, adding more salt if necessary.

Use a sausage stuffer to stuff the meat mixture into casings, following the manufacturer's directions. Twist into 6-inch lengths and place in a large pot. Cover with cold water and heat until the water reaches 170°F—do not boil. Cook for 3 minutes, then remove the sausages with a slotted spoon and cool completely. The sausages, wrapped tightly, will keep for 1 month in the freezer, or 5 days in the refrigerator.

MAKE THE MUSTARD SAUCE: In a small bowl, whisk all the ingredients together.

GRILL THE BOUDIN AND MAKE THE SALAD: Heat a large stovetop cast-iron grill pan over medium-high heat and put the sausages in the pan. Cook until well marked on all sides and heated through, about 8 minutes total.

Meanwhile, in a large bowl, combine 2½ cups of the lentils, the frisée, and just enough mustard sauce to coat the ingredients. Toss to combine. Divide the salad among 6 to 8 serving plates. Slice the sausages on the bias and arrange the slices of 1 sausage on top of each salad. Drizzle with mustard sauce and serve immediately.

NOTE: *Your butcher can supply you with sausage casings. If you have to buy a lot of them (they aren't expensive), submerge the unused casings in a salt solution, cover tightly, and refrigerate them—they'll keep for several months. Casings are either packed in coarse salt or in a salty brine: If yours are covered in salt, soak them in cold water for at least 1 hour, drain, and rinse several times before using, by slipping an end over the sink faucet and running cold water through them; if they're in a brine, just rinse them well.*

CHICKEN AND POMEGRANATE CHILI

THE CARDINALS HAVE MOVED
3 TIMES, FROM CHICAGO TO
ST. LOUIS TO ARIZONA.

CHEF: Eddie Matney, Eddie Matney's Restaurant, Phoenix

WINE SUGGESTION: MacMurray SC Pinot Noir

SERVES 4

PREP TIME
02:00+

CHILI

- 2 tablespoons olive oil
- 1 pound boneless, skinless chicken breasts, cut into chunks
- 1 pound boneless, skinless chicken thighs, cut into chunks
  Salt and freshly ground black pepper
- 1 onion, chopped
- 2 carrots, chopped
- 2 celery stalks, chopped
- 6 garlic cloves, crushed
- 2 tablespoons ancho chile powder
- 2 bay leaves
- 2 cups pomegranate juice
- 2 cups low-sodium chicken broth

CHICKPEA POLENTA CAKES

- 2 tablespoons olive oil, or more if needed
- 1 onion, chopped
- 2 garlic cloves, chopped
- 1 cup falafel mix (see *Notes*)
- 1 cup coarse polenta
- 3 cups low-sodium chicken broth
- 1 cup crumbled farmer cheese (see *Notes*)
  Salt and freshly ground black pepper
  Fresh pomegranate seeds

MAKE THE CHILI: Preheat the oven to 350°F.

In a large flameproof baking dish, heat the oil on top of the stove over medium-high heat. Season the chicken with salt and pepper, put in the dish, and cook, turning occasionally, until browned, about 5 minutes. Add the onion, carrots, celery, and garlic and sauté for 5 minutes. Add the chile powder, bay leaves, pomegranate juice, and broth and bring to a boil.

Remove the dish from the heat and cover with aluminum foil, making sure to seal the dish tightly. Bake for about 2 hours, until the chicken is cooked through and the sauce is thick.

MAKE THE CHICKPEA POLENTA CAKES: Meanwhile, in a medium saucepan, heat 1 tablespoon of the oil over medium heat. Add the onion and garlic and sauté until softened, about 5 minutes. Add the falafel mix and polenta and sauté for 5 minutes. Add the broth, 1 cup water, the cheese, and salt and pepper to taste and simmer until the liquid is absorbed, 18 to 22 minutes. Remove from the heat and pour the mixture onto a rimmed baking sheet, smoothing the top with a rubber spatula. Let cool completely, about 2 hours, then cut into triangles.

In a large sauté pan, heat the remaining 1 tablespoon oil over high heat. Working in batches if necessary to avoid crowding the pan, add the triangles, and cook until golden brown on each side, 5 to 7 minutes; add more oil to the pan if needed.

Divide the chickpea polenta cakes among 4 serving plates and spoon the chili over them. Garnish with pomegranate seeds and serve immediately.

NOTES: *Falafel mix, made up of dried ground chickpeas and other beans, dehydrated vegetables, and spices, can be found in Middle Eastern markets.*

Farmer cheese is a fresh cheese made by draining and pressing cottage cheese into a loaf form until it's dry and firm enough to slice or crumble. If farmer cheese is unavailable, substitute queso fresco or queso blanco, which can be found in the refrigerated Mexican foods section of many supermarkets and in Latino markets.

RED LENTIL HUMMUS
AND ROASTED WINTER VEGETABLE SANDWICHES

PREP TIME
02:00+

CHEF: **Bill Cardwell** and **Dave Owens,** Cardwell's at the Plaza, St. Louis

WINE SUGGESTION: McWilliam's Chardonnay

RED LENTIL HUMMUS

- 4 tablespoons extra-virgin olive oil
- 1 cup minced onion
- 2 tablespoons minced garlic
- 2 cups red lentils (see *Notes*), rinsed and drained
- 1⁄8 teaspoon red pepper flakes
- 2 teaspoons salt
- 2 tablespoons grated lemon zest
- 3 tablespoons fresh lemon juice
- 1⁄4 cup tahini (see *Notes*)
- 1⁄8 teaspoon ground cayenne pepper
- 2 tablespoons minced fresh dill

DRESSING

- 2 teaspoons salt
- 1½ tablespoons extra-virgin olive oil
- 1⁄4 cup white wine vinegar
- 1⁄3 cup roasted garlic purée
- 1½ tablespoons grated peeled ginger
- 1½ tablespoons honey
- 1 tablespoon tomato paste
- 1 tablespoon brown sugar
- 3⁄4 teaspoon chili powder
- 3⁄4 teaspoon ground cumin
- 1⁄2 teaspoon ground turmeric
- 1⁄4 teaspoon red pepper flakes
- 1½ tablespoons fresh lemon juice

ROASTED VEGETABLES

- 1⁄2 cup diced carrot
- 1⁄2 cup diced onion
- 1⁄2 cup diced parsnip
- 1⁄2 cup diced celery root (see page 168)
- 1⁄2 cup diced turnip
- 1⁄4 cup olive oil
  Salt and freshly ground black pepper
- 1 pound peeled and seeded winter squash (such as 1 butternut squash)

SANDWICHES

  Two 12-inch walnut wheat baguettes
- 8 ounces aged Gouda cheese, thinly sliced

MAKE THE RED LENTIL HUMMUS:

In a heavy saucepan, combine 1 tablespoon of the oil, the onion, and garlic and cook over medium-low heat until softened but not browned, about 6 minutes. Add the lentils, red pepper flakes, 1⁄2 teaspoon of the salt, and 3 cups water and bring to a boil over high heat. Lower the heat and simmer, uncovered, until the lentils are very soft, 10 to 12 minutes. Let cool to room temperature.

Put the lentil mixture in a food processor with the lemon zest, lemon juice, tahini, the remaining 3 tablespoons oil, the remaining 1½ teaspoons salt, and the cayenne. Process until smooth, then transfer to a bowl and fold in the dill. Set aside.

MAKE THE DRESSING: In a medium bowl, whisk all the ingredients together.

FROM 1999–2001 THE RAMS WERE THE
FIRST NFL TEAM TO SCORE AT LEAST
500 POINTS IN 3 CONSECUTIVE SEASONS.

SERVES 4

MAKE THE ROASTED VEGETABLES:
Preheat the oven to 350°F.

In a baking dish or roasting pan, toss the diced vegetables with 2 tablespoons of the oil and salt and pepper to taste. Roast until just tender and beginning to caramelize, 15 to 20 minutes.

Add the dressing and toss to combine, then return the vegetables to the oven and roast until well browned, 5 to 8 minutes, watching carefully to make sure they do not burn. Set aside.

Meanwhile, cut the winter squash into ¼-inch slices. Brush with the remaining 2 tablespoons oil and sprinkle with salt and pepper, then arrange in a single layer on a baking sheet. Roast until tender, about 15 minutes. Leave the oven on.

MAKE THE SANDWICHES: Split the baguette pieces and smear the cut sides with hummus. Layer half of the cheese slices on the bottom pieces, top with the squash and roasted vegetables, then the remaining cheese slices and the top bread pieces. Wrap the sandwiches in aluminum foil and put in the oven for 15 minutes, or until warmed through and the cheese is melted. Unwrap, cut each sandwich in half, and serve immediately.

NOTES: *Red lentils are actually salmon-colored and turn golden as they cook. If you can't find red lentils, use yellow or brown lentils (which may need to be cooked slightly longer).*

Tahini is a paste made from sesame seeds—look for Middle Eastern tahini (it's less bitter than East Asian tahini, which is made from unhulled seeds) in cans or jars in the international foods section of the supermarket. Tahini is an essential ingredient in traditional chickpea hummus and is often also used in baba ganoush. If tahini is unavailable, substitute natural (unsweetened) peanut butter and reduce the quantity to 2 tablespoons.

SEARED TEQUILA CHICKEN SKEWERS

PREP TIME
01:00+
MARINATE 4 HOURS

CHEF: **Eddie Matney,** Eddie Matney's Restaurant, Phoenix

WINE SUGGESTION: McWilliam's Shiraz

CHICKEN

- ¼ cup tequila
- Juice of 1 lime
- 1 garlic clove, chopped
- 1 tablespoon chopped fresh cilantro
- 12 chicken tenders
- Salt and freshly ground black pepper
- Olive oil

CHORIZO GRAVY

- 2 tablespoons olive oil
- 1 pound fresh chicken chorizo or other chicken sausage, casings removed
- 2 stalks celery, chopped
- 2 garlic cloves, chopped
- 1 onion, chopped
- 2 cups low-sodium chicken broth
- 2 teaspoons dried oregano, preferably Mexican oregano
- 1 teaspoon ground cumin
- Salt and freshly ground black pepper
- 2 tablespoons red wine or water
- 1 tablespoon cornstarch

MASHED POTATOES

- 3 pounds Yukon gold potatoes, with skins, quartered
- 2 cups (4 sticks) unsalted butter, cut into pieces
- 1 cup sour cream
- ½ cup heavy cream
- 1 tablespoon Worcestershire sauce
- 1 tablespoon minced garlic
- 2 teaspoons salt
- 1 teaspoon freshly ground black pepper

- 12 bamboo skewers
- Fresh cilantro sprigs

FOUNDED IN 1899, THE CARDINALS
ARE THE OLDEST CONTINUOUSLY RUN
PROFESSIONAL FOOTBALL TEAM.

SERVES 4

MARINATE THE CHICKEN: In a large bowl, combine the tequila, lime juice, garlic, and cilantro. Add the chicken and toss to coat. Cover the bowl with plastic wrap and put in the refrigerator to marinate for 4 to 6 hours.

MAKE THE CHORIZO GRAVY: In a medium sauté pan, heat the oil over medium heat and add the chorizo, celery, garlic, and onion. Cook, stirring to break up the sausage meat, for 10 minutes. Add the broth, oregano, cumin, and a pinch of salt and pepper. Bring to a boil, then reduce the heat and simmer for 30 minutes.

In a small bowl, stir together the wine and cornstarch, then add it to the gravy, stirring constantly. Simmer for 5 minutes, season to taste with salt and pepper, then remove from the heat and cover to keep warm until ready to serve.

MAKE THE MASHED POTATOES: Put the potatoes in a large pot with cold water to cover. Bring to a boil over high heat and cook until the potatoes are tender, 15 to 20 minutes. Drain well and return the potatoes to the pot. Add the remaining ingredients and mash with a potato masher until smooth. Cover to keep warm and set aside.

COOK THE CHICKEN: Thirty minutes before cooking the chicken, soak the 12 bamboo skewers in a pan of water. Remove the chicken from the marinade and thread the pieces onto the skewers. Sprinkle lightly with salt and pepper.

Preheat the oven to 350°F.

Heat a large sauté pan over high heat and coat the bottom lightly with oil. Working in batches if necessary to avoid crowding the pan, add the chicken skewers and cook, undisturbed, for about 1½ minutes, until well browned; turn and cook the other side until browned. Transfer to a baking sheet and bake for about 5 minutes, until just cooked through.

Divide the mashed potatoes among 4 serving plates, mounding them in the center. Arrange 3 chicken skewers around the potatoes like a teepee, drizzle the gravy around the plate, and top with cilantro sprigs. Serve immediately.

HERB-CRUSTED MAHI MAHI
WITH CRAB AND MUSHROOMS AND LOBSTER BUTTER SAUCE

PREP TIME
01:00+

CHEF: **Dave "D.K." Kodama,** Sansei, Honolulu

SERVES 2

LOBSTER BUTTER SAUCE

- 1 tablespoon olive oil
- 1 fresh lobster body (tail and claws reserved for another use), split, coarsely chopped, and rinsed well
- 1 cup diced onions
- ½ cup diced carrot
- ½ cup diced celery
- ¼ cup dry white wine
- 1 sprig fresh tarragon
- ¼ cup tomato paste
- 1 cup heavy cream
- ½ cup (1 stick) chilled unsalted butter, cut into ½-inch pieces

  Salt and freshly ground black pepper

MAHI MAHI AND MUSHROOMS

- Two 6-ounce pieces mahi mahi (or use tuna or bluefish)
- 2 tablespoons unsalted butter, melted

  Salt and freshly ground black pepper
- 2 tablespoons mixed chopped fresh herbs such as parsley, basil, thyme, and chives
- 1 cup coarsely chopped spinach
- 2 tablespoons olive oil
- ¼ cup diced onion
- 1 teaspoon minced garlic
- 1 cup stemmed and sliced shiitake mushrooms
- 1 cup crabmeat, picked over

The luxurious lobster butter sauce is based on a rich stock made with a chopped fresh lobster body. Save the tail and claws to steam for Lobster and Brie Mac and Cheese (see page 156).

MAKE THE LOBSTER BUTTER SAUCE: In a large pot, heat the oil over medium-high heat. Add the lobster and sauté until the shells turn red, about 5 minutes. Add the onions, carrot, and celery and sauté until they begin to brown, about 5 minutes.

Add the wine and cook until almost evaporated, about 2 minutes, then add the tarragon and stir in the tomato paste. Pour in enough cold water to cover the ingredients (about 3 cups), bring to a low simmer, and simmer for 30 minutes. Pour through a fine-mesh sieve set over a clean saucepan and discard the solids. Place the pan over high heat and bring to a boil. Cook until reduced by half, 8 to 10 minutes. Add the cream and boil until reduced by one-third, 8 to 10 minutes. Whisk in the butter, a piece at a time, then season with salt and pepper to taste. Cover to keep warm and set aside.

MAKE THE MAHI MAHI AND MUSHROOMS: Brush the top of each piece of fish with butter, season with salt and pepper, and sprinkle with the herb mixture, gently pressing the herbs onto the fish so they adhere. Divide the spinach between 2 serving plates and set aside.

In a large sauté pan, heat the oil over medium-high heat. Add the fish, herb side down, and cook until golden brown on the bottom, about 4 minutes. Using a thin metal spatula, turn the fish over and cook until just cooked through, 2 to 4 minutes longer. Arrange the fish, herb side up, over the spinach on the serving plates.

Return the pan to medium-high heat and add the onion, garlic, and mushrooms. Sauté until the onion is just tender, about 4 minutes. Add the crabmeat and sauté until heated through. Season with salt and pepper to taste. Spoon the crab mixture over the fish and ladle the lobster butter sauce around and over the fish. Serve immediately.

PATRICK WILLIS's
LEMON AND CRACKED PEPPER CHICKEN
WITH BROCCOLI

#52 LINEBACKER
6'1", 240 POUNDS
UNIVERSITY OF MISSISSIPPI, b. 1-25-85

PREP TIME
00:30

CHEF: Patrick Willis

SERVES 2

1½   pounds chicken tenders

2   garlic cloves, chopped

Juice and grated zest of 1 lemon

¾   teaspoon cracked black pepper

Salt

1   pound broccoli, cut into florets, or 1 small bunch broccoli rabe, tough stems removed

1   tablespoon olive oil

Thin strips of lemon zest

2   lemon wedges

Patrick says, "My grandmother is a phenomenal cook. I was told that at a young age my Dad would always sit in the kitchen and watch her cook. I'm the oldest of eight kids, and he taught all of us to cook when we were really young."

In a medium bowl, combine the chicken, garlic, lemon juice, grated lemon zest, cracked pepper, and ½ teaspoon salt and toss to evenly coat the chicken. Set aside.

Bring a large pot of water to a boil. Add the broccoli and bring back to a boil; boil for 2 to 3 minutes, until almost tender. Drain in a colander and set aside.

In a large sauté pan, heat the oil over high heat. Add the chicken in a single layer and cook, without disturbing, for 3 minutes. Turn and cook for 2 to 3 minutes on the other side, until nicely browned and just cooked through. Remove to 2 serving plates.

Return the pan to high heat and add the broccoli and ½ cup water. Cook, stirring, until just tender and heated through and the water is almost

evaporated, 1 to 2 minutes. Season with salt to taste. Using tongs or a slotted spoon, transfer the broccoli to the plates and pour the pan sauce over the chicken and broccoli. Garnish with the strips of lemon zest and the lemon wedges and serve immediately.

LARRY FITZGERALD'S
YANKEE POT ROAST

#11 WIDE RECEIVER
6'3", 226 POUNDS
UNIVERSITY OF PITTSBURGH, b. 8-31-83

CHEF: **Larry Fitzgerald**

SERVES 4

PREP TIME
00:30
SLOWCOOK 3–8 HOURS

---

4 to 6 small carrots, peeled

4 to 6 very small new Yukon gold or red potatoes

1 onion, cut into large chunks

1 garlic clove, crushed

One 2- to 3-pound beef chuck roast, trimmed of excess fat

Salt and freshly ground black pepper

1 tablespoon olive oil

½ cup red wine

1 cup low-sodium beef broth

1 bay leaf

1 tablespoon tomato paste

Coarse sea salt and cracked black pepper

Larry says, "I'm a big crockpot guy. I'll cut up my vegetables and just throw them in the pot with a lean roast. So when I get home I can have a pot roast. I'm eventually going to have a family to cook for, and I want to be able to pull my own weight in the kitchen."

Put the carrots, potatoes, onion, and garlic in a 4- to 6-quart slow cooker.

Season the beef generously with salt and pepper. Heat the oil in a heavy sauté pan over medium-high heat and add the beef. Cook until browned on all sides, 8 to 10 minutes. Transfer to the slow cooker on top of the vegetables.

Return the pan to medium-high heat and add the wine, stirring to scrape up any browned bits from the bottom of the pan. Boil for 1 minute, then pour the wine over the beef in the slow cooker and add the broth. Tuck the bay leaf into the liquid, and dot the liquid around the beef with the tomato paste. Cook on the low setting for 6 to 8 hours, or on high for about 3 hours, until the vegetables and meat are tender.

Remove the meat to a carving board and cut or pull it into large chunks. Arrange on a platter with the vegetables. Season the cooking liquid with salt and pepper and spoon some of it over the meat and vegetables. Serve immediately, with small bowls of coarse salt and cracked pepper.

ORANGE AND ROCK SHRIMP RISOTTO

WITH ROASTED SQUASH

ARROWHEAD STADIUM HAS
SOLD OUT 149 STRAIGHT GAMES
SINCE 1991.

PREP TIME
02:00+

CHEF: Debbie Gold, The American Restaurant, Kansas City

WINE SUGGESTION: Frei Brothers RR Chardonnay

SERVES 4

ROASTED SQUASH

- 2½ **pounds winter squash such as butternut or acorn squash**
- ¼ **cup honey**
- 2 **tablespoons unsalted butter**

  One 2-inch piece of ginger, peeled and thinly sliced

  Salt and freshly ground black pepper

RISOTTO

- 2 **navel oranges**
- ½ **fennel bulb, trimmed**
- 1 **large celery stalk**
- 3 **tablespoons olive oil**
- 1 **small Spanish onion, diced**
- 1 **pound Arborio rice**
- ¾ **cup white wine**

  About 6 cups shrimp stock or low-sodium chicken broth, warmed

- 6 **ounces fresh peeled and deveined rock shrimp, cleaned of any shell pieces**
- 1 **tablespoon unsalted butter, at room temperature**
- 2 **tablespoons minced fresh chives**
- 1 **tablespoon minced fresh flat-leaf parsley**

  Salt and freshly ground black pepper

MAKE THE ROASTED SQUASH: Preheat the oven to 450°F and position a rack in the middle of the oven. Line a rimmed baking sheet with aluminum foil.

Cut the squash in half and scoop out the seeds. Arrange on the prepared baking sheet, cut sides up.

In a small saucepan, combine the honey, butter, ginger, and ¼ cup water. Bring to a simmer over medium heat. Brush the mixture over the squash and drizzle any remaining mixture on top. Sprinkle with salt and plenty of pepper. Bake for 45 minutes to 1 hour, until golden brown and tender. Scrape the squash from the skin and put it in a blender. Purée until smooth. Transfer to a small saucepan and set aside.

MAKE THE RISOTTO: Zest the oranges. Remove the skin of the oranges. Holding an orange over a bowl to catch the juices, cut between the membranes, separating the sections. Repeat with the second orange. Set the zest, juice, and sections aside in a bowl.

Coarsely chop the fennel and celery. Put in a food processor and pulse until finely chopped.

In a medium nonreactive saucepan, heat the oil over medium heat. Add the fennel-celery mixture and the onion and sauté until softened, about 5 minutes. Add the rice and stir to coat it with the oil. Reduce the heat to medium-low and add the wine. Cook, stirring constantly, until almost completely absorbed. Add ¼ cup of the stock; cook, stirring constantly and keeping the liquid at a simmer, until most of the stock is absorbed. Continue cooking and adding broth, about ¼ cup at a time, stirring constantly and letting each addition be absorbed before adding the next, until the rice is cooked through but still holds its shape, 20 to 25 minutes.

Add the shrimp, then gently stir in the butter, chives, parsley, and orange zest, juice, and sections. Season with salt and pepper to taste. Rewarm the squash purée and divide it and the risotto among 4 serving plates. Serve immediately.

DARREN MCFADDEN'S
TURKEY NECKS
WITH SPECKLED GRITS
AND GRAVY

#20 RUNNING BACK
6'2", 205 POUNDS
UNIVERSITY OF ARKANSAS, b. 8-27-87

PREP TIME
01:30+

CHEF: Darren McFadden

SERVES 2 TO 4

---

3 tablespoons vegetable oil
4 turkey necks
   Salt and freshly ground black pepper
2 onions, sliced
1 carrot, roughly chopped
1 celery stalk, roughly chopped
1 teaspoon peppercorns
1 bunch parsley stems
1 bay leaf
1⅓ cups speckled grits (see *Note*)
2 tablespoons all-purpose flour

In some families, the turkey neck—which contains long shreds of flavorful dark meat—is roasted alongside the rest of the bird. In other families, the neck is used to make a rich broth for gravy. And then there are those, like Darren McFadden, who appreciate turkey necks year-round.

In a heavy skillet, heat 1 tablespoon of the oil over medium-high heat. Season the turkey necks with salt and pepper to taste and add them to the skillet. Cook until well browned on all sides, about 10 minutes total. Transfer to a large saucepan or pot and add 1 of the onions, the carrot, celery, peppercorns, parsley stems, and bay leaf. Add water to just cover. Bring to a boil, then skim the foam from the surface, lower the heat, and simmer until the turkey is very tender, 1 to 1½ hours, skimming occasionally. Remove the turkey to a plate, reserving the cooking liquid.

While the turkey is simmering, rinse the grits in cold water and pour off the bran that rises to the surface; drain. Put the grits in a small saucepan with

1½ teaspoons salt and 4 cups water. Bring to a boil, then lower the heat and simmer, uncovered, for about 30 minutes, stirring occasionally and adding more water if necessary, until tender. Cover to keep warm and set aside.

When the turkey is done, put the remaining onion and 2 tablespoons oil in the skillet and cook over medium heat until the onion is very soft and caramelized, about 10 minutes. Sprinkle in the flour and cook, stirring, for about 2 minutes, until the flour is no longer white. Pour the turkey cooking liquid through a fine-mesh sieve into the skillet (discard the solids) and stir to scrape up the browned bits from the bottom of the pan. Simmer the gravy, stirring constantly, until thickened, about 5 minutes. Return the turkey necks to the skillet and turn to coat them with the gravy; cook to heat through. Serve immediately with the grits.

NOTE: *Outside the South, speckled grits are available in specialty food stores and by mail order.*

SHAWNE MERRIMAN'S
SHEPHERD'S PIE

#56 LINEBACKER
6'4", 272 POUNDS
UNIVERSITY OF MARYLAND, b. 5-25-84

CHEF: Shawne Merriman

SERVES 6

PREP TIME
01:00+

MASHED POTATO TOPPING

6	large russet potatoes, peeled and cut into 1-inch pieces
½	tablespoon unsalted butter
⅓	cup milk
	Salt and freshly ground black pepper

FILLING

1½	pounds lean ground beef
1	large onion, diced
1	celery stalk, diced
1	teaspoon minced garlic
	Two 15-ounce cans tomato sauce
	One 1-pound bag of frozen mixed vegetables
1	teaspoon dried thyme
1	teaspoon dried oregano
	Salt and freshly ground black pepper
½	teaspoon paprika

Shawne's chef Melanie Harper shared one of the linebacker's favorite dishes. "He makes the cleanup process very easy," she says. "There is never anything left on his plate."

MAKE THE MASHED POTATO TOPPING: Put the potatoes in a large pot and add cold water to cover; add a generous pinch of salt, bring to a boil, and cook until tender, about 10 minutes. Drain, then return the potatoes to the pot and place over low heat for 1 minute to evaporate excess water. Mash the potatoes until smooth and beat in the butter, milk, and salt and pepper to taste. Set aside.

MAKE THE FILLING: Preheat the oven to 350°F.

Put the meat, onion, celery, and garlic in a large sauté pan over medium heat and cook, stirring with the back of a wooden spoon to break up the meat, until the meat is no longer pink and the vegetables are softened, about 8 minutes. Drain in a colander and transfer to a 9-by-13-inch baking dish. Stir in the tomato sauce, frozen vegetables, thyme, oregano, and

salt and pepper to taste. Spread the mashed potatoes evenly over the filling (you may need to use your hands for this), then sprinkle the top with the paprika. Cover the dish with aluminum foil and bake for 20 minutes, then uncover and bake for 20 minutes longer, or until the topping is lightly browned and the filling is bubbly. Serve immediately.

BARLEY MUSHROOM RISOTTO

ON NOVEMBER 11, 2001, SHAUN ALEXANDER RUSHED FOR 266 YARDS, INCLUDING A TEAM-RECORD 88-YARD TOUCHDOWN.

CHEF: **Kaspar Donier,** Kaspar's, Seattle

WINE SUGGESTION: Frei Brothers RR Chardonnay

SERVES 4

PREP TIME
01:00+

¾ cup barley

Salt

2 tablespoons unsalted butter

3 tablespoons chopped onion

½ teaspoon chopped garlic

2 cups sliced mushrooms

1 cup low-sodium chicken broth

¼ cup heavy cream

1 cup grated Monterey Jack cheese

2 tablespoons chopped fresh parsley

Freshly ground pepper

This easy risotto-like dish features barley instead of rice, so it doesn't require constant stirring. The barley can be cooked a day or two in advance and covered and refrigerated; you can then put the rest of the meal together in about 10 minutes. Serve with a lightly dressed green salad, or spinach sautéed with garlic and olive oil, and a loaf of rustic bread.

In a medium saucepan, combine the barley and 2¼ cups water and bring to a boil. Add ½ teaspoon salt, lower the heat, and simmer, uncovered, for about 45 minutes, or until the liquid is absorbed.

In a large sauté pan, melt the butter over medium heat. Add the onion and garlic and sauté until the onion is transparent, 4 to 6 minutes. Add the mushrooms and sauté for 2 minutes. Add the broth, cream, and barley and cook until heated through.

Stir in the cheese and parsley and season to taste with salt and pepper. Divide the risotto among 4 serving plates and serve immediately.

GARGANELLI PASTA WITH BROCCOLI
AND SPICY FENNEL SAUSAGE

SAN FRANCISCO IS THE ONLY TEAM
TO GO UNDEFEATED (5–0) IN
MULTIPLE SUPER BOWLS.

PREP TIME
00:30+
MARINATE 12 HOURS

CHEF: Paul Arenstam, Americano, San Francisco

WINE SUGGESTION: Frei Brothers RR Chardonnay

SERVES 8

SAUSAGE

2	pounds boneless pork shoulder, trimmed
	Salt and freshly ground black pepper
1	tablespoon olive oil
2	onions, diced
12	garlic cloves, chopped
1	bunch fresh flat-leaf parsley
3	tablespoons fennel seeds
2	tablespoons red pepper flakes
	Cracked black pepper

PASTA

2	pounds dried garganelli pasta (see *Notes*)
¼	cup extra-virgin olive oil
1	onion, thinly sliced
3	garlic cloves, minced
1	bunch broccoli di Cicco, tough stems removed, or 4 cups small broccoli florets (see *Notes*)
2	tablespoons dry white wine
	Zest of 2 lemons
2	tablespoons unsalted butter
	Salt and freshly ground black pepper
1	tablespoon fresh lemon juice
2	tablespoons grated pecorino cheese

MAKE THE SAUSAGE: Cut the pork into 1-inch cubes and put it in a large bowl. Season generously with salt and pepper. Cover and let marinate in the refrigerator for 12 hours.

Heat a large sauté pan over medium heat. Add the oil, onions, and garlic and sauté until the onions are softened, about 5 minutes. Remove to a bowl and let cool completely.

Using a meat grinder fitted with the medium die, grind the pork. Add the sautéed onion mixture, the parsley, fennel, and red pepper flakes. Mix thoroughly and season with salt and cracked pepper to taste. Fry a small piece of the mixture in a skillet to check for seasonings. Set aside.

MAKE THE PASTA: Cook the pasta in a large pot of boiling salted water for about 12 minutes, or until al dente; drain, reserving the cooking water. Put the pasta in a large serving bowl.

Meanwhile, in a large skillet, heat ¼ cup of oil over medium heat. Add the onion and garlic and sauté until the onions are just starting to soften, about 4 minutes. Shape the sausage mixture into small, free-form chunks, no bigger than 1 inch, and add to the skillet; cook, turning frequently, until the sausage is browned all over, about 5 minutes. Add the broccoli and sauté for 1 minute. Add the wine, ½ cup of the pasta cooking water, the lemon zest, butter, and salt and pepper to taste. Toss with the pasta.

Sprinkle the lemon juice and cheese over the pasta and serve immediately.

NOTES: *Garganelli are ridged tubes formed from square pieces of pasta rolled on the diagonal. Penne rigate makes a fine substitute.*

Broccoli di Cicco, an heirloom variety of sprouting broccoli, has small heads and side shoots that mature at different times rather than as a single large central head. Roughly chopped blanched broccoli rabe would be another appropriate substitution here.

PROFITEROLES
WITH SPICED RUM ICE CREAM
AND CHOCOLATE SAUCE

THE LOS ANGELES RAMS WERE THE FIRST
NFL TEAM BASED ON THE WEST COAST.
THEY ARE NOW THE ST. LOUIS RAMS.

PREP TIME
01:00+
CHILL OVERNIGHT

CHEF: Bill Cardwell and **Dave Owens,** Cardwell's at the Plaza, St. Louis

WINE SUGGESTION: Barefoot Bubbly

SERVES 8

PROFITEROLES

- ½ cup vegetable oil
- ¼ teaspoon salt
- 1⅓ cups all-purpose flour
- 5 large eggs

SPICED RUM ICE CREAM

- 2 large eggs
- ½ cup sugar
- 3 cups half-and-half
- 4 ounces white chocolate, chopped
- 1 tablespoon spiced rum
- ½ teaspoon vanilla extract

CHOCOLATE SAUCE

- 1 cup heavy cream
- 2 cups chopped dark chocolate
- 1 cup brewed espresso

Peanut brittle

To simplify this recipe, use purchased ice cream (rum or chocolate). Extra profiteroles can be frozen in an airtight container for several months.

MAKE THE PROFITEROLES: Preheat the oven to 375°F. Line 2 baking sheets with parchment paper.

In a medium saucepan, combine 1 cup water with the oil and salt. Bring to a boil over high heat. Lower the heat to medium, add the flour, and cook, stirring constantly with a wooden spoon, until the flour is thoroughly incorporated and the dough forms a ball and pulls away from the sides of the pan as you stir, 3 to 5 minutes. Transfer the dough to a large bowl and use an electric mixer to beat on low speed for 2 minutes to cool the dough slightly.

One at a time, add the eggs, beating well after each addition. Scrape the dough into a pastry bag fitted with a large plain tip (or use a heavy-duty zip-top bag with one corner cut off) and pipe half-dollar-sized rounds onto the prepared baking sheets. Bake for 30 to 35 minutes, or until puffed and golden. Remove from the oven. Split the profiteroles in half crosswise and return them to the turned-off oven to dry for 10 minutes. Cool on wire racks.

MAKE THE SPICED RUM ICE CREAM: In a medium bowl, whisk the eggs and sugar together until smooth. Set aside.

In a small saucepan, heat the half-and-half until warm but not boiling. Stir about ¼ cup of the half-and-half into the egg mixture, then stir the egg mixture into the saucepan. Cook over low heat, whisking frequently, until the mixture reaches 145°F on a candy thermometer. Remove from the heat and pour the custard through a fine-mesh sieve into a bowl.

In a microwave-safe bowl, heat the white chocolate in a microwave oven on low power 5 to 10 seconds at a time, until just softened. Stir into the custard, along with the rum and vanilla. Cover and refrigerate overnight, then freeze in an ice-cream maker according to the manufacturer's instructions. Put in the freezer until firm.

MAKE THE CHOCOLATE SAUCE: In a small saucepan, bring the cream to a simmer, then remove from the heat and stir in the chocolate and espresso.

Arrange 3 profiteroles on each of 8 serving plates and remove the tops. Fill with the rum ice cream, drizzle with sauce, and garnish with a piece of brittle. Serve immediately.

EXOTIC FRUIT SOUP
WITH HIBISCUS FLOWER GRANITA

IN THE 1982 AFC CHAMPIONSHIP AGAINST
THE BENGALS, THE CHARGERS GENERATED A
TEAM RECORD OF 661 TOTAL YARDS.

PREP TIME
01:00+
FREEZE 2–4 HOURS

CHEF: **Jeff Thurston,** The Prado at Balboa Park, San Diego

WINE SUGGESTION: Barefoot Bubbly

SERVES 8

GRANITA

1 cup sugar

1¼ cups dried hibiscus flowers
(see *Notes*)

1 tablespoon fresh lime juice

FRUIT SOUP

4 cups mirin (see *Notes*)

¾ cup sugar

1 vanilla bean, seeds scraped from
the pod

¼ cup peeled and sliced ginger

2½ star anise pods

½ cinnamon stick

1 tablespoon ground coriander

½ teaspoon freshly ground black
pepper, or more to taste

1 tablespoon fresh lime juice

1 cup diced pineapple

½ cup diced mango

½ cup diced papaya

1 ruby red grapefruit, peeled and cut
into sections (see *Notes*)

¾ cup strawberries, diced

Seeds from 1 pomegranate

1 tablespoon chopped fresh cilantro

1 tablespoon chopped fresh mint

MAKE THE GRANITA: In a medium saucepan, bring 5 cups water and the sugar to a boil, stirring to dissolve the sugar, then remove from the heat. Add the hibiscus flowers and steep for 20 minutes. Pour through a fine-mesh sieve set over bowl and stir in the lime juice. Transfer to a shallow pan and freeze, raking the mixture every 30 minutes with a fork, until thoroughly frozen, 2 to 4 hours.

MAKE THE FRUIT SOUP: Meanwhile, in a large nonreactive saucepan, combine 7 cups water with the mirin, sugar, vanilla bean and seeds, ginger, star anise, cinnamon, coriander, and pepper. Bring to a boil, then reduce the heat to low and cook for 20 minutes. Pour through a fine-mesh sieve set over a bowl. Add the lime juice and put the soup in the refrigerator to chill completely.

Divide the pineapple, mango, papaya, grapefruit, strawberries, and pomegranate seeds among 8 large chilled martini glasses or soup plates. Ladle the soup over the fruit. Garnish with cilantro and mint and place a heaping spoonful of the granita on top. Serve immediately.

NOTES: *Dried hibiscus is used to make bright pink agua de Jamaica, a sweet and refreshing cold infusion popular throughout Latin America. Look for dried hibiscus at health food stores and Mexican markets.*

Mirin, a sweet Japanese rice wine, can be found in Asian markets, health food stores, and sometimes in the international foods section of supermarkets.

To section grapefruit: Peel the grapefruit. Cut between the membranes, separating the sections.

WARM BITTERSWEET-CHOCOLATE CUPCAKES

THE BRONCOS' ALL-TIME LEADING RUSHER IS FORMER RUNNING BACK TERRELL DAVIS, WHO AMASSED 7,607 YARDS.

CHEF: Kevin Taylor, Restaurant Kevin Taylor, Denver

WINE SUGGESTION: Barefoot Bubbly

SERVES 8

PREP TIME
00:30+

CUPCAKES

- ¼ **cup sugar, plus some for the muffin pans**
- ½ **cup heavy cream**
- 1 **tablespoon unsweetened cocoa powder**
- 2 **tablespoons unsalted butter**
- 5 **ounces good-quality bittersweet chocolate, chopped**
- 2 **large eggs**
- ¼ **cup ground pecans**
- 1 **teaspoon vanilla extract**

ICING

- ¼ **cup heavy cream**
- 2 **ounces good-quality bittersweet chocolate, chopped**

- 8 **scoops vanilla ice cream**

MAKE THE CUPCAKES: Preheat the oven to 350°F. Butter 8 cups in a muffin pan and dust with sugar.

In a small saucepan, combine the cream, cocoa powder, and butter and bring to a boil over medium heat. Remove from the heat and add the chocolate, stirring until melted.

In a large bowl using an electric mixer, beat the eggs and sugar until stiff peaks form. Gently fold in the chocolate mixture, pecans, and vanilla until just combined; do not overmix the batter. Fill the muffin cups two-thirds full with batter. Bake for 10 to 15 minutes, until a toothpick inserted in the center comes out clean. Let cool in the pan on a wire rack for 10 minutes, then turn the pan upside down to remove the cupcakes.

MAKE THE ICING: While the cupcakes are baking, put the cream in a small saucepan and bring to a boil. Remove from the heat and add the chocolate, stirring until melted. Set the chocolate mixture aside until cooled but still warm, stirring occasionally to prevent a skin from forming. Dip the top of each cupcake into the icing.

Serve the cupcakes warm, with the ice cream on the side.

PETER KING'S
ORANGE-GLAZED PUMPKIN COOKIES

FOOTBALL NIGHT IN AMERICA

PREMIER PRO FOOTBALL WRITER PETER KING HAS WRITTEN SPORTS ILLUSTRATED'S "INSIDE THE NFL" FOR 17 YEARS.

PREP TIME
01:00+

CHEF: Peter King, Reporter, Football Night in America

MAKES ABOUT 42 COOKIES

COOKIES

2½	cups all-purpose flour
1	teaspoon baking powder
1	teaspoon baking soda
1	teaspoon ground cinnamon
½	teaspoon freshly grated nutmeg
½	teaspoon salt
½	cup (1 stick) unsalted butter, softened
1½	cups sugar
1	cup canned pure pumpkin purée
1	large egg
1	teaspoon vanilla extract

GLAZE

2	cups confectioners' sugar, sifted
3	tablespoons milk
1	tablespoon unsalted butter, melted
½	teaspoon vanilla extract
½	teaspoon pure orange oil (see *Note*)

MAKE THE COOKIES: Preheat the oven to 350°F. Butter 2 baking sheets or line them with parchment paper.

Sift the flour, baking powder, baking soda, cinnamon, nutmeg, and salt into a medium bowl.

In a large bowl, using an electric mixer, beat the butter and sugar until smooth. Beat in the pumpkin, egg, and vanilla until smooth. Using a wooden spoon, gradually stir in the flour mixture until blended. Drop by rounded tablespoonfuls onto the prepared baking sheets. Bake for 15 to 18 minutes, rotating the pans halfway through the baking time, until firm around the edges. The centers will be soft to the touch. Cool for 2 minutes on the baking sheets, then remove to wire racks and cool completely.

MAKE THE GLAZE: In a small bowl, combine all the ingredients and stir until smooth. When the cookies are cool, use a dull knife or spatula to spread glaze on top of the cookies. The cookies will keep, in an airtight container at room temperature, for 3 days.

NOTE: *Orange oil, available at specialty food stores, is preferable to orange extract here because it imparts a more intense orange flavor and won't discolor the glaze at all. But you can substitute extract if necessary.*

"At Football Night in America, the most important meal is the late breakfast, which generally consists of a giant omelet filled with many ingredients, topped off by at least one slice of pumpkin loaf from Starbucks. However, pumpkin loaf is not quite as good as the single-best dessert item during football season, the pumpkin cookies made by Peter King's wife, Ann. They're chewy, they're topped with a light icing, and they would make even a dying man smile. He'll occasionally bring two or three boxes to the studio. People descend on them like hungry wolves." — BOB COSTAS

**#85 DEFENSIVE END
(RETIRED)
UNIVERSITY OF FLORIDA, b. 2-26-50**

JACK YOUNGBLOOD'S
KAHLÚA CAKE

CHEFS: **Jack Youngblood** and wife, **Barb Youngblood**

SERVES 6 TO 8

PREP TIME
01:00+

CAKE

1   box yellow cake mix

     One 3.9-ounce package instant chocolate pudding

½   cup sugar

1   cup vegetable oil

4   large eggs

¼   cup Kahlúa

¼   cup vodka

GLAZE

¼   cup Kahlúa

½   cup confectioners' sugar, plus additional for serving

Jack says, "This is my absolute favorite dessert that my wife, Barb, bakes. I request it for all special occasions, and if I'm lucky I get to lick the batter bowl!"

MAKE THE CAKE: Preheat the oven to 350°F. Butter a 10-inch (12-cup) Bundt pan.

In a large bowl using an electric mixer, combine all the ingredients with ¾ cup water and beat for about 2 minutes, until smooth. Pour the batter into the prepared pan and bake until a toothpick inserted in the center of the cake comes out clean, about 55 minutes. Invert the cake onto a serving plate.

MAKE THE GLAZE: While the cake is baking, in a small bowl, whisk together the Kahlúa and confectioners' sugar until smooth. Pour the glaze over the warm cake and let cool completely. Dust with confectioners' sugar, slice into wedges, and serve.

THROWING A SUPER BOWL PARTY IS LIKE SHOOTING FISH IN A BARREL: YOU DON'T HAVE TO WORK HARD TO LURE THEM IN.

The traditional Super Bowl party is beloved for its lack of pretension and its focus on guilty pleasures, from hot, cheesy dips to fried appetizers and meats you can eat with your fingers. Most advice for partygivers centers on keeping the food warm, the beer cold, and both close to the television.

As a holiday of our own invention, the Super Bowl party is open to interpretation. Hosts can surprise guests with an elegant spread of warm bruschetta and cheese-filled phyllo triangles while still offering as much pleasure and comfort as traditional pre-game favorites. A Super Bowl party doesn't have to be a large-scale bash. The event can be a family occasion, a special meal that's not too fussy but still stands out as a more-than-ordinary dinner.

The real draw of a Super Bowl party may be neither the finger foods nor the game itself, but the excuse to gather your favorite people in the dull dregs of winter when everyone needs it the most.

SUPER
BOWL

MENU 1:
RETRO, FUN, AND EASY

This is an easy-going menu for a gathering of friends in front of the TV, and happily accepts your own football-season favorites into the mix—your signature guacamole or spinach dip would feel right at home here. Finger licking is encouraged, especially with the chilaquiles (basically chips and dip in one bubbling casserole)—they can be scooped out of the dish onto sturdy paper plates. Your guests will welcome the cool, sweet taste of Chris Chambers's fruit bowls, full of berries and melon. And then they'll dig in to the small, flavor-packed barbecued hot beef sandwiches from John Madden's repertoire.

At halftime, finish up the gumbo and dirty rice and let guests help themselves. The unusual and over-the-top brownie-crusted pecan pie is a reason for celebration in itself—and just what fans on the wrong side of the night's scoreboard will appreciate.

APPETIZERS
* **RED BEAN CHILAQUILES**
* **CHRIS CHAMBERS'S FRUIT BOWLS**
* **JOHN MADDEN'S BARBECUED HOT BEEF SANDWICHES**

MAIN COURSE
* **CHICKEN GUMBO WITH CAJUN DIRTY RICE**

DESSERT
* **PECAN PIE WITH BROWNIE CRUST AND VANILLA SAUCE**

RED BEAN CHILAQUILES

AT THE 2000 AFC PLAYOFFS AGAINST THE DOLPHINS, THE JAGUARS SCORED 62 POINTS, THE SECOND MOST IN NFL PLAYOFF HISTORY.

CHEF: Jamey Evoniuk, b.b.'s, Jacksonville

WINE SUGGESTION: Red Rock Merlot

SERVES 8 TO 10

PREP TIME
01:00+

- 10 plum tomatoes, quartered
- 1 yellow onion, cut into 8 wedges
- 2 jalapeño chiles
- ¼ cup fresh cilantro leaves
- 1 teaspoon salt
- Eight 6-inch corn tortillas
- 3 tablespoons olive oil or canola oil
- 3 garlic cloves, minced
- Two 15-ounce cans kidney beans, drained and rinsed
- ½ cup shredded queso asadero or Monterey Jack cheese
- 1 scallion, sliced

Most of this dish can be prepared well in advance if you're making it for a game-day party: Roast the vegetables up to 2 days ahead of time; crisp the tortillas early on the day you plan to serve the chilaquiles (or, in a pinch, use good-quality tortilla chips); sauté the garlic and beans that morning as well, and store them in the fridge. Just before guests arrive, assemble the casserole, then pop it in the oven during the pregame broadcast.

Preheat the broiler to high. Position a rack 4 inches from the heat source. On a baking sheet lined with aluminum foil, arrange the tomatoes, onion wedges, and chiles. Broil until the skins blacken, 4 to 5 minutes. Turn the vegetables over and broil until blackened, 3 to 4 minutes. Transfer to a bowl, cover, and let stand for about 10 minutes.

Peel the tomatoes. Wearing gloves, peel and seed the chiles. Place the tomatoes, chiles, and onion in a blender or food processor and pulse until coarsely puréed. Add the cilantro and ½ teaspoon of the salt and pulse to make a chunky sauce. Set aside. The sauce can be made up to 2 days in advance, covered and refrigerated.

Set the oven temperature to 400°F. Stack the tortillas and cut them into 6 wedges, making 48 wedges total. Place them in a single layer on a baking sheet and bake until crisp, 4 to 5 minutes. Remove from the oven and set aside.

Set the oven temperature to 350°F.

In a large frying pan, heat 2½ tablespoons of the oil over medium-high heat. Add the garlic and sauté until golden, 1 to 2 minutes. Stir in the beans and the remaining ½ teaspoon salt and cook until heated through, about 3 minutes. Remove from the heat.

Grease a large rectangular baking dish with the remaining ½ tablespoon oil. Spread ½ cup of the tomato sauce in the dish. Layer 16 of the tortilla wedges on top and cover with one third of the bean mixture. Repeat layering, and top with the remaining sauce. Sprinkle with the cheese and bake until the top is browned and bubbly, 25 to 30 minutes.

Sprinkle with the scallion and serve, scooping portions straight from the dish.

CHRIS CHAMBERS's
FRUIT BOWLS

#89 WIDE RECEIVER
5'11", 210 LBS.
UNIVERSITY OF WISCONSIN, b. 8-12-78

PREP TIME
00:30

CHEF: Chris Chambers

SERVES 6 TO 8

4 apples
3 navel oranges
1 pint strawberries
½ pint raspberries
½ pint blackberries
½ pint blueberries
Fresh mint sprigs (optional)

Chris says, "Going back to high school, I was always told you need to eat a certain amount of carbohydrates before a game because it's going to give you energy. But I also eat some kind of steak before a game. I like steak and eggs before a game, and some kind of fruit. That's my game day breakfast." Unadorned, easy-to-eat fruit is always welcome on a table of game-day noshes, but you could also offer a simple yogurt dressing to dollop on top: Whisk together one 5.3-ounce container of Greek (thick, strained) yogurt, 1 teaspoon vanilla extract, and honey to taste. Alternatively, skewer whole strawberries and chunks of apple, pineapple, papaya, and banana and serve the yogurt dressing on the side as a dipping sauce.

Core the apples and cut them into 8 wedges each, then cut the wedges crosswise into chunks; put in a large serving bowl. Peel the oranges. Holding them over the bowl to catch the juices, cut between the membranes to separate into segments. Put the segments in the bowl. Hull and quarter the strawberries, then add them to the bowl. Rinse the raspberries, blackberries, and blueberries and pat them dry. Add the berries to the bowl and toss gently to combine. Garnish with mint, if desired, and serve immediately.

JOHN MADDEN'S
BARBECUED
HOT BEEF SANDWICHES

AS HEAD COACH, MADDEN GUIDED THE RAIDERS TO 7 AFC WESTERN DIVISION TITLES AND A VICTORY IN SUPER BOWL XI.

CHEF: John Madden, Analyst, Sunday Night Football

SERVES 10

PREP TIME
06:00+

2	tablespoons unsalted butter
2	onions, chopped
2	garlic cloves, chopped
½	cup chopped celery
2	cups ketchup
3	tablespoons cider vinegar
3	tablespoons Worcestershire sauce
1	teaspoon hot sauce
¼	cup packed brown sugar
1½	teaspoons chili powder
½	teaspoon dry mustard
2	dashes paprika
2	teaspoons salt
½	teaspoon freshly ground black pepper
3	pounds cooked shredded roast beef
	10 to 12 hamburger buns

John says, "This is the first recipe that we tested for my cookbook, John Madden's Ultimate Tailgating, and the minute I bit into it, I knew we were off to a good start."

In a large skillet, heat the butter over medium heat. Add the onions and sauté until tender and lightly browned, about 8 minutes.

Put the onions, 1½ cups water, and all the remaining ingredients except the buns in a 4- to 6-quart slow cooker. Cover and cook on the low setting for 6 to 8 hours. Pile the meat on the buns and serve immediately.

CHICKEN GUMBO
WITH CAJUN DIRTY RICE

IN 1999 THE JAGUARS COMPILED A RECORD
OF 14–2, THE BEST REGULAR-SEASON
RECORD IN THE NFL THAT YEAR.

PREP TIME
01:00+

CHEF: Shane Cheshire, First Street Grille, Jacksonville Beach

WINE SUGGESTION: McWilliam's Shiraz

SERVES 4

GUMBO

- ¼ cup vegetable oil
- ½ large onion, diced
- 1 to 2 datil or habanero chiles, thinly sliced (see *Note*)
- ½ red bell pepper, seeded and chopped
- ½ green bell pepper, seeded and chopped
- 3 garlic cloves, thinly sliced
- ½ cup (1 stick) unsalted butter
- 1½ cups all-purpose flour
- 1½ cups low-sodium chicken broth
- One 6-ounce bottle New Orleans–style hot sauce
- 5 plum tomatoes, diced
- 3 bay leaves
- 8 ounces boneless, skinless chicken breast, cut into ½-inch pieces
- 1 fresh chorizo sausage link, cut into ¼-inch-thick rounds
- 3 tablespoons filé powder (see page 140)
- 2 tablespoons fresh thyme leaves
- 10 okra pods, cut into ½-inch rounds

DIRTY RICE

- 1 pound beef liver or chicken livers
- Flour for dredging
- ½ cup vegetable oil
- 3 small shallots, minced
- 2 tablespoons Cajun spice blend
- 1 cup white wine
- 2 cups hot cooked white long-grain rice
- Salt

- Pickled okra pods

MAKE THE GUMBO: Put the oil, onion, chiles, and bell peppers in a large, heavy pot and cook over medium heat, stirring frequently, until softened, about 5 minutes. Add the garlic and cook, stirring, for 3 minutes. Add the butter and stir until it is melted, then sift in the flour and stir to combine. Reduce the heat to low and cook, turning the flour mixture over slowly and constantly, until it has turned dark brown, about 10 minutes.

Gradually whisk in the broth and hot sauce, then add the tomatoes, bay leaves, chicken, chorizo, filé powder, thyme, and okra. Bring to a simmer and cook until the chicken is cooked through and the okra is tender, about 10 minutes.

MAKE THE DIRTY RICE: Dredge the liver in flour and shake off the excess. Heat the oil in a sauté pan over medium heat, then add the liver and shallots. Cook, turning the liver frequently and stirring the shallots, until the shallots are tender, about 3 minutes. Add the spice blend and wine and cook until the wine is completely evaporated. Remove from the heat.

Transfer the liver to a cutting board and chop it coarsely. In a large bowl, gently toss the rice together with the liver and shallot mixture, and season with salt to taste.

Serve the gumbo and dirty rice family style in large bowls, with the pickled okra on the side.

NOTE: *Datil chiles are extremely hot cousins of the habanero and Scotch bonnet chiles, though some say their flavor is fruitier than either. Substitute habaneros, but be judicious.*

PECAN PIE
WITH BROWNIE CRUST AND VANILLA SAUCE

DENVER BEAT ATLANTA 34-19 AT THE FALCONS' LONE SUPER BOWL APPEARANCE IN 1999.

CHEF: Kirk Parks, Rathbun's, Atlanta

WINE SUGGESTION: Barefoot Bubbly

SERVES 8

PREP TIME
02:00+

BROWNIE CRUST

2	large eggs
1	teaspoon vanilla extract
10	tablespoons unsalted butter
1¼	cups sugar
¾	cup unsweetened cocoa powder
¼	teaspoon salt
½	cup all-purpose flour

PECAN FILLING

1	cup packed light brown sugar
1	cup light corn syrup
4	large eggs
1	tablespoon vanilla extract
½	cup (1 stick) unsalted butter, melted
3	tablespoons whiskey (optional)
4	cups chopped pecans

VANILLA SAUCE

½	cup heavy cream
1	cup milk
½	vanilla bean, split
3	large egg yolks
½	cup sugar

MAKE THE BROWNIE CRUST: Preheat the oven to 325°F.

In a small bowl, beat the eggs and vanilla, and set aside. Put the butter, sugar, cocoa powder, and salt in a large metal bowl. Set the bowl over a pan of simmering water and stir until the butter is melted and the mixture is warm; remove the bowl from the pan. Whisking constantly, add the egg mixture and continue to whisk until thoroughly incorporated. Beat in the flour, then spread the batter evenly in a 9-inch round cake pan that is 2 inches deep. Bake for 15 minutes, then cool to room temperature. Leave the oven on.

MAKE THE PECAN FILLING: In a large bowl using an electric mixer, beat the sugar and corn syrup, until very smooth, about 3 to 4 minutes. Add the eggs and vanilla and beat until just combined. Add the butter and the whiskey, if using, and beat until just combined. Fold in the pecans, then pour the mixture into the baked and cooled brownie crust. Bake for 45 minutes, until firm in the center, then cool to room temperature on a wire rack.

MAKE THE VANILLA SAUCE: In a small saucepan, combine the cream and milk. Scrape the vanilla bean and add the seeds and bean to the pan. Bring just to a simmer, then remove from the heat and let steep for 30 minutes. Remove the vanilla bean.

In a medium bowl, whisk the egg yolks and ¼ cup of the sugar until smooth. Stir the remaining ¼ cup sugar into the milk mixture and bring to a bare simmer. Whisk about ½ cup of the milk mixture into the egg mixture, then slowly pour the egg mixture into the saucepan and whisk to combine. Cook over low heat, stirring constantly, until thick enough to coat the back of the spoon; do not boil. Pour through a fine-mesh sieve set over a bowl, then set the bowl in a larger bowl of ice water and cool to room temperature. (The sauce can be made up to 1 day in advance and refrigerated, covered. Bring to room temperature before serving.)

Serve slices of the pie drizzled with the sauce.

MENU 2:
A VIP BOX
DINNER

Sometimes you want to get a little fancy, and there's no reason Super Bowl Sunday can't dress up in its Oscar-night best once in a while. You'll need a fair amount of help in the kitchen if you want to offer the full menu here, although feel free to pare down the selection of appetizers to two or three. You can enlist a neighborhood teenager to help pass platters of appetizers during the party, or simply set the platters out on a big table as a buffet.

The pork can simmer away unattended in the oven during the first half, and the parsnip purée can be made earlier in the day and reheated in the microwave. Invite everyone to fill their own dinner plates, and offer a simple green salad with vinaigrette and thick slices of crusty Italian bread.

Make the chocolate cake early on the day of the game (make two of them for an all-out bash). If you like, make or buy a team-logo stencil and set it on top of the cake when you dust it with sugar for a sophisticated version of the ubiquitous football-field-decorated sheet cake. Offer the shortbread cookies or purchased truffles in cellophane bags as a parting gift.

APPETIZERS

- ★ **SPICY MISO CHIPS WITH TUNA**
- ★ **BRUSCHETTA WITH WHITE BEANS, ARUGULA, AND PARMESAN**
- ★ **BEEF CARPACCIO ROLLS WITH ROASTED GARLIC AÏOLI**
- ★ **CHICKEN LIVER MOUSSE WITH WARM CROSTINI**
- ★ **GOAT CHEESE AND WALNUT PHYLLO TRIANGLES**

MAIN COURSE

- ★ **CITRUS-GLAZED PORK WITH PARSNIP-CHIVE PURÉE**

DESSERT

- ★ **FLOURLESS CHOCOLATE CAKE WITH CHOCOLATE SAUCE**
- ★ **POPPY SEED SHORTBREAD BARS**

SPICY MISO CHIPS WITH TUNA

THE ONLY PERSON TO HAVE COACHED
THE JETS AND THE GIANTS IS
BILL PARCELLS.

CHEF: Shin Tsujimura, *Nobu New York, New York City*

WINE SUGGESTION: Whitehaven Sauvignon Blanc   **MAKES 20 TO 30 HORS D'OEUVRES**

PREP TIME
00:30

½   cup mirin (see page 216)

2   tablespoons sake

⅓   cup white miso paste (see *Notes*)

1   tablespoon sugar

¼   cup rice vinegar

1   tablespoon prepared Japanese
     hot mustard (see *Notes*)

2   tablespoons chile-garlic sauce
     (see *Notes*)

8   ounces sashimi-grade tuna

     20 to 30 good-quality unsalted
     potato chips

     Chopped fresh cilantro
     or chives

The miso sauce can be prepared several days in advance and kept, tightly covered, in the refrigerator until just before serving. Top with the potato chips at the last minute so they don't become at all soggy.

In a small saucepan, combine the mirin and sake and bring to a boil over high heat. Boil for 30 seconds to evaporate some of the alcohol, then reduce the heat to low. Add the miso and sugar and stir to combine. Cook over low heat, stirring, until the miso paste and sugar are dissolved. Remove from the heat and cool to room temperature, then add the vinegar, mustard, and chili-garlic sauce.

Finely dice the tuna and put it in a medium bowl. Toss with just enough of the sauce to coat the tuna, about 10 teaspoons. Spoon a bit of the tuna onto each potato chip, garnish with cilantro, and serve immediately.

NOTES: *Miso is available in the refrigerated section of Asian markets and health food stores.*

Japanese hot mustard comes in a tube and is available at Japanese markets. It can be used on its own, mixed with mayonnaise as a spread for sandwiches, or mixed with a bit of soy sauce and used for dipping. Substitute any spicy, smooth-textured mustard.

Chile-garlic sauce is similar to sambal oelek (see page 35), but includes garlic. It's available at Asian markets.

BRUSCHETTA
WITH WHITE BEANS, ARUGULA, AND PARMESAN

BEARS LEGENDS RED GRANGE, GEORGE HALAS, AND BRONKO NAGURSKI WERE IN THE FIRST HALL-OF-FAME CLASS IN 1963.

PREP TIME

SOAK OVERNIGHT

CHEF: Susan Goss, West Town Tavern, Chicago

WINE SUGGESTION: Frei Brothers RR Chardonnay

SERVES 8

- ¾ cup dried white beans, soaked overnight in water to cover by 3 inches (see *Note*)
- 3 sprigs fresh thyme
- 1 bay leaf
- 1 teaspoon salt
- ¼ cup olive oil, plus more for brushing
  Freshly ground black pepper
- 2 baguettes
- 2 garlic cloves, cut in half
  Shaved Parmesan cheese
- 2 cups baby arugula leaves
  White truffle oil (optional)
  Coarse sea salt

Drain the beans, return to the pan, and cover with fresh water. Add the thyme and bay leaf. Bring to a boil, then lower the heat and simmer for about 45 minutes, or until softened. Add the salt and let stand for 15 minutes. Drain the beans, discard the herbs, and mash the beans coarsely with a fork. Add the olive oil and season with pepper to taste.

Slice the baguettes and brush the slices on one side with oil. Then rub them with the cut side of the garlic cloves. Place on a baking sheet and bake until golden brown, about 5 minutes. Let cool, then mound the beans on the bruschetta and arrange a few cheese shavings over the beans. Top with some arugula leaves, drizzle with truffle oil, if using, and sprinkle with coarse sea salt. Place on a serving platter and serve immediately.

NOTE: *To cut down on prep time, use one 15-ounce can of white beans (cannellini, navy, or Great Northern) instead of cooking dry beans: Drain them well, and rinse in a colander under cold running water. Mash them in a microwave-safe bowl, mix with the oil and salt and pepper to taste, then warm in a microwave oven just before serving. The bean topping is also good at room temperature.*

BEEF CARPACCIO ROLLS

WITH ROASTED GARLIC AÏOLI

BUFFALO REACHED AN NFL-RECORD
4 CONSECUTIVE SUPER BOWLS
BETWEEN 1991 AND 1994.

CHEF: Paul Jenkins, Tempo Restaurant, Buffalo

WINE SUGGESTION: Red Rock Merlot

SERVES 8

PREP TIME

02:00

REFRIGERATE OVERNIGHT

BEEF CARPACCIO ROLLS

One 1-pound beef sirloin, halved and well trimmed

Salt and coarsely ground black pepper

1 cup plus 3 tablespoons olive oil

¼ cup capers, drained, plus some for garnish

Leaves from ½ bunch fresh flat-leaf parsley

1 bunch arugula, torn into pieces

1 tablespoon balsamic vinegar

Grated Parmesan cheese

ROASTED GARLIC AÏOLI

1½ cups mayonnaise

2 heads garlic, roasted

1 tablespoon fresh lemon juice

Salt and freshly ground white pepper

MAKE THE CARPACCIO ROLLS: Season the beef generously with salt and pepper. In a blender, combine 1 cup of the oil, the capers, and parsley and blend until smooth. Season with salt and pepper to taste. Place the beef in a large, heavy-duty zip-top bag and add the marinade. Seal the bag and turn the beef to fully coat with the marinade. Refrigerate overnight.

Remove the meat from the marinade and pat almost dry. Discard marinade. Let the meat rest at room temperature for 20 minutes. Heat 2 tablespoons oil in a large, heavy skillet over medium-high heat. Add the beef and sear on all sides, turning with tongs about every 2 minutes, about 12 minutes total. Remove from the heat to a plate and cool completely. Wrap in plastic wrap and freeze for 1 hour or refrigerate overnight.

MAKE THE ROASTED GARLIC AÏOLI: Meanwhile, in a blender, combine the mayonnaise, roasted garlic, and lemon juice and blend until smooth. Season with salt and white pepper to taste. Refrigerate until ready to serve. The aïoli can be prepared 1 day ahead and kept refrigerated.

ROLL THE CARPACCIO: Using a very sharp knife, slice the meat as thinly as possible. Place each slice between two sheets of waxed paper or plastic wrap and pound until paper-thin.

In a large bowl, toss the arugula with the oil and vinegar and season with salt and pepper to taste.

Arrange a slice of beef on a flat work surface. Place some arugula at the end of the beef closest to you and roll up tightly; place seam side down on a serving platter. Repeat with the remaining beef. If you're not serving right away, cover with plastic and refrigerate until ready to serve.

Top the carpaccio rolls with aïoli and garnish with capers and cheese. Serve immediately.

CHICKEN LIVER MOUSSE
WITH WARM CROSTINI

THE RAIDERS ARE THE ONLY TEAM TO PLAY IN THE SUPER BOWL IN FOUR DIFFERENT DECADES.

PREP TIME
01:00+
SOAK OVERNIGHT

CHEF: **Douglas Keane,** Jardinière, San Francisco

WINE SUGGESTION: Don Miguel Gascon

SERVES 8

1	pound chicken livers, trimmed
4	cups whole milk
1	tablespoon olive oil, plus more for brushing
2	large shallots, minced
1	cup port wine
6	large egg yolks
¾	cup rendered chicken fat (see *Note*)
1	cup heavy cream
	Salt and freshly ground black pepper
2	baguettes

Although some time is required for soaking the livers and chilling the mousse, you can get started two days before kickoff; just before serving, make the crostini, spread with the mousse, and you're ready to go.

Put the chicken livers in a large bowl. Pour the milk over the chicken livers, cover with plastic, and refrigerate overnight.

Drain the chicken livers and rinse well under cold running water. Transfer to paper towels to drain.

In a medium saucepan, heat 1 tablespoon of the oil over medium heat. Add the shallots and sauté until softened, 3 to 5 minutes. Add the port, increase the heat, and simmer until reduced to a syrup, about 10 minutes. Remove from the heat and cool.

Preheat the oven to 350°F.

Transfer the port reduction to a food processor. Add the chicken livers and process until smooth. With the machine running, slowly add the egg yolks and chicken fat through the hole in the lid and process until thickened. Strain through a fine-mesh sieve into a bowl. Add the cream and season with salt and pepper to taste.

Spoon the mousse into a 2-quart round baking dish and place in a roasting pan. Set the roasting pan in the oven and pour enough boiling water into the pan to come halfway up the sides of the baking dish. Bake for about 50 minutes, until set and a small knife inserted in the center comes out clean. Remove the baking dish from the pan and cool on a wire rack. Cover with plastic and refrigerate until cold, about 2 hours.

Shortly before serving, remove the mousse from the refrigerator. Preheat the oven to 350°F.

Slice the baguettes and brush the slices on one side with oil. Place on a baking sheet and bake until golden brown, about 5 minutes. Spread a small amount of the mousse over the warm crostini, arrange on a serving platter, and serve.

NOTE: *Ask your butcher for rendered chicken fat, or schmaltz or make your own by slowly heating chicken skin and the fat from around the cavity in a saucepan until it melts, then straining it. Goose or duck fat, available in tins at specialty food shops, are fine substitutes.*

GOAT CHEESE AND WALNUT PHYLLO TRIANGLES

CHEF: Don Pintabona, Tribeca Grill, New York City

WINE SUGGESTION: Bridlewood Syrah

MAKES 16 TRIANGLES

PREP TIME
01:00+

- 8 ounces frozen phyllo sheets, defrosted (see *Note*)
- ½ cup mascarpone cheese
- ½ cup goat cheese
- 1 teaspoon minced garlic
- ¼ cup ground walnuts
- ¼ cup bread crumbs
- 1 tablespoon minced fresh chives
- 1 tablespoon minced fresh parsley
- 1 large egg, beaten

  Salt and freshly ground black pepper

  Melted and cooled unsalted butter

Fill and fold the triangles early in the day and refrigerate them, covered, on the baking sheet. Bake them just before serving. Alternatively, bake the flaky triangles a day in advance and put them in a 400°F oven for a few minutes to warm through and crisp up.

Preheat the oven to 425°F.

Using a sharp knife, cut the phyllo into 4 equal-sized strips. Stack the strips and keep the stacks separated between sheets of waxed paper. Cover the phyllo with a dampened kitchen towel.

In a medium bowl, combine the mascarpone, goat cheese, garlic, walnuts, bread crumbs, chives, and parsley. Add the egg and season with salt and pepper to taste.

On a work surface, remove 1 strip of phyllo, brush lightly with butter, and place a second strip on top. Brush the second strip with butter and place about a teaspoon of the filling in the lower right-hand corner of the phyllo about ½ inch from the edge. Fold up the right corner to form a triangle, and continue to fold the filled triangle up the length of the strip, like folding a flag. Brush the triangle with butter. Continue filling and folding until the phyllo and filling are used up, placing the triangles on baking sheets as they are formed. You should have about 16 phyllo triangles. Bake until lightly golden, about 15 minutes. Arrange on a serving platter and serve immediately.

NOTE: *Phyllo dough can be found in the frozen foods section of your supermarket, usually near the frozen pie shells. Let it defrost in the refrigerator overnight before using.*

CITRUS-GLAZED PORK
WITH PARSNIP-CHIVE PURÉE

PREP TIME
`03:00+`

CHEF: Kent Rathbun, Abacus Restaurant, Dallas

WINE SUGGESTION: McWilliam's Shiraz

PORK

Sixteen 3- to 4-ounce pieces pork cheek or shoulder meat

1	tablespoon salt
1	tablespoon cracked black pepper
1	tablespoon granulated garlic
2	cups all-purpose flour
¼	cup vegetable oil
2	cups chopped onion
1	cup chopped celery
1	cup chopped carrot
¼	cup coarsely chopped garlic
¼	cup coarsely chopped shallots
2	bay leaves, preferably fresh
3	tablespoons chopped rosemary leaves
2	tablespoons chopped thyme leaves
4	cups orange juice
4	cups grapefruit juice
1	cup veal demi-glace (see *Note*)
	2 to 4 tablespoons cornstarch
1	tablespoon unsalted butter
2	tablespoons grated orange zest

PARSNIP-CHIVE PURÉE

4	pounds parsnips, peeled and chopped
½	cup (1 stick) unsalted butter
4	garlic cloves, chopped
4	shallots, chopped
2	cups heavy cream
	Salt
¼	cup chopped fresh chives

Pork cheek is an inexpensive cut that, like pork belly, is becoming increasingly popular with creative chefs. When slowly braised to break down the connective tissue that would otherwise make the meat tough, it becomes tender and intensely flavorful. If you can't find pork cheeks, use chunks of well-marbled pork shoulder.

MAKE THE PORK: Preheat the oven to 275°F.

Put the pork in a large bowl and toss with the salt, pepper, and granulated garlic. Spread the flour on a large plate and dredge the pork in the flour; set the pork aside on a separate plate.

DALLAS WAS THE FIRST TEAM IN NFL HISTORY TO WIN 3 SUPER BOWLS IN 4 YEARS.

SERVES 8

In a large, heavy nonreactive pot, heat the oil over medium-high heat. Dredge the pork in flour again. Working in batches to avoid crowding the pot, add the pork to the oil and cook until golden brown on all sides, about 10 minutes. Remove the pork from the pot and set aside.

To the pot, add the onion, celery, carrot, garlic, and shallots and cook over medium heat until caramelized, about 20 minutes. Add the bay leaves, rosemary, thyme, orange juice, grapefruit juice, and demi-glace and bring to a boil.

Meanwhile, put the pork pieces in a roasting pan large enough to hold them tightly packed in a single layer. Pour the vegetable-citrus mixture over the pork, cover the pan tightly with aluminum foil, and bake for 2½ to 3 hours, until the pork pieces are very tender but still hold their shape. Carefully remove the pork with a slotted spoon and arrange the pieces on a large serving platter, discarding the vegetables; cover with foil to keep warm.

Strain the braising liquid through a fine-mesh sieve into a large saucepan. Bring to a boil, then lower the heat and simmer until the sauce is reduced by half, skimming the clear fat and any foam or impurities from the surface frequently. In a small bowl, combine 2 tablespoons cornstarch and ¼ cup water, then whisk the mixture into the sauce. Simmer for 5 more minutes; if the sauce is too thin, add more cornstarch-water mixture and cook 5 minutes longer. Pour the sauce through a very-fine-mesh sieve into a bowl, then whisk in the orange zest and butter.

MAKE THE PARSNIP-CHIVE PURÉE: While the pork is in the oven, blanch the parsnips in a large pot of boiling water for about 4 minutes, until just starting to soften; drain.

In a medium saucepan, melt ¼ cup of the butter over medium heat. Add the garlic and shallots and sauté until the shallots are translucent, about 5 minutes. Add the parsnips and cream. Bring to a simmer and cook until the parsnips are very soft, about 8 minutes.

Transfer to a blender and blend until smooth, then return the purée to the saucepan and set aside until ready to serve.

When the pork and sauce are ready, heat the parsnip purée over low heat until thick and reheated (it should be the consistency of loose whipped potatoes). In a small saucepan, melt the remaining ¼ cup butter over medium-high heat and cook until it is brown and has a nutty aroma, about 5 minutes. Whip the browned butter into the purée, season with salt to taste, and whip in the chives. Serve immediately, with the pork.

NOTE: *Demi-glace is a meat or fish stock that's been cooked for many hours; the result is a thick and highly flavorful seasoning agent used in sauces, particularly in French cuisine. You can find half-pint containers of demi-glace in the frozen foods section of specialty grocers and some supermarkets.*

FLOURLESS CHOCOLATE CAKE
WITH CHOCOLATE SAUCE

IN 1993 CAROLINA BECAME THE
29TH NFL FRANCHISE, AND THE FIRST
EXPANSION TEAM SINCE 1976.

PREP TIME
01:00+
REFRIGERATE OVERNIGHT

CHEF: **Tobin McAfee,** Sir Edmond Halley's, Charlotte

WINE SUGGESTION: Barefoot Bubbly

SERVES 8 TO 12

FLOURLESS CHOCOLATE CAKE

- ¾ **cup (1½ sticks) unsalted butter, cut into small pieces**
- 1 **pound bittersweet chocolate, chopped**
- 5 **large eggs, separated**
  Pinch of salt
- 2 **tablespoons sugar**

CHOCOLATE SAUCE

- ¾ **cup half-and-half**
- 1 **tablespoon unsalted butter**
- 8 **ounces semisweet chocolate chips**
- 1 **tablespoon instant espresso powder**

  Confectioners' sugar
  Whipped cream

MAKE THE FLOURLESS CHOCOLATE CAKE: Preheat the oven to 325°F. Butter an 8-inch round cake pan and line the bottom with parchment paper.

Combine the butter and chocolate in the top of a double boiler placed over barely simmering water and stir until the chocolate is melted. Remove from the heat and beat in the egg yolks. In a separate bowl using an electric mixer, beat the egg whites and salt until soft peaks form. Beat in the sugar until stiff peaks form. Using a rubber spatula, fold one-quarter of the egg whites into the chocolate, then fold in the remaining egg whites. Transfer the batter to the cake pan and smooth the top, spreading evenly. Set the cake pan in a roasting pan and pour in enough boiling water to come halfway up the sides of the cake pan. Bake for about 30 minutes, or until the cake has risen slightly and the edges are just starting to set. Cool completely on a wire rack, then cover with plastic and refrigerate overnight.

MAKE THE CHOCOLATE SAUCE: Meanwhile, in a small saucepan, combine the half-and-half and butter over medium heat. Heat until small bubbles appear along the edges, but do not boil. Remove from the heat, add the chocolate and espresso powder, and stir until the chocolate melts, the espresso powder is dissolved, and the mixture is smooth. Set aside to cool. The sauce can be made up to 2 days ahead and kept refrigerated; bring to room temperature before serving.

Remove the cake from the refrigerator 1 hour before serving. To unmold, run a thin knife around the sides of the pan to loosen the cake. Invert onto a plate and peel off the parchment paper. Invert again onto a serving plate and dust with confectioners' sugar. Cut into 8 to 12 slices and place on dessert plates. Top each slice with a dollop of whipped cream and drizzle with chocolate sauce. Serve immediately.

POPPY SEED
SHORTBREAD BARS

IN A GAME AGAINST THE EAGLES ON
SEPTEMBER 30, 2007 THE GIANTS AMASSED
12 SACKS—A SINGLE-GAME RECORD.

CHEF: **Don Pintabona,** Tribeca Grill, New York City

WINE SUGGESTION: Barefoot Bubbly

MAKES 24 BARS

PREP TIME

00:45+

½ **cup (1 stick) unsalted butter**

½ **cup confectioners' sugar**

2 **teaspoons grated orange zest**

2 **tablespoons poppy seeds**

1 **cup all-purpose flour**

¼ **teaspoon salt**

Preheat the oven to 300°F. Butter an 8-inch square baking ban.

In a large bowl using an electric mixer, cream the butter and confectioners' sugar until light-colored and very fluffy. Beat in the orange zest and poppy seeds, then beat in the flour and salt. Firmly press the dough into the baking pan and bake until pale gold, about 30 minutes. Cool on a wire rack for 15 minutes, then cut into 24 bars and let cool completely in the pan. Gently retrace the cuts and separate into bars. Arrange on a serving platter and serve.

MENU 3:
FAMILY NIGHT

In the weeks after the holidays, you don't need a good excuse to gather the family or close friends for a special meal, but the Super Bowl provides one anyway. A beautiful (yet surprisingly unfussy) salad, elegant lamb chops, and a satisfying, cherry-studded bread pudding are sure to chase away the winter doldrums.

APPETIZERS

BABY SPINACH SALAD WITH CANDIED PECANS, SHIITAKE CHIPS, AND BLUE CHEESE

MAIN COURSE

SUMAC-SEARED LAMB CHOPS WITH TWICE-BAKED EGGPLANT

DESSERT

CHERRY AND WHITE CHOCOLATE BREAD PUDDING

KARL MECKLENBURG'S GINGER COOKIES

THE STALEYS BECAME THE BEARS IN 1922 BECAUSE THEY SHARED WRIGLEY FIELD WITH THE CUBS.

BABY SPINACH SALAD
WITH CANDIED PECANS, SHIITAKE CHIPS, AND BLUE CHEESE

CHEF: Susan Goss, Zinfandel, Chicago

WINE SUGGESTION: Frei Brothers RR Chardonnay

SERVES 6

PREP TIME

01:00+

CANDIED PECANS

1	large egg white, lightly beaten
½	cup sugar
1	teaspoon ground cinnamon
½	teaspoon ground ginger
¼	teaspoon ground allspice
¼	teaspoon ground coriander
½	teaspoon salt
2	cups pecan halves

SHIITAKE CHIPS

24	large shiitake mushrooms (about 8 ounces)
2	tablespoons olive oil
	Salt and freshly ground black pepper

RED WINE SYRUP

1	cup red wine
1	tablespoon dark brown sugar

SPINACH SALAD

¼	cup olive oil
2	tablespoons fresh lemon juice
	Salt and freshly ground black pepper
12	ounces baby spinach leaves
3	ounces blue cheese, crumbled

MAKE THE CANDIED PECANS: Preheat the oven to 300°F.

Line a baking sheet with parchment paper.

In a large bowl, beat the egg white until foamy. In a small bowl, combine the sugar, cinnamon, ginger, allspice, coriander, and salt and beat into the egg white. Add the pecans and stir until coated. Remove the pecans with a slotted spoon and place on the baking sheet. Discard the remaining egg white mixture. Bake until the pecans are golden brown, about 30 minutes. Cool completely on the baking sheet. The pecans may be made up to a week ahead and stored, tightly covered, at room temperature.

MAKE THE SHIITAKE CHIPS: Increase the oven temperature to 400°F.

Remove and discard the stems from the mushrooms and in a large bowl, toss the caps with the oil. Season with salt and pepper to taste. Arrange the caps on baking sheets, leaving a little space between them. Roast for 20 to 30 minutes, until lightly browned and crisp. Remove from the oven and cool to room temperature. The shiitake chips can be made up to 2 hours ahead, kept at room temperature.

MAKE THE RED WINE SYRUP: Meanwhile, in a medium saucepan, combine the wine and brown sugar over low heat. Cook, stirring, to dissolve the sugar, then raise the heat to medium and bring to a simmer. Simmer until reduced by three-quarters, about 10 minutes. Watch carefully toward the end that the syrup doesn't scorch. Transfer to a bowl and cool to room temperature. The syrup can be made up to 2 days ahead; bring to room temperature before using.

MAKE THE SPINACH SALAD: In a medium bowl, whisk together the oil and lemon juice until thickened. Season with salt and pepper to taste. In a large bowl, toss the spinach with the dressing.

Divide the salad among 6 serving plates. Sprinkle with the cheese and pecans. Place 4 shiitake chips on top and drizzle with the syrup. Serve immediately.

SUMAC-SEARED LAMB CHOPS
WITH TWICE-BAKED EGGPLANT

IN 1944 THE WARTIME CARDINALS
AND STEELERS PLAYED AS
ONE TEAM, CALLED CARD-PITT.

PREP TIME
01:00+

CHEF: **Eddie Matney,** Eddie Matney's Restaurant, Phoenix

WINE SUGGESTION: MacMurray SC Pinot Noir

SERVES 4

EGGPLANT

1   large eggplant, unpeeled, cut into 1-inch-thick rounds

2   tablespoons olive oil

1   russet potato, cooked and mashed

1   tablespoon unsalted butter, melted

2   tablespoons half-and-half or milk

4   fresh basil leaves, chopped

3   ounces soft goat cheese

2   ounces cream cheese

    Salt and freshly ground black pepper

¼   cup grated Parmesan cheese

LAMB CHOPS

12   lamb chops

2   tablespoons olive oil

1   tablespoon ground sumac (see *Note*)

    Salt and freshly ground black pepper

    Fresh basil leaves

    Shaved Parmesan cheese

MAKE THE EGGPLANT: Preheat the oven to 350°F.

Brush the eggplant slices with the oil and arrange them in a single layer on a baking sheet. Bake for 30 to 40 minutes, until soft and browned. Lower the oven temperature to 325°F.

Roughly chop the eggplant and put it in a large bowl. In a medium bowl, combine the mashed potato, butter, and half-and-half and mash until smooth, then add it to the eggplant with the basil, goat cheese, and cream cheese; mash with a potato masher until smooth and thoroughly combined. Season with salt and pepper to taste. Spoon into an 8-inch baking dish and sprinkle with the Parmesan. Bake for 30 minutes, until hot and bubbly.

MAKE THE LAMB CHOPS: Meanwhile, rub the lamb chops with the oil, then sprinkle with the sumac and salt and pepper to taste. Let rest for 10 minutes.

Heat a large cast-iron grill pan or a large sauté pan over high heat. Add the chops and cook for 2 to 3 minutes per side for medium-rare.

Spoon a mound of eggplant into the center of a large serving platter and arrange the chops around it with the bones pointing up toward the center, like a teepee. Garnish with the basil leaves and shaved Parmesan. Serve immediately.

NOTE: *The dried fruit of the sumac shrub (related to but different from the genus that includes poison ivy, oak, and sumac) is used extensively in Turkey, Greece, and the Levant. The deep reddish-brown spice has a distinctive sour flavor, and in addition to being used as a rub for meat, the crushed berries are sometimes steeped in warm water, which is strained and used in marinades, dressings, or cold drinks. Look for sumac in Middle Eastern markets, or substitute dried ground lemon zest (mixed with a bit of sweet paprika for color).*

CHERRY AND WHITE CHOCOLATE BREAD PUDDING

IN 2006 THE SAINTS SOLD OUT THE
SUPERDOME FOR THE ENTIRE SEASON,
A FIRST IN FRANCHISE HISTORY.

PREP TIME

LET STAND 1 HOUR

CHEF: Christopher Wilson, Emeril's Restaurant, New Orleans

WINE SUGGESTION: Barefoot Bubbly

SERVES 6

3   large eggs

2   cups heavy cream

1   cup milk

¾   cup packed light brown sugar

1   teaspoon vanilla extract

½   teaspoon ground cinnamon

4   cups ½-inch cubes day-old white bread

4   ounces white chocolate, finely chopped

¾   cup dried cherries

2   tablespoons unsalted butter, melted

Emeril's suggests serving this sumptuous bread pudding with white chocolate whiskey sauce, but you can use any chocolate sauce you prefer: Try the one on page 238, or a good-quality purchased sauce.

Butter a 9-inch square baking pan.

In a large bowl, beat the eggs. Beat in the cream, milk, brown sugar, vanilla, and cinnamon. Add the bread, chocolate, and dried cherries, then stir in the melted butter. Pour into the baking pan and let stand for 1 hour.

Preheat the oven to 350°F.

Put the pudding in the oven and bake until just set, about 45 minutes. Cool on a wire rack until just warm, about 20 minutes, then cut into rectangles and serve.

KARL MECKLENBURG'S
GINGER COOKIES

**# 77 LINEBACKER
(RETIRED)
UNIVERSITY OF MINNESOTA, b. 9-1-60**

CHEFS: Karl Mecklenburg and his wife, **Kathi Mecklenburg**

MAKES ABOUT 6 DOZEN COOKIES

PREP TIME
00:30+
REFRIGERATE 1 HOUR

2	cups sugar, plus more for rolling
1½	cups (3 sticks) unsalted butter
½	cup light molasses
2	large eggs
4½	cups all-purpose flour
1	tablespoon baking soda
2	teaspoons ground cinnamon
1	teaspoon ground ginger
1	teaspoon ground cloves
½	teaspoon freshly grated nutmeg
½	teaspoon salt

Karl says, "This is my wife Kathi's recipe from an old Broncos cookbook that was compiled when I was playing. It's not the holidays without her ginger cookies."

In a large bowl using an electric mixer, combine the sugar, butter, molasses, and eggs.

In a separate bowl, sift together the flour, baking soda, cinnamon, ginger, cloves, nutmeg, and salt. Gradually add the flour mixture to the sugar mixture and mix until thoroughly incorporated. Cover the bowl with plastic wrap and refrigerate for 1 hour.

Preheat the oven to 350°F.

Shape the dough into 1-inch balls, roll them in sugar, and place on ungreased baking sheets about 1 inch apart. Bake for about 10 minutes, until just firm in the center. Remove to wire racks to cool. Serve.

FEEDING AMERICA
AND TASTE OF THE NFL
TACKLE HUNGER
IN THE UNITED STATES

EVERY DAY, HUNDREDS OF THOUSANDS OF AMERICANS HAVE TROUBLE PUTTING FOOD ON THEIR FAMILY'S TABLE. BUT THE FACE

of hunger in this country might surprise you. "People going hungry today are providing service in restaurants; they're taxi drivers; they're hairdressers," says Vicki B. Escarra, president and CEO of Feeding America. "They're average Americans who just can't make ends meet, even with a salary of $30,000. The idea that we're dealing only with homeless people is wrong. These are working families."

Since 1979, Feeding America—known until 2008 as America's Second Harvest—has made getting food to families that need it its first and only mission. Through a network of more than 200 food banks in every state—plus Washington, D.C., and Puerto Rico—Feeding America helps some 25 million people every year, 12 million of them children. Food collected during drives, purchased, or donated by farmers, producers, wholesalers, and others is distributed directly to those in need by volunteers and staff.

Since 1992, Feeding America has benefited from a historic partnership that has brought together food, football, families, and charity. The catalyst for this combination is Taste of the NFL, a non-profit event that has funneled the great charitable impulses of the NFL, its players, fans, and chefs from every NFL city toward this organization.

Taste of the NFL debuted at Super Bowl XXVI, a cold-weather championship weekend in January 1992. Wayne Kostroski, a far-sighted restaurateur in the host city, Minneapolis, had pushed a fresh idea. Why not gather regional food from each of the then 28 NFL teams? Kostroski suggested to receptive NFL executives. Assemble NFL players and alumni, star chefs, a premier music act, and paying guests for a star-studded Super Bowl bash with all the glitter of other major NFL gala events, but with a charitable purpose.

Left and opposite: Feeding America funds food banks across the country. The volunteers pictured here and thousands of others help serve more than 25 million people each year. **Below:** Taste of the NFL founder Wayne Kostroski with contributing chef Eddie Matney at Super Bowl XLII.

Starting with one thousand guests at $75 a ticket in 1992, Taste of the NFL—the "Party with a Purpose"—now attracts 3,000 guests who buy tickets for $500 and up during each Super Bowl. Through local and national media, Taste's call for food bank support reaches millions of people around each Super Bowl.

The enthusiastic chefs and player representatives in each NFL city have helped transform that first modest party into a nationally known event that generates hundreds of thousands of dollars for food banks—and spreads the message of helping the hungry to millions of fans. "You walk around and taste each of the teams' dishes, made by our top chefs from each NFL city," Kostroski says. "The players have chosen to be there, and guests will always be looked in the eye as players greet you."

Since its inception, Taste of the NFL has generated more than $10 million for hunger relief groups. Feeding America has always been the primary beneficiary of the event, an acknowledgment that the charity is at front lines of the fight against hunger.

The organization helps people most of us would call "average Americans." Close to 40 percent of Feeding America's clients live in a household where at least one person is working, more than 3 million are senior citizens, and some 43 percent live in suburban or rural areas.

Feeding America counts more than 1 million volunteers for its affiliated relief agencies at churches, senior citizens' homes, boys and girls' clubs, and other community institutions. Feeding America is one of the most efficient charities in the country, delivering results to its clients and its

donors. Ninety-eight cents out of each dollar collected goes toward feeding the hungry. "For a charity it's the very best," Escarra says. "It's incredibly lean and well organized."

Taste of the NFL presently holds 10 regional events a year, before and during the regular football season, bringing the message of local food charity to an ever larger group of fans. "We're very thankful and proud to have Wayne and the rest of Taste of the NFL being great partners for us, not only nationally but locally," Escarra says.

Proceeds from the sale of this book help fight hunger through Feeding America. You can help America's food banks by visiting **www.feedingamerica.org.** For details on Taste of the NFL and its events, please visit **www.TasteoftheNFL.com.**

THE CHEFS

Every year, chefs from around the country donate their time and recipes to help fight hunger through Taste of the NFL, the annual "Party with a Purpose" that benefits American food banks. We thank them for their efforts and their great dishes.

Paul Arenstam is executive chef of Americano Restaurant at Hotel Vitale in San Francisco, where his dishes showcase the abundance of the neighboring Ferry Plaza Farmer's Market. An ardent proponent of organic and sustainable ingredients, he has been featured in *Gourmet*, *Food & Wine*, *Bon Appétit*, and the *New York Times*.

Marty Blitz is chef and proprietor of Mise en Place in Tampa, Florida. He is known for his seasonal approach to cooking, using the freshest ingredients available as he changes his menu daily for lunch and dinner. In 2001, Mise En Place was rated number one for food in the Central Florida/Gulf Coast Restaurants edition of the Zagat Survey. The James Beard House also named Blitz a Rising Star.

Bob Brody is Director of Food and Beverage at Pechanga Resort & Casino in Temecula, California, which offers eight dining establishments, including four gourmet restaurants. He was formerly executive chef of Trellises Garden Grille at the Town and Country Resort in San Diego.

Bill Cardwell is executive chef and owner of Cardwell's at the Plaza in St. Louis, which features a carefully crafted American menu devoted to local, seasonal ingredients. The restaurant is continually ranked among the region's top restaurants by the likes of *Esquire*, *Food & Wine*, *Wine Spectator*, and *Gourmet*.

Charles Charbonneau is executive chef of The Augustine Grille at the Sawgrass Marriott Golf Resort & Spa in Ponte Vedra Beach, Florida. He honed his craft at the Culinary Institute of America and has since worked for Hyatt Hotels, Ritz-Carlton Hotels, and Interstate Hotels & Resorts, where he served as corporate chef.

Shane Cheshire is executive chef and at The Sun Dog in Neptune Beach, Florida. He was formerly executive chef of First Street Grille and The Homestead Restaurant, both in Jacksonville, Florida.

Stephen Cole is the former chef and owner of Café Allegro in Kansas City, Missouri, which he sold in 2002. The restaurant received an Award of Excellence from *Wine Spectator* and Best Food and Best Restaurant recognition from the Zagat Restaurant Survey.

Sanford D'Amato is chef and owner of Sanford Restaurant in Milwaukee, which was named one of the 50 Best Restaurants in America by *Gourmet* in 2006. He has appeared on such programs as *Dining Around* on the Food Network; *Great Chefs, Great Cities*; and CBS's *Always in Good Taste*.

Jean-Robert de Cavel is chef de cuisine and owner of Jean-Robert at Pigall's in Cincinnati, which serves French-American cuisine in a modern Parisian setting. In 2003 it was named one of the Top 75 New Restaurants in the World by *Condé Nast Traveler*. De Cavel has been featured in *Wine Spectator, Bon Appétit, Gourmet,* and *Esquire*.

Andy DiVincenzo was chef and owner of Billy Ogden's in Buffalo, NY, a local institution that received countless four-star reviews during its existence. DiVincenzo was dedicated to many charitable causes, including Taste of the NFL.

Frank DiVincenzo proudly carries on the culinary legacy started by his late brother, Andy, with whom he worked closely for more than two decades. He has been active in many charitable causes, including Kids Escaping Drugs, the Make-a-Wish Foundation, March of Dimes, and Camp Good Days and Special Times.

Kaspar Donier is chef and owner of Kaspar's Special Events & Catering in Seattle, where he takes advantage of the freshest local seafood available to create innovative dishes. He has been featured in national magazines and on television and radio and is a four-time nominee for the James Beard Award for Best Chef: Northwest.

Jamey Evoniuk is chef and co-owner of Heirlooms Culinary Café and Market in Jacksonville, Florida, a restaurant and catering business specializing in fresh, local ingredients and Heirloom vegetables. Evoniuk was previously an executive chef at many high-end restaurants, including b.b.'s, also in Jacksonville.

Bobby Flay is a critically acclaimed chef, restaurateur, award-winning cookbook author, and television personality. His restaurants include Mesa Grill (three locations), Bar Americain, and Bobby Flay Steak. Flay is the host of *Boy Meets Grill* on the Food Network and is also Food Correspondent for *The Early Show* on CBS.

Jeffrey "J.G." Gaetjen is executive chef at Kinkead's in Washington, D.C., an American brasserie-style restaurant specializing in fresh seafood. He began working with owner Bob Kinkead at Twenty-One Federal in 1991, where he was sous chef. In his pursuit of culinary excellence, her strives to create eye-appealing, succulent dishes using quality ingredients.

Tom Gladbach is executive chef at Wildfire in Eden Prairie, Minnesota, an upscale steakhouse with a 1940s supper club atmosphere. He was formerly executive chef at Tejas in Edina, Minnesota.

Debbie Gold is chef and owner, along with her husband, Michael Smith, of 40 Sardines in Overland Park, Kansas, which is known for its focus on fresh, straightforward flavors from around the world. *Esquire* named Gold a Chef to Watch in 1997, and in 1999 she and Smith won the James Beard Foundation Award for Best Chef: Midwest.

Susan Goss is chef and owner of West Town Tavern in Chicago, which serves contemporary comfort food in a neighborhood setting. She has been widely heralded for her culinary work there, as well as at her former restaurants, Something Different in Indianapolis and Zinfandel Restaurant in Chicago.

Jonathan Hale is executive chef of Blue Point Coastal Cuisine in San Diego, a sophisticated San Francisco–style supper club, where he selects only the best seafood and meats from coast to coast each day to create his signature dishes. In 2003, Blue Point was named Best Seafood Restaurant by the San Diego Restaurant Association.

Tony Hanslits is Director of Culinary Education at The Chef's Academy in Indianapolis. Previously he was executive chef and co-owner of Tavola di Tosa Italian Restaurant and Tosa EuroCafe. Hanslits and his recipes have appeared in numerous publications, and in 2004 he was a finalist in *Italian Cooking & Living* magazine's competition held in New York.

Greg Hardesty is chef and owner of Elements in Indianapolis, a sophisticated and intimate restaurant serving modern American fare using the best artisanal products from Indiana and around the world. Elements was named restaurant of the year by *Indianapolis Monthly* in 2003.

Blake Hartwick is executive chef of Bonterra Dining & Wine Room and Las Ramblas Café in Charlotte, North Carolina. He attended Johnson & Wales University in Charleston, South Carolina, and has also worked at some of the region's best restaurants, including Bistro 100, Carpe Diem, and Sonoma, where he was the sous chef.

Mark Haugen is chef and owner of Tejas in Edina, Minnesota. There, he brings a creative background in classical French cuisine, which he applies to indigenous Southwestern cooking styles and flavors. He is also a co-owner of the Cuisine Concepts group and serves as chef director of Taste of the NFL.

David Holben is executive chef of Del Frisco's Double Eagle Steak House in Dallas. Previously, he was executive chef at Culpepper Steak House, also in Dallas. In 1990, *Food & Wine* named him one of America's Best New Chefs.

John Howie is chef and owner of Seastar Restaurant and Raw Bar in Bellevue, Washington. He originated the use of planks for restaurant service and is the author of *The Cedar Plank Cookbook* and *The Plank Cookbook*. He has also been featured on CBS's *The Early Show*, CNN, and the Food Network.

Paul Jenkins began his culinary career at a Buffalo hot dog stand. His more than 25 years as a chef since then have included work at Oliver's Restaurant and the Buffalo Club. He is the co-creator of Tempo, a Mediterranean-Italian restaurant in downtown Buffalo.

Victor Jones is the longtime chef at Sterling's of Avondale in Jacksonville, Florida, which offers eclectic, upscale American cuisine, with an emphasis on fresh season specialties. The restaurant has been the winner of ten consecutive Golden Spoon Awards from *Florida Trend* magazine.

Douglas Keane is executive chef and owner of Cyrus in Healdsburg, California, where he specializes in an ambitious culinary style that he refers to as "contemporary luxury" cuisine. The restaurant received two stars from *The Michelin Guide* and was named one of *Gourmet's* Top 50 Restaurants, while Keane was named *Esquire's* Chef of the Year and *Food & Wine's* Best New Chef.

Bob Kinkead is chef and owner of Kinkead's in Washington, D.C., an American brasserie-style restaurant featuring fresh seafood and daily changing menus. Since opening in 1993, Kinkead and the restaurant have won nearly every major award in the food service industry, including the James Beard Award. He is also the author of *Kinkead's Cookbook*.

Dave "D.K." Kodama is chef and owner of Sansei Seafood Restaurant & Sushi Bar in Honolulu. Since opening in 1996, the restaurant has been collecting rave reviews and culinary honors, including a 90 rating in *Wine Spectator*, inclusion as one of *Bon Appétit's* Favorite Asian Restaurants, and recognition as one of the best sushi bars in *Travel + Leisure*.

Emeril Lagasse is a renowned chef, restaurateur, TV personality, and author. He's the chef-proprietor of nine restaurants—in New Orleans, Las Vegas, Orlando, Miami, and Gulfport, Mississippi—all of which consistently win critical praise and top ratings. As the star of *Essence of Emeril* and *Emeril Live* on the Food Network, he has hosted over 1600 shows. He is also the best-selling author of 12 cookbooks.

Dennis Leary is chef and owner of Canteen in San Francisco, an intimate, 20-seat restaurant in the Commodore Hotel offering personally prepared, unique, accessible food. Previously, he was executive chef at Rubicon, also in San Francisco, for five years.

Stephen Lewandowski is executive chef of Tribeca Grill in New York City, where his elegant, innovative cuisine finds a perfect complement in the restaurant's superb wine list, winner of *Wine Spectator's* Grand Award. The wine dinners he co-hosts with wine director David Gordon have won critical acclaim.

Nancy Longo is chef and owner of Pierpoint in Baltimore, which has received high praise from the likes of *Travel + Leisure*, *Condé Nast Traveler*, *Saveur*, and the *New York Times*. She has been featured on ABC News' *Primetime* and appeared as a guest on the Food Network.

Lachlan Mackinnon-Patterson is chef and owner of Frasca Food and Wine in Boulder, Colorado, where he applies his culinary talents to create innovative, yet traditional, northern Italian dishes. In 2005, he was named one of *Food & Wine's* Best New Chefs, and in 2008 he won the James Beard Foundation Award for Best Chef: Southwest.

Bob Malone is chef and owner of The Camelot, with locations in Warrendale and Wexford, Pennsylvania. He was formerly the executive chef at the Treesdale Golf & Country Club in Gibsonia, Pennsylvania.

Eddie Matney is chef and owner of Eddie's House in Scottsdale, Arizona. He has been celebrated for his multicultural, multiethnic culinary style in a number of prestigious publications, including *Food & Wine*, *USA Today*, and *Bon Appétit*.

Tobin McAfee is chef and owner of Sir Edmond Halley's in Charlotte, North Carolina, where he puts his own creative spin on traditional English pub fare. He participates in many charitable activities, including Share Our Strength's Taste of the Nation and the Southern Cooking benefit for the homeless.

Jack McDavid is chef and owner of Jack's Firehouse in Philadelphia. He specializes in creating exciting, original dishes with the freshest locally grown, handpicked ingredients. He can be seen on the Food Network's *Grillin' and Chillin'* and has lent his support to numerous charities, including Taste of the NFL, Taste of the Nation, and Meals on Wheels.

Michael Meffe is executive chef at Peter Shear's Downtown in Canton, Ohio. He was previously executive chef at Jacob Good in Akron, and Nemo Grill in Avon, Ohio. He enjoys preparing global cuisine with French and Asian influence.

Michael Mina is a chef and founder and CEO of The Mina Group, a San Francisco–based restaurant management company that operates high-end, innovative restaurants, including Michael Mina in San Francisco, Nobhill, Seablue, and Stripsteak in Las Vegas, and Arcadia in San Jose. Mina was named Chef of the Year by *Bon Appétit* in 2005.

Paul Minnillo is chef and owner of Baricelli Inn in Cleveland, which has received numerous industry awards and is consistently ranked as a top restaurant in The Zagat Survey. Minnillo also founded the Baricelli Cheese Co., which airfreights artisan cheeses directly from France, and is a consulting chef for Continental Airlines.

Bruce Molzan is chef and owner of Ruggles Grill in Houston, which is known for its upscale, inventive take on traditional Southwestern fare.

He has been featured in numerous publications, elected to Who's Who in Food and Wine in Texas, and once competed in the Bocuse d'Or, which names America's top native-born chef.

Paul O'Connell is chef and owner of Chez Henri in Cambridge, Massachusetts, an eclectic French bistro with a Latin twist. His funky yet sophisticated menus have impressed both patrons and food critics alike, garnering acclaim from such publications at *Bon Appétit* and *Esquire*.

Dave Owens works on new products at Bissinger's, the St. Louis–based chocolate company. He was formerly a chef at Cardwell's at the Plaza and Terrene, both in St. Louis.

Kirk Parks is pastry chef at NAVA in Atlanta. He has garnered many awards, including The James Beard Foundation Award for Baker of the Year: Southwest. He has also been featured in *Southern Living*, *Bon Appétit*, *Gourmet*, and *Food & Wine*, and on many local TV programs.

Don Pintabona is chef and owner of Dani in New York City and was formerly executive chef at the Tribeca Grill. After the attacks of 9/11, he spearheaded "Operation Chefs With Spirit," a campaign that fed over 600,000 hot meals to relief workers at the World Trade Center site. He is also the author of two books, the *Tribeca Grill Cookbook* and *The Shared Table: Cooking with Spirit for Family and Friends*.

Brian Polcyn is chef and proprietor of Five Lakes Grill in Milford, Michigan, which serves seasonal, contemporary American cuisine. He has been recognized by such publications as the *New York Times*, *Gourmet*, and *Bon Appétit* and has received three gold medals and one silver medal from the American Culinary Federation.

Dustin Pritchett is chef de cuisine at the Sunset Grill in Nashville, where he has worked since 2001. He began his career in Montana, where worked at Chico Hot Springs, Uncle Looies, Livingston Bar & Grill, and Rumours.

Kent Rathbun is chef and owner of Abacus in Dallas, Shinsei in Dallas, and Jasper's, with several locations throughout Texas. He has appeared on such programs as the Food Network's *Iron Chef America*, *Chef du Jour*, and *Ready, Set, Cook!*; CBS's *The Early Show*; and NBC's *Today*. He has been nominated four times for the James Beard Foundation Award for Best Chef: Southwest.

Kevin Rathbun is chef and owner of Rathbun's, Kevin Rathbun Steak, and Krog Bar, all in Atlanta. Since opening in 2004, Rathbun's has received numerous accolades, including being named Best New Restaurant 2004 by *Esquire* and Best New American Restaurant 2004 by *Travel + Leisure*.

Megan Roen Forman is assistant pastry chef at Sucré New Orleans, which offers up pastries, one-of-a-kind chocolates, and gelatos. She was formerly the pastry chef at Bayona, also in New Orleans.

Chris Rossi is executive chef and owner of Citron in Oakland, California, which combines authentic French and Mediterranean dishes in a distinctive upscale atmosphere. Trained in the European apprentice style, he began cooking while still in high school with Paula La Duc Catering and Wente Vineyards Restaurant, later opening the Steelhead Brewery and Café Zenon in Oregon.

Chris Schlesinger is chef and owner of the East Coast Grill & Raw Bar in Cambridge, Masschusetts. In 1996 he received the James Beard Award for Best Chef: Northeast. He is the coauthor, along with John Willoughby, of many cookbooks, including *Let the Flames Begin*, *License to Grill*, and *The Thrill of the Grill*.

Michael Smith is chef and owner, along with his wife, Debbie Gold, of 40 Sardines in Overland Park, Kansas, which is known for its focus on fresh, straightforward flavors from around the world. In 1999 he and Gold won the James Beard Foundation Award for Best Chef: Midwest.

Susan Spicer is chef and owner of Bayona in New Orleans, which serves up her legendary eclectic global cuisine. In 1993, she was the recipient of the James Beard Award for Best Chef: Southeast Region. She is the author of *Crescent City Cooking: Unforgettable Recipes from Susan Spicer's New Orleans*.

Allen Susser is chef and owner of Chef Allen's in Aventura, Florida, which features his signature New World Cuisine. He was the recipient of the James Beard Foundation Award for Best Chef: Southeast and is the author of the books *New World Cuisine and Cookery*, *The Great Citrus Cookbook*, and *The Great Mango Cookbook*.

Neal Swidler was formerly executive chef at NOLA and chef de cuisine at Emeril's Delmonico, both in New Orleans.

Kevin Taylor is chef and owner of Restaurant Kevin Taylor and Primo Ristorante, both located in the Hotel Teatro in Denver. He also operates Kevin Taylor's at the Opera House and Palettes at the Denver Art Museum. Restaurant Kevin Taylor has received numerous awards, including the Mobil Travel Guide Four Star Award and *Wine Spectator*'s Award of Excellence. *Travel + Leisure* also named it one of the 50 Best Hotel Restaurants.

Jeff Thurston is executive chef of The Prado at Balboa Park in San Diego. Under his creative direction, the restaurant won honors as San Diego's Best New Restaurant and has been named one of America's Top Restaurants by *Gourmet*. Thurston was also named Chef of the Year by the California Restaurant Association.

Shin Tsujimura is executive chef at NOBU Fifty-Seven in New York City, which, like the original downtown-New York location, is renowned for a style of cooking that mixes both Japanese influences and Peruvian ingredients and sensibilities. The restaurant was awarded three stars by the *New York Times* in 2005.

Brian Uhl is executive chef at Midtown Café and is owner and executive chef at CABANA, both in Nashville. He specializes in wild game dishes in the framework of contemporary cuisine. His innovative cooking has been recognized in *Bon Appétit*, *Food Arts*, the *New York Times*, and *GQ*.

Rocco Whalen is chef and owner of Fahrenheit in Cleveland. His mature cooking style has been recognized by *Esquire*, who named him a Chef to Keep Your Eye On, and *Gourmet*, who included Fahrenheit in its Guide to America's Best Restaurants.

Christopher Wilson was formerly chef de cuisine at Emeril's Restaurant in New Orleans, and is currently Director of Culinary Operations for the Emeril's group of restaurants.

Anthony Zello is chef at Bigelow Grille, located in the Doubletree Hotel in Pittsburgh. The restaurant received a four-star rating from the *Pittsburgh Post-Gazette* and was voted one of the Top 25 Best Restaurants in the city by *Pittsburgh Magazine* in 2007 and 2008.

INDEX

PHOTOGRAPHY CREDITS:

AFP/Getty Images: 230; Iain Bagwell: cover, 135, 227, 228; Kate Baldwin: 61, 171; Scott Boehm/Getty Images: 4–5, 222; Kevin Chelko (Beth Buzogany and Teresa Chelko, stylists): 14, 21, 25, 36, 40, 56, 64, 68, 82, 89, 94, 108, 111, 112, 117, 119, 120, 123, 126, 131, 137, 138, 144, 173, 174, 177, 190, 194, 196, 203, 207, 213, 236; Chromepix/Newscom: 54; Colin Cooke: 45, 157; Tim Defrisco/Getty Images Sport: 245; Tony Dejak/AP Images: 62–63; Courtesy Tom Donoghue: 247; Ken Epstein: 200; Courtesy Feeding America: 246, 247; Michael Fabus/Getty Images Sport: 104; Focus on Sport/Getty Images: 225; Steve Freeman/NBC Sports: 10, 129; Getty Images: 240; Sam Greenwood/Getty Images/Newscom: 141; Otto Greule, Jr./Getty Images/Newscom: 205; Drew Hallowell/Getty Images Sport: 49; Michelle Havens: 26, 66; Michael C. Hebert, New Orleans Saints: 148; Kevin Ross Hedden: 2, 180, 215, 243; Ann Heisenfelt/AP Images: 114–15; Harry How/Getty Images/Newscom: 101; Icon Sports Media/Newscom: 224; IOS Photos/Newscom: 185, 208, 209; Jed Jacobsohn/Getty Images: 8, 43; M. Jensen: 34, 92, 96, 169; Donn Jones, Tennessee Titans: 147; Rich Kane/Wirepix/Newscom: 48, 75; Todd Kirkland/Icon SMI/Newscom: 163; Don Lansu/Wirelmage/Newscom: 99; LBF Photography: 19, 31, 51, 53, 73, 81, 85, 102, 128, 132, 143, 150, 158, 160, 165, 187, 210; Steve Levin/National Football League/Getty Images: 105; Andy Lyons/Getty Images/Newscom: 87; Jim McIsaac/Getty Images/Newscom: 55; Miami Dolphins: 58; Joe Murphy/Wirelmage/Newscom: 149; Courtesy NBC Sports: 11, 22, 74, 90, 182; Newscom: 86; Joseph Poellot/Wirelmage/Newscom: 107; Joseph Rogate/Wirelmage/Newscom: 39; Jim Scherzi (Dave Lenweaver, stylist): 16, 29; Jim Scherzi (Kathy Bahn, stylist): 94; Brad Schloss/Icon SMI/Newscom: 152; Eric Seals/Detroit Free Press/MCT: 6–7; Keith Seaman: 189; Paul Spinelli/Getty Images Sport: 12–13, 154, 220–21; Allen Dean Steele/Wirelmage/Newscom: 38; Rick Stewart/Getty Images Sport: 184; Rick Stewart/Getty Images/Newscom: 98; Damon Tarver/Cal Sport Media/Newscom: 204; Derek Till: 183; Dilip Vishwanat/Getty Images Sport: 166–67; Zuma Press/Newscom: 146

The Sunday Night Football Cookbook © 2008 NBC Universal, Inc.

Chef recipes provided courtesy of Taste of the NFL/Hunger Related Events. All recipes and photographs are copyright their makers. All rights reserved. No part of this book may be reproduced in any form or by any electronic means, including information storage and retrieval systems, without permission in writing from the publisher, except by a reviewer who may quote brief passages in a review.

NBC and NBC Sports are trademarks of NBC Universal, Inc. NFL Team Names/logos are trademarks of the teams indicated. All other NFL-related trademarks are trademarks of the National Football League.

The information in this book has been carefully researched and tested, and all efforts have been made to ensure accuracy. Neither the publisher nor the producer nor the creators can assume responsibility for any accident, injuries, losses, or other damages resulting from the use of this book.

The National Football League, its member professional football clubs, NFL Enterprises LLC, NFL Properties LLC, NFL Ventures, L.P., NFL Ventures, Inc., its affiliates, and each of their respective subsidiaries, affiliates, shareholders, officers, directors, agents, representatives and employees (collectively the "NFL Entities") will have no liability or responsibility for any claim arising in connection with use of this book or the recipes contained therein. The NFL Entities have not endorsed, offered or sponsored this book in any way.

John Madden's recipes adapted from *John Madden's Ultimate Tailgating.* © 1998 Red Bear, Inc. Used with permission.

Photography credits appear on page 255.

Published by
Time Inc. Home Entertainment
135 West 50th Street, New York, NY 10020

Library of Congress Control No. 2008905662

ISBN-13: 978-1-60320-797-3
ISBN-10: 1-60320-797-X

Printed in the United States of America

11 10 09 08   10 9 8 7 6 5 4 3 2 1

ACKNOWLEDGMENTS

This book could not have been made without the gracious assistance of everyone at Taste of the NFL and Hunger Related Events, including Wayne Kostroski, Max Kittel of epmthree, Liz Brown, Kristin Christensen, and Mark Haugen.

Thanks to Dick Ebersol and Ken Schanzer for their consistent support and guidance of our efforts to make *Sunday Night Football* his night, her night and their night.

Thanks to Tiki Barber, Jerome Bettis, Cris Collinsworth, Bob Costas, Peter King, Andrea Kremer, John Madden, and Al Michaels.

Thanks to the team at NBC Sports: Wendy Bass, Justin Byczek, Dave Dore, Lindsay Fitz, Adam Freifeld, Fred Gaudelli, Lyndsay Iorio, Wade Junco, Mike McCarley, Brian Matthews, Jon Miller, and Brian Walker.

Thanks to the team at the NFL: Frank Supovitz, Cathy Yancy, Brian McCarthy, Craig Ellenport, and David Weinberg.

Thanks to: Steve Goodman and Lara Potter of the NFL Players Association; RJ Gonser and John Caplin of CAA Sports; Denise White, Lindsey Waterhouse and Lauren Renschler of EAG; Linda Boff, Deborah Meyer and Caryn Dubelko of iVillage; Ellen Stone of Bravo; and Faith Hill and her team of Sandra Westerman and Paul Freundlich.

Thanks to the many NFL teams, agents and publicists who helped facilitate contributors, including: Sandy Montag, Melissa Baron, Jared Winley, Mark Lepselter, David Studley, Melanie LeGrande, Jim Christman, Mark Dalton, Brian Cleek, and Andrew Ree.

Thanks to Kim Niemi, Melissa Bloom, Richard Fraiman, Peter Harper, Nina Fleishman, Tom Mifsud, and Jodi Bannerman.

Thanks also to Susan Haspel and Heather Auer of NBC Community Affairs; Wendy MacGregor and Philip Zepeda of Feeding America; the Ad Council, including Heidi Arthur, Rowena Tse, James Baumann and Dena Graham.

Time Inc. Home Entertainment thanks Victoria Alfonso, Alexandra Bliss, Glenn Buonocore, Margaret Hess, Suzanne Janso, Brynn Joyce, Robert Marasco, Brooke Reger, Mary Sarro-Waite, Ilene Schreider, Adriana Tierno, and Alex Voznesenskiy.

Melcher Media thanks Eileen Baumgartner, Daniel del Valle, Max Dickstein, Coco Joly, Jason Klarman, Lauren Nathan, Lia Ronnen, Holly Rothman, Jessi Rymill, Ellen Stone, Shoshana Thaler, Rebecca Wiener, Betty Wong, Megan Worman, Lauren Zalaznick.

NFL PLAYERS

Many of the NFL players featured in this book appear through the courtesy of NFL PLAYERS, the licensing and marketing subsidiary of the NFL Players Association. For more information, please visit www.NFLPlayers.com.

E.&J. Gallo Winery.

Gallo's commitment to the non-profit event and hunger-related charities has been running for 10 years, focused on donations to Taste of the NFL and the creation of a wine list for each year's event. This year, Gallo has also provided wines to match the chefs' contributions to *The Sunday Night Football Cookbook*.

The Sunday Night Football Cookbook was produced by

MELCHER MEDIA

Melcher Media
124 West 13th Street, New York, NY 10011
www.melcher.com

Publisher: Charles Melcher
Associate Publisher: Bonnie Eldon
Editor in Chief: Duncan Bock
Editor: David E. Brown
Associate Editor: Lindsey Stanberry
Production Director: Kurt Andrews
Designed by Gary Tooth/Empire Design Studio

Time Inc. Home Entertainment:
Richard Fraiman, Publisher; Steven Sandonato, General Manager; Carol Pittard, Executive Director, Marketing Services; Tom Mifsud, Director, Retail & Special Sales; Peter Harper, Director, New Product Development; Laura Adam, Assistant Director, Brand Marketing; Helen Wan, Associate Counsel; Holly Oakes, Senior Brand Manager, TWRS/M; Anne-Michelle Gallero, Design & Prepress Manager; Susan Chodakiewicz, Book Production Manager; Nina Fleishman, Assistant Manager, Product Marketing.